THE ZEN MASTER HAKUIN

Prepared for the Columbia College Program of
Translations from the Oriental Classics
Wm. Theodore de Bary, Editor

NUMBER LXXXVI OF THE *Records of Civilization:*
Sources and Studies EDITED UNDER THE AUSPICES OF
THE DEPARTMENT OF HISTORY, COLUMBIA UNIVERSITY

The Zen Master Hakuin:
Selected Writings

Translated by
Philip B. Yampolsky

Hakuin, 1686 - 1769

COLUMBIA UNIVERSITY PRESS
NEW YORK and LONDON 1971

Philip B. Yampolsky is an Adjunct Associate Professor of Japanese and Librarian of the East Asian Library at Columbia University

Portions of this work were prepared under a grant from the Carnegie Corporation of New York and under a contract with the U.S. Office of Education for the production of texts to be used in undergraduate education. The texts so produced have been used in the Columbia College Oriental Humanities program and have subsequently been revised and expanded for publication in the present form. Copyright is claimed only in those portions of the work not submitted in fulfillment of the contract with the U.S. Office of Education. Neither the Carnegie Corporation nor the U.S. Office of Education is the author, owner, publisher, or proprietor of this publication, and neither is to be understood as approving by virtue of its support any of the statements made or views expressed therein.

RECORDS OF CIVILIZATION: SOURCES AND STUDIES

Edited under the Auspices of the Department of History,
Columbia University

For Yuiko

❇ FOREWORD

❇ *The Zen Master Hakuin: Selected Writings* is one of the Translations from the Oriental Classics by which the Committee on Oriental Studies has sought to transmit to Western readers representative works of the major Asian traditions in thought and literature. Our intention is to provide translations based on scholarly study but written for the general reader rather than primarily for other specialists.

Of the major traditions of Oriental thought Chinese and Japanese Buddhism is the least well represented by competent translations, despite the quantity of secondary writing on the subject. Professor Yampolsky has already contributed importantly to filling this gap by his translation of the *Platform Sutra of the Sixth Patriarch*, a basic text of the early Ch'an (Zen) school. The present work is of a quite different sort, representing the more fully developed and authenticated Zen tradition in Japan. Hakuin is probably the leading figure in the history of Japanese Rinzai Zen, and the man most responsible for the flourishing of the school into modern times.

The selections given here are also quite in contrast to the earlier "scripture" attributed to the Sixth Patriarch, which invokes his authority in doctrinal matters and sectarian disputes. Hakuin's letters are rather an intimate revelation of his personal religious experience. This difference, however, has not necessarily made the translator's work any easier. Much of the meaning is implicit, not explicit, and cannot be determined with certainty. Therefore we owe much thanks to Professor Yampolsky for his willingness to undertake the often hazardous task of interpreting these texts for Western readers.

Wm. Theodore de Bary

✿ PREFACE

✿ The translations offered here are meant to serve as a general introduction to Hakuin. They are not intended, as the lack of detailed annotation will indicate, to represent an exhaustive study of the man and his works. In selecting material for translation I have been guided by several factors. Those works of a technical character, designed primarily for Zen students, were eliminated at once as requiring too much explanatory apparatus to be of interest to the general reader. While many of Hakuin's shorter pieces have gained considerable popularity in Japan, they are often written in imitation of songs and recitations current in the author's time, and are thus dull and repetitious when rendered into English. I have thus confined myself to the translation of three pieces that consist of letters to various acquaintances of Hakuin. Although composed in an epistolary style, they are in effect sermons, dealing primarily with Zen.

Hakuin has up to now been studied neither by Buddhist specialists nor by students of the language and literature of his period, so that my translations suffer from the absence of scholarly works to which I might have turned for assistance. Hakuin writes in an exceptionally difficult style and there are many places where the translation must be regarded as tentative. In addition, he quotes freely from canonical texts and from other writers. Very frequently his quotations are in error or are very vaguely identified. I have made no exhaustive attempt to identify these quotations; when the source is fairly readily obtainable, I have supplied the information, but when this is not the case, I have so indicated or left the quotations unannotated.

Hakuin's works have appeared in numerous popular editions; however these are usually very lightly edited and annotated, if at all. I have found the version known as *Hakuin zenji shū*, edited by Tokiwa Daijō in the *Dai-Nihon bunko* series (Tokyo, 1938) to be by far the most reliable, and have depended largely on the texts as given there. Readers familiar with Zen in English translation may note the failure to refer to R. D. M. Shaw, *The Embossed Tea Kettle* (London, 1963). I have not found this work of sufficient accuracy to justify reference to it.

I have used the following rules in transliterating proper names, book titles, and technical terms: names of Chinese monks and other figures mentioned in the text are given in Chinese romanization, with Japanese readings for those prominent in Buddhism provided in the notes; in the introduction I give the Chinese reading with the Japanese in parentheses; in the main body of the text names of Buddhas and bodhisattvas are given in Japanese romanization (examples: Shakamuni, Amida, Birushana); names of Indian figures other than Buddhas and bodhisattvas are rendered in Sanskrit romanization; Buddhist terms mentioned in the text are given in their romanized Japanese reading, except for Sanskrit terms that have been adopted into English; names of books are in the romanized language of the original with the exception of those commonly known by their English titles.

The preparation of these translations has been made possible in part by a contract with the United States Department of Health, Education, and Welfare, under the provisions of Title IV, Public Law 85–864, as amended, Section 602. I am much indebted to Mr. Kazuhiro Furuta of Kyoto and to Professor Seizan Yanagida of Hanazono University for their kindness in answering numerous questions, and to the Reverend Jōgaku Fukutani for her helpful suggestions. My colleague Professor Yoshito Hakeda, and Professor Abe Masao have read portions of the manuscript and have furnished important advice. The editing of the manuscript was in the hands of Miss Anita Feldman of the Columbia University Press. Her care, patience, and meticulousness have eliminated numerous errors and inconsistencies and her insistence on a more elaborate explanation of various historical and technical details has been of great assistance to my work. My wife Yuiko has been of extensive help to me in unraveling the complexities of Hakuin's syntax. Were it not for her assistance, many more errors than are now present would have found their way into the translation. For whatever mistakes in translation and interpretation remain, I must bear the responsibility.

Philip B. Yampolsky

❋ CONTENTS

✸ ABBREVIATIONS

HOZ   *Hakuin oshō zenshū*. Tokyo, 1967. 8 vols. Reprint edition.

HZS   *Hakuin zenji shū*. Edited by Tokiwa Daijō, Tokyo, 1938 (*Dai-Nihon bunko: Bukkyō hen*).

T   *Taishō shinshū dai-zōkyō*. Tokyo, 1914–1922. 85 vols.

ZD   *Zen Dust*, by Miura Isshū and Ruth Sasaki. Kyoto, 1966.

ZZ   *Dai-Nihon zoku-zōkyō*. Kyoto, 1905–1912. 750 vols.

THE ZEN MASTER HAKUIN

INTRODUCTION:
HAKUIN AND
RINZAI ZEN

❀ The mid-Tokugawa period priest Hakuin is known as the reviver of Rinzai Zen. All present-day Rinzai Masters trace themselves to him. The system developed by Hakuin and his disciples, their approach toward Zen as a school of Buddhism, and their procedures for mastering it, constitute the Zen of the Rinzai monasteries of today. Hakuin based his teaching on that of the Sung Master Hsü-t'ang Chih-yü (Kidō Chigu, 1185-1269), as transmitted to Japan, maintaining in his school of Zen the Sung Master's emphasis on koan study and on a lifelong devotion to Zen practice.

In order to elucidate the role that Hakuin played in the revivification of this school of Zen, it is necessary to trace briefly the history and development of Zen in Japan. For present purposes we may ignore the several recorded instances of the introduction of Zen teachings during the Nara and Heian periods and turn our attention to the Zen of the Kamakura period.

Zen tradition speaks of twenty-four schools and of forty-six transmissions of Zen to Japan.[1] This traditional classification is of relatively late date, and it certainly does not include the names of all the monks who traveled between China and Japan. It does include Japanese monks who went to China to study and Chinese monks, largely refugees from the Mongol invaders, who brought their teachings to Japan. Not all of these schools and transmissions

[1] For a discussion of the origins and developments of this tradition, see Ogisu Jundō, "Nihon Zenshū nijūshi-ryū shiden kō," *Nihon Bukkyō gakkai nempō*, no. 21 (1955), pp. 273-89.

founded schools of Zen in Japan, since some of their monks remained in retirement; but the others, for longer or shorter periods, played a significant role in the Zen of Japan. This brief introduction cannot provide in full detail the complicated story of these various transmissions, but some discussion of them is essential to our understanding of the process whereby Zen developed, grew, declined, and was revived in Japan.

It is customary for Japanese historians to assign the initial introduction of Zen to Eisai (1141–1215)[2] because he was the first to found a Zen temple. A Tendai monk, Eisai first visited China in 1168 on a brief trip to the holy places of his school of Buddhism. In 1186 he set out again for a lengthier stay, returning in 1191 with the sanction of the Rinzai Master Hsü-an Huai-ch'ang (Kian Eshō). In 1194 he attempted to found a Zen temple in Kyoto, but was officially forbidden to do so as a result of pressure exerted by the traditional Buddhist schools, chiefly the Tendai center at Mount Hiei.[3] He did, however, found a temple devoted to Zen in Kyushu, and later, under the patronage of the Kamakura military government, established temples in that city and in Kyoto. It would be a mistake, however, to consider Eisai as anything more than the founder of temples at which Zen was taught. He was primarily a Tendai man, whose objective seems to have been to restore the Tendai school to its earlier religious eminence in Japan and to revive a strict adherence to Buddhist precepts. Of the many books he wrote only one is devoted to Zen; the rest largely concern Tendai and its esoteric aspects. The Yōjō-ryū, the school that he established, is strictly in the Tendai tradition, although the teaching at the temples he founded combined Tendai esoteric doctrines and Zen. His disciples, too, all taught a combination of Tendai esotericism and Zen.[4]

At the same time that Eisai was propagating Zen teachings along with those of the Tendai, another monk originally from Hiei-zan was active in promoting a Zen school. This man, Dainichi Nōnin (no dates), was a self-enlightened Zen Master.

---

[2] His name is perhaps more properly read Yōsai.

[3] *Hyakurenshō*, 10 (*Kokushi taikei* [Tokyo, 1931], 11, 125).

[4] Eisai's position in Japanese Zen is excellently described in Yanagida Seizan, *Rinzai no kafu* (Tokyo, 1967), pp. 5–91.

To defend his teaching from charges of illegitimacy, he sent two of his disciples to China with a written presentation of his understanding of Zen. This was acknowledged by a prominent Sung Rinzai Master, who sent portraits, verse, and a statement in praise of Nōnin in return. The pressures that led to the banning of Eisai's Zen in 1194 affected Nōnin's teachings as well, and it is probable that his school had at one time a considerable influence. Indeed, when Nichiren in his *Kaimokushō* complains that Pure Land and Zen doctrines are flooding the country, he specifically condemns the Pure Land teachings of Hōnen and the Zen doctrines of Nōnin.[5] Nōnin's school, referred to as *Nihon Daruma-shū* by others, was later propagated by Nōnin's disciple Kakuan at a monastery at Tōnomine in present-day Nara Prefecture. The school did not last for long, as its buildings were twice burned by monks associated with the old sects in Nara. Significantly, a large number of the disciples of this school later joined the group that developed into the Sōtō school of Zen in Japan. Among them was Koun Ejō (1198–1280), later to become the Second Patriarch of the Japanese Sōtō Sect.

The first to teach a representative Zen school of the Sung period was the famous Dōgen (1200–1253).[6] Originally associated with the Tendai Sect, he studied in China, returning to Japan in 1227. He had received his instruction under a Master associated with the Ts'ao-t'ung or Sōtō school. The numerous teachers of Zen who were active in China at that time differed in methods of instruction, emphasis, and involvement with literary and political enterprises, but the distinction so clearly marked now in Japan between Rinzai and Sōtō as separate religious sects was scarcely in evidence. Dōgen was sharply critical of much of the Zen he encountered in China, and it was not until he met a strict teacher, T'ien-t'ung Ju-ching (Tendō Nyojō, 1163–1228), who was committed to a traditional style of Zen, that he found himself temperamentally at home. The precise details of Dōgen's four years under Ju-ching are not known, but it must be presumed that it involved

[5] T84, p. 232b.

[6] For a brief discussion of Nōnin's school and its relationship with Dōgen's group, see Ōkubo Dōshū, "Dōgen Zenji no genshi sōdan to Nihon Daruma-shū to no kankei," *Dōgen Zenji kenkyū* (Tokyo, 1941), pp. 77–125.

a large amount of the koan study that marked Sung Zen. Dōgen himself later compiled a collection of three hundred koans,[7] and it is probable that he used them to a certain extent in his teaching.

For various reasons, largely concerned with internal doctrinal disputes in the Sōtō Sect, Dōgen's major work, the *Shōbō genzō*, received only very limited distribution over the centuries. It was guarded as a secret treasure and was distributed only in a very limited form in manuscript; several variant manuscript versions of the work exist. So efficient were Sōtō Sect authorities in protecting it from public view that they were able to ban the printing of this work from 1722 until 1796.[8] In 1796 the publication of the 95-chapter version was begun and it was not completed until 1811. Although several Tokugawa-period Sōtō scholars studied the teachings and praised the founder of the school, appreciation of Dōgen's position in the history of Japanese thought has had to wait for twentieth-century scholarship.

When Dōgen returned from China in 1227 he sought at once to establish a temple devoted solely to the propagation of Buddhism by the Zen method in which he had been trained. But he made no attempt to found a Sōtō school; this was the work of his descendants. Finding the atmosphere of Kyoto not conducive to his aims, Dōgen transferred his activities to the remote area of Fukui where he established a monastery in 1243. Here he devoted himself to the strict instruction of his disciples. But with the premature death of Dōgen the group lost its focus and internal conflicts led to a split. Dōgen's followers soon introduced such esoteric elements as prayers and incantations into the teaching.[9] By the time of the Fourth Patriarch, Keizan Jōkin (1268–1325), Sōtō Zen was no longer centered in Fukui, but had begun to spread throughout the country.[10] As the years passed Sōtō became

[7] The authenticity of this collection has been a subject of debate, but has recently been established. See ZD, pp. 198–99.

[8] See Yokozeki Ryōin, *Edo jidai Tōmon seiyō* (Tokyo, 1938), p. 909.

[9] For the influence of Shingon Buddhism on the early Japanese Sōtō Masters see Kōchi Eigaku, "Keizan Zenji no Mikkyōteki hairyo to sono raiyu," *Shūgaku kenkyū* no. 2 (1960), pp. 42–49.

[10] The spread of Sōtō Buddhism is described in Suzuki Taizan, "Sōtō Zen no gufu to sono gegosha," *Kokumin seikatsushi kenkyū* (Tokyo, 1960), IV, 223–76. Suzuki has written several other works on the subject.

one of the great proselytizing sects, together with the Shin and Nichiren schools. It continued to include much borrowed from esoteric Buddhism and directed its efforts toward founding temples and converting the farmers and the populace in general.

The thirteenth and fourteenth centuries saw the gradual growth of Rinzai Zen in Kamakura and Kyoto. Many of the Japanese monks who went to China came from a Tendai or Shingon background and on their return advocated a Zen that contained esoteric elements. Others brought back with them a strict Sung koan Zen. Many of the Chinese monks who arrived demonstrated a literary proclivity that was prominent in some Sung schools. Because of the difficulty in communication between the Chinese and Japanese most instruction was carried on in writing, and this practice further contributed to the literary emphasis characteristic of these schools. All the Zen that arrived at this time was of the Rinzai school, with the exception of that brought by two Sōtō monks;[11] these monks made no effort, however, to found their own schools, and instead associated themselves with Rinzai temples in Kyoto. Zen monks soon gained the patronage of both the Imperial Court and the Shogunate in Kamakura and later in Kyoto, allowing them to escape the pressures exerted by the established schools of Buddhism.

Monks moved frequently between Kamakura and Kyoto, yet in this early period of Japanese Zen a certain difference is already discernible between the Zen of the two cities. That introduced to Kyoto was more apt to be mixed with esoteric doctrines which would appeal to the well-educated courtiers. Prominent among the monks centered in Kyoto were Enni Ben'en (Shōitsu Kokushi, 1202–1280) and another famous monk, Shinchi Kakushin (Hattō Kokushi, 1207–1298) who founded a temple in Wakayama but had frequent contact with the Kyoto court. Both of these men combined Zen with esoteric doctrines, Shinchi adding Pure Land elements as well. The situation in Kamakura was somewhat different; a large number of the monks who went there were refugees from China. Because of the very significant language barrier, and because their converts were largely found among the more poorly educated warriors, the

[11] Tung-ming Hui-jih (Tōmyō E'nichi, 1273–1340) and Tung-ling Yung-yü (Tōryō Yōyo, d. 1365).

Chinese monks had to adapt their koan teaching to a form more suitable to their new Japanese believers. Prominent among these Chinese monks were Lan-hsi Tao-lung (Rankei Dōryū, 1213–1278) and Wu-hsüeh Tsu-yüan (Mugaku Sogen, 1226–1286).

Of most concern, however, to the story of Rinzai Zen in Japan is the school founded by Nampo Jōmyō (Daiō Kokushi, 1235–1309). It is this school to which Hakuin traces his lineage; it is this school that Hakuin was to revive some five hundred years after it was introduced to Japan. Nampo began his studies under Lan-hsi in Kamakura, traveling to China in 1259, where he studied under Hsü-t'ang Chih-yü. On his return in 1267 he spent several years in Kamakura and some thirty years in Kyushu. Later he spent considerable time in Kyoto and ended his days in Kamakura. Nampo's teachings seem to have followed quite faithfully those of his Chinese Master. He emphasized the koans and did not add extraneous elements derived from other Buddhist schools, as was often the practice among his contemporaries. Of Nampo's many disciples, the best known was his successor Shūhō Myōchō (Daitō Kokushi, 1282–1338). Shūhō never attempted to go to China; he devoted himself to study under his Master in Japan. Shūhō attempted to follow the traditions of the famous T'ang Masters, and after completing his training lived for many years in retirement before emerging as a teacher. A strict disciplinarian, he was probably the first to organize a systematic program of koan study in Japan. He founded a temple, the Daitoku-ji, in Kyoto, and his heir Kanzan Egen (Musō Daishi, 1277–1360), the founder of another temple, the Myōshin-ji, continued his tradition. This school of Zen became known as the Ō-Tō-Kan school[12] and it persisted throughout the vicissitudes of the following centuries. Its teachings are preserved today in the Zen of Hakuin.

Zen had received strong support from the Hōjō family in Kamakura, and although the ascendancy of the family was destroyed in 1333, Zen continued to gain popularity with the Kyoto court and the Ashikaga shoguns. The most famous of the

[12] The name Ō-Tō-Kan derives from a contraction of the names of the three early leaders of the school—Daiō Kokushi (Nampo Jōmyō), Daitō Kokushi (Shūhō Myōchō), and Kanzan Egen.

Zen Masters of the early Muromachi period was Musō Soseki (Shōkaku Kokushi, 1275–1351). Musō, who also had an early background in esoteric Buddhism, studied under a number of Zen teachers in Kyoto and Kamakura. As did Shūhō, he lived in retirement during his early years, but later emerged to become one of the most active of Zen masters. He is credited with having converted seven emperors to Zen, and, extending his influence from religion to governmental matters, he actively encouraged the Ashikaga shoguns in their trade relations with the continent. In his teaching Musō sought to combine Zen with the esoteric doctrines.

The school founded by Musō and his disciples became intimately involved in what is known as the *Gozan bungaku* movement, or the "Literature of the Five Mountains." The Hōjō regents had, in imitation of the Sung temple system, set up in order of rank five temples or "mountains," with ten subsidiary temples, in both Kamakura and Kyoto. This was a complicated method of assigning rank and priority to the many Zen temples in the two cities. This system, with many internal shifts and changes, was continued by the Ashikaga shoguns. All the different schools of Zen became involved, to a greater or lesser degree, with the literary movement associated with this system of temple ranking. Later the literature that flourished in the temples of these schools came to be known as *Gozan bungaku.*

The enormous literature of Zen in both China and Japan is almost exclusively a literature designed to explicate the teaching of Zen specifically and of Buddhism as a whole. The Literature of the Five Mountains, however, represents a departure from this pattern. Musō was himself quite aware of the dangers to Zen which were present in this literary trend. In a piece known as *Sanne-in yuikai* he warns:

I have three grades of disciples: those who devote themselves to casting aside the myriad circumstances and investigate their own selves alone are of the highest grade; those whose practice is not pure and who are fond of all sorts of studies are of the middle grade; those who of themselves darken the luminescence of their own spirits and relish merely the spittle of the Buddhas and the Patriarchs are of the lowest grade. Those who befuddle their minds in non-Buddhist works and devote their efforts to literary endeavors are nothing but shaven-headed laymen and are not fit to be classed even with those of the lowest grade.[13]

If one can judge by later developments in Gozan literature, it would appear that in spite of Musō's strictures against those who devoted themselves to literary endeavors, it was the "shaven-headed laymen" who came to dominate Zen in the Muromachi period. The monks in the temples were all poets and literary figures. The poetry they dealt with was all written in Chinese and was of a highly pedantic and unimaginative type requiring extensive study to master its elaborate rules. The Zen gardens gained in popularity; art objects were imported from China and Korea; Chinese poetry, historical works, and Neo-Confucian texts were studied. Education was virtually in Zen hands. In the temples secret records of koan interviews, known as *missan-chō*,[14] were produced in abundance, and the use of koans, particularly those derived from the *Pi-yen lu*,[15] became a literary and educational device rather than a method for the practice of Zen. All schools of Zen became involved in these activities. The Zen priests were essentially poets and they began to leave the temples and enter into lay life. As the monks concerned themselves with worldly affairs, the lay world took more interest in Zen. But it was no longer a lay world of high-born courtiers and officials, for education was more generally available in the Muromachi period. The interest in poetry, art, theatre, and in the tea ceremony reflects this higher educational level more than it does an interest in Zen. Although the pervasive Zen atmosphere which surrounded

[13] Quoted in Yanagida, *Rinzai no kafu*, p. 188.
[14] Suzuki has published and discussed several of these works. See D. T. Suzuki, *Zen shisōshi kenkyū* (Tokyo, 1943), I, 291–376.
[15] The *Pi-yen lu*, known in Japan as the *Hekigan roku*, is a collection of a hundred lectures by Yüan-wu K'o-ch'in (Engo Kokugon, 1063–1135) on an earlier collection of koans. It was first printed in 1128 and was brought to Japan in the latter part of the Kamakura period. It soon gained great popularity and was used in all schools of Rinzai Zen

the arts had much to do with the activities of the monks in the temples, it had little to do with Zen as a teaching.[16]

It might not be too much of an exaggeration to say that when Zen flourishes as a teaching it has little to do with the arts and that when the teaching is in decline its association with the arts increases. To a certain extent this can be seen in the literary schools of Sung China. In Japan it is more evident. The traditional Zen schools of the T'ang, some of the Zen schools of the Sung, the Zen taught by Dōgen and the Ō-Tō-Kan school in Japan, and, as we shall see, the Zen of Hakuin, advocated a lifetime devotion to the study and practice of Zen. They taught that once one has gained the initial awakening, one must devote one's self to a continued practice and deepening of one's experience and understanding. There is no room for art here; there is no room for secular literature. The ultimate purpose of the Zen Master is one thing alone: to produce a disciple to carry on the teaching, be he a "whole man or half a man," as the Zen Masters express it, and thus to preserve the teaching.

The great artistic expression of the Muromachi and later periods shows a major concern for Zen. Yet at this time no Zen of the kind here described was being taught. In some of the things Zen Buddhism teaches, with the methods it uses, and the intensity of its discipline and practice, there are elements that appeal to the Japanese artistic temperament. But the type of Zen in which this temperament found sustenance was one that was scarcely representative of traditional Zen Buddhist teaching. There were, however, individual Zen monks of great stature who left their marks in this period of the history of Japanese Zen. Among them Ikkyū Sōjun (1394–1481) is perhaps the most celebrated. Hakuin himself was lavish in his praise of this monk, stating that in Ikkyū's time Zen had yet to decline. Yet Ikkyū has always been regarded as a Zen eccentric, a literary figure who virtually rejected the monastic disciplines, and about whom many legends and anecdotes have been handed down. Furthermore, it is perhaps significant that Ikkyū left no heirs to continue his teaching.

[16] For an excellent discussion of the Zen of this period, see Yanagida, *Rinzai no kafu*, pp. 184–97.

The fifteenth century saw a succession of civil disorders that culminated in the Ōnin Wars of 1467–1477. Kyoto was destroyed and the great temples with it. With the destruction of the religious establishments in Kyoto, Rinzai Zen began to move throughout the country and temples associated with Gozan Bungaku schools came to be founded. Perhaps the most active main temple in this respect was the Myōshin-ji, which established branch temples in numerous localities. The sixteenth century saw continued warfare, until finally the country was brought to peace at the beginning of the seventeenth century. We hear little of Zen during this period, although the names of Zen Masters and monks still appear in the temple histories and lineage records.

Soon after the country was unified under the Tokugawa, the government adopted a policy of state support of Buddhism, with strict regulations governing the various schools. Whereas this contributed to the much-deplored degeneration of the Buddhist temples and monasteries, it also served to encourage intellectual studies and to turn the monks to a new examination and investigation of their religion. With the establishment of Edo as the eastern capital, there was a shift of religious focus from the Kansai district centered around the capital in Kyoto to the Kantō district in the east of Japan; there was also an increased activity throughout the whole country. Rinzai Zen, which had formerly directed its attention to the Kyoto court and the higher strata of society, turned now to the general populace for its support. There arose such teachers as Bankei Yōtaku (1622–1693) and Shidō Bu'nan (1603–1676), who preached a popular Buddhism, highly simplified and quite unrelated in terms of teaching method and content to the Zen that had preceded them. Zen was beginning to emerge from the Chinese influences that had dominated it and to acquire something of a Japanese tinge.

In 1654 Yin-yüan Lung-ch'i (Ingen Ryūki, 1592–1673) arrived in Japan, bringing with him a brand of Rinzai Zen that was colored with the accretions of Pure Land thought that had developed during the Ming dynasty. His arrival and the subsequent founding of the Ōbaku school served as a stimulus to the almost dormant Rinzai Zen of Japan. The well-known priest Gudō Tōshoku (1577–1661) indignantly refused to welcome

Yin-yüan at the Myōshin-ji, one of the few temples that actively continued a Rinzai tradition. The Myōshin-ji, of course, was associated with the Ō-Tō-Kan school of Zen. It is likely, however, that Yin-yüan came to Japan for the purpose of preserving what he believed to be the true Rinzai teaching, which was threatened in China by the invading Manchu hordes, and not to found a new sect of Zen.[17]

A monk by the name of Daishin Gitō (1657–1730), writing around 1680, declared that as of that time nineteen of the so-called twenty-four schools of Zen had vanished and that only five remained: those of Dōgen, Enni, Lan-hsi, Wu-hsüeh, and Nampo.[18] Of these five the Zen of Dōgen and that of Nampo and the Ō-Tō-Kan school, as handed down by Hakuin, are the only ones that survive today.

Hakuin makes his appearance in the mid-Tokugawa period. His biography is well known; however, it is based largely on Hakuin's own works, in many of which he describes his own career. His disciple Tōrei Enji (1721–1792) used much of this material in compiling a chronological account of his Master's life.[19] There is, however, very little corroborative evidence of any kind. Thus, we must take Hakuin's word, and his disciple's, for his career.

The lack of corroborative evidence may give rise to occasional reservations about the accuracy of some of the details, but not of the cumulative impression that the life of this remarkable man makes. His life was devoted primarily to the teaching and practice of Zen. It is in the tradition of the old T'ang Masters and of Japanese monks like Nampo. This tradition he handed down to his followers and it has persisted in Rinzai Zen monasteries. But while Hakuin returned to the strict koan study of the Sung period, he added new elements and began to organize his materials into a

[17] For a discussion of the content of Yin-yüan's Zen, see Furuta Shōkin, *Nihon Bukkyō shisōshi no sho-mondai* (Tokyo, 1964), pp. 165–73.

[18] Cited in Ogisu Jundō, "Nihon Zenshū nijūshi-ryū shiden kō," *Nihon Bukkyō gakkai nempō*, no. 21 (1955), p. 288.

[19] Hakuin's autobiography appears in *Itsumade gusa*, *Orategama*, and other works. For a collated edition of Tōrei's *Hakuin nempu*, which contains some material by Hakuin himself, see Rikukawa Taiun, *Kōshō Hakuin oshō shōden* (Tokyo, 1963), pp. 443–546.

course of study. While basing himself on a Chinese tradition, he created a living Zen that would be attractive to the Japanese. Furthermore, he put much emphasis on the propagation of a popular Buddhism for laymen, a Buddhism acceptable to ordinary farmers, as well as to high-born courtiers or officials. This popular Buddhism was at times quite unrelated to the strict Zen he taught his disciples.

Hakuin was born in 1686 to a commoner family of low status, in Hara, in present-day Shizuoka Prefecture. He was a Kantō man (that is, he came from an eastern district closer to Edo than to Kyoto), and although he turned back to Kyoto Zen for his teaching, he remained always an independent, active proponent of the popular-type, mass-appeal Buddhism that had arisen in Edo with such men as Shidō Bu'nan and Suzuki Shōsan (1579–1655). At an early age he turned to Buddhism, although he describes a period when he lost his faith in its efficacy and devoted himself to secular literature. This period is reflected in his voluminous writings in both Chinese (*kambun*) and Japanese, which demonstrate his wide knowledge of Chinese literature and the various popular Japanese genres of the time. At the age of twenty-two he set out to pursue his studies in earnest, visiting various temples and gaining what he believed to be a degree of awakening. Toward the end of his twenty-fourth year he visited the Zen Master Shōju Rōjin (Dōkyō Etan, 1642–1721). Shōju was the heir of Shidō Bu'nan, who was in turn the heir of Gudō Tōshoku. Gudō was in the Myōshin-ji tradition and traced his Zen ancestry to Kanzan, Shūhō, and Nampo. Hakuin stayed with Shōju only eight months; all we know of this Zen Master we know from Hakuin, who quotes him extensively. Hakuin most probably did not receive Shōju's sanction[20] of his understanding of Zen; he himself writes that it was not until much later that he awakened to the import of Shōju's teaching. Hakuin never visited Shōju again; nor did he make mention in his writings of his con- nection with Shōju until after the latter's death. It is nevertheless

---

[20] In an inscription erected at Shōju's temple by Tōrei, the latter states that Hakuin, among others, received Shōju's sanction. This, however, is not very impressive evidence. For the text of this inscription, see Rikukawa, *Kōshō Hakuin oshō shōden*, p. 42.

accepted that Hakuin was Shōju's heir, and thus of the Ō-Tō-Kan line of transmission.[21]

After leaving Shōju Hakuin wandered about from temple to temple, practicing and perfecting his Zen. When he was thirty-two he returned to his temple, the Shōin-ji in his native town of Hara. Here he devoted himself to teaching a growing band of disciples. He frequently traveled about Japan, using the donations he received for preaching and lecturing to print the large number of works he composed and to support the disciples who studied under him. He passed away in January of 1769.

Whatever suspicions one may entertain about the authenticity of Hakuin's lineage, these have little bearing on the type of Zen he taught. Hakuin insisted that, for Zen meditation practice, the practitioner must have three basic qualities: an overriding faith, a great doubt when facing the koans, and a strong aspiration and perseverance. The student's first task was to see into his own true nature (kenshō). To this end Hakuin championed the *Mu* koan and later in his life the *Sekishu no onjō*, the "Sound of the Single Hand," a koan which he himself devised.[22] The method by

---

[21] Some of the questions raised above (and many others) are found in an extraordinary book, *Gendai sōji-Zen hyōron*, by Fukunaga Shūho (Tokyo, 1926). The work is a polemic attack on Hakuin and his school, filled with unsubstantiated charges and accusations. Contained are detailed answers and other materials relating to all the koans used in the Hakuin school. The book has been unofficially suppressed and copies are very hard to obtain.

[22] Both the *Mu* and the Sound of the Single Hand koans are given as subjects for meditation to the beginning student once he has mastered the initial meditation techniques. In the *Mu* koan, which itself is a Zen story beginning with the passage: "A monk asked Chao-chou, 'Does a dog have Buddha-nature?' Chao-chou answered, '*Mu!*'" the practitioner is required to meditate (always under the guidance of his teacher) until he arrives at the state in which, in Hakuin's own words, "within his heart there is not the slightest thought or emotion, only the single word *Mu*" (see Translation, "Orategama zokushū," p. 144). This koan is found in the famous collection *Wu-men kuan* (Mumonkan in Japanese, T48, 292–99), first printed in 1228. The collection gained great popularity in Japan and the koans it contains are widely used in Zen study. The Sound of the Single Hand was devised by Hakuin himself. He describes it and expounds its value in *Yabukōji* (see Translation, pp. 163 ff). For a discussion of the history of the koan, see ZD, pp. 3–32. For an outline of the organization and progression of koan study, see also ZD, pp. 35–76.

which koans are to be solved is, of course, by disciplined *zazen*, or meditation sitting, accompanied by private interviews with the teacher (*sanzen*), in which the Master gives guidance and eventually sanction to the student's understanding of a particular koan. But this is only the first step. In his *Yasen kanna* Hakuin quotes the famous Sung Master Ta-hui Tsung-kao (Daie Sōkō, 1089–1163) as having stated that he had experienced eighteen great awakenings and an uncountable number of small ones during his lifetime.[23] Thus, once the initial awakening has been obtained, the student must go on with the practice after awakening. This unremitting practice is, in effect, the koan system.

It is difficult to obtain an exact picture of the early role of the koans in Japan. We know that they were used by Shūhō Myōchō (Daitō Kokushi), for a koan collection compiled by him remains.[24] Surely they played a significant role in the teachings of the early Zen Masters who came from China. That koans were used throughout the Muromachi and Momoyama periods is demonstrated by the many records of koan interviews (*missanchō*) that remain. Exactly how they were used or in what number is not certain, but records indicate a system of approximately three hundred koans, centering around the *Pi-yen lu* koan collection. Reference is found to a system involving the study of one hundred koans before beginning the *Pi-yen lu* (*hekizen*), then the hundred koans in the *Pi-yen lu*, and a hundred koans after the *Pi-yen lu* (*hekigo*). It is unclear just what this system involved, and the "hundred koans" in each instance appears to be an approximate number.[25] Also involved was the custom of requiring the student to add verse comments, drawn mainly from Chinese poetry, indicating his understanding of a particular koan. This custom was maintained, in a modified form, in the Zen taught by Hakuin.

With the spread of the Rinzai schools throughout the country there came a tendency to devise a form that would have a greater popular appeal. This type of Zen made little use of the koan and

[23] HOZ5, 364.

[24] *Daitō Kokushi hyakunijissoku.* A reproduction of a manuscript edition under this title was published by D. T. Suzuki (Tokyo, 1944).

[25] For a discussion see D. T. Suzuki, *Zen shisōshi kenkyū*, I, 296–303.

at times even rejected it. It was against this kind of Zen that Hakuin revolted, at least in terms of its suitability for the practicing monk. Although Hakuin devoted considerable effort, particularly in his writings, toward the lay world, for the monastery environment he insisted on a strict and lengthy term of study, centering on the koan.

The exact details of the koan system Hakuin used are not clearly known. As mentioned earlier, it emphasized the use of the *Mu* koan and later the Sound of the Single Hand for the initial awakening, with an intensive program of koan study for the practice after awakening. This program was later organized by Hakuin's disciple Tōrei and by the latter's disciples Inzan Ien (1751–1814) and Takuju Kōsen (1760–1833) into a formalized system of koan study. There are variations in the methods used by Inzan and Takuju, but essentially they are compatible. The programs of study require a progression through a specified series of koans. Frequently the order and type of the koan will vary. As the student's understanding advances, koans investigated at an earlier stage may be investigated again, until eventually those few who survive the intensive, rigorous, and exhausting course of study are themselves sanctioned as teachers. Then follows a period of several years' self-imposed isolation until the student is ready to emerge as a teacher.

In addition to the formal meditation, the practitioner is required, together with the body of monks, to live in an extremely regulated monastic atmosphere, with set rules for proper procedure in all his activities. An important feature of the monk's life is the work period in which the temple buildings and grounds are cared for, vegetables grown, and other tasks accomplished. This work, as Hakuin conceived it, was a part of the koan study. Thus he emphasized practice in the midst of activity, be it in the work of the temple or in the bustle of the lay world. In *Orategama* we read:

I am not trying to tell you to discard completely quietistic meditation and to seek specifically for a place of activity to carry on your practice. What is most worthy of respect is a pure koan meditation that neither knows nor is conscious of the two aspects, the quiet and the active.

This is why it has been said that the true practicing monk walks but does not know he is walking, sits but does not know he is sitting.

For penetrating to the depths of one's own true self-nature and for attaining a vitality valid on all occasions, nothing can surpass meditation in the midst of activity.[26]

Producing a disciple to carry on the teaching has always been an essential requirement of Zen. The lineages of many famous monks throughout the history of the school have become extinct after a generation or two because they had no disciples to hand down their teachings. In the Ming edition of the *Ching-te ch'uan-teng lu* a famous passage in the biography of Po-chang reads: "He whose view is equal to that of his teacher diminishes by half his teacher's power. He whose view exceeds that of his teacher is qualified to transmit the teaching."[27] Hakuin was very much aware of the need to produce such a disciple and he did, in fact, sanction several. Frequently he alludes to this need in his writings; the following passage from *Orategama* illustrates Hakuin's awareness of the necessity to train a disciple, despite the great difficulty of producing one "qualified to transmit the teaching."

Attaching to his arm the supernatural talisman that wrests life from death, he lets reverberate in his mouth the talons and teeth of the Cave of the Dharma, smashes the brains of monks everywhere, and pulls out the nails and knocks out the wedges. Without the least human feeling he produces an unsurpassedly evil, stupid, blind oaf, be it one person or merely half a person, with teeth sharp as the sword trees of hell and a gaping mouth like a tray of blood. Thus will he recompense his deep obligation to the Buddhas and the Patriarchs.[28]

Here the Master, armed with spiritual powers and techniques to instruct others, produces a splendid disciple, described, with typical Zen irony, as an "evil, stupid, blind oaf."

Hakuin recognizes the need for a Buddhism directed toward the people in general. Although his chief preoccupation was with the monks who were studying under him, he also showed a major concern for the common people, as well as for the spiritual

---

[26] See Translation, "Orategama I," p. 33–34.   [27] T51, p. 249, n. 27.
[28] See Translation, "Orategama I," p. 39.

welfare of the feudal lords and their retainers. He addressed works to each of these three groups. Directed toward the monks are books designed principally as aids to their study: *Kaian koku go* contains verse comments on the *Daitō-roku* [Record of Daitō]; the *Sokkō-roku kaien fusetsu* consists of lectures on the *Hsü-t'ang-lu* [Record of Hsü-t'ang]; the *Keisō dokuzui* comprises Hakuin's own recorded sayings, in the traditional style of such works; other books are chiefly autobiographical statements designed to encourage his students.[29]

His advice to various feudal lords makes up much of his writing. This advice is given in letter form, with the same passages often repeated in two or more letters. When printed, several letters are usually grouped together under various titles, generally the names of unpretentious plants and flowers. Not all of these letters, however, are addressed to feudal lords; two in the well-known *Orategama* are directed toward a nun of the Hoke (Nichiren) Sect and an ailing priest. Much of the material contained in them deals with the efficacy of the Zen Hakuin preaches, but some works are cautionary expositions on the functions of a good ruler, conventionally Confucian in tone. He advocates a humane government and the proper treatment of the farmers. But no matter what the principal subject of the letter may be, Hakuin invariably adds passages extolling the virtues of his own school of Buddhism. The advice he gives is often praiseworthy, but one wonders how the wealthy young lord of Okayama Castle reacted on being told to abandon his income of a million *koku* and the luxuries of his mansion, and to "clean up the garden, change the water in the basins, and with a laughing face wash the feet of your retainers' horses."[30]

At other times Hakuin, in an effort to encourage his audience, makes statements to which he himself can scarcely give much credence. In *Orategama* he describes the advantage the warrior has over the monk in the practice of Zen:

A warrior must from the beginning to the end be physically strong. In his attendance on his duties and in his relationships with others the

---

[29] See Appendix for a listing of Hakuin's works.
[30] See Translation, "Hebiichigo II," p. 220.

most rigid punctiliousness and propriety are required. His hair must be properly dressed, his garments in the strictest order, and his swords must be fastened at his side. With this exact and proper deportment, the true meditation stands forth with an overflowing splendor. Mounted on a sturdy horse, the warrior can ride forth to face an uncountable horde of enemies as though he were riding into a place empty of people. The valiant, undaunted expression on his face reflects his practice of the peerless, true, uninterrupted meditation sitting. Meditating in this way, the warrior can accomplish in one month what it takes the monk a year to do; in three days he can open up for himself benefits that would take the monk a hundred days.[31]

Hakuin's concern with the common people is indicated by the large number of brief pieces, written in imitation of popular songs or modeled on popular recitations of the day, that he composed. One curious practice that Hakuin strongly advocated for both commoner and samurai was the recitation of the *Emmei jikku Kannon gyō*, the "Ten-Phrase Kannon Sutra for Prolonging Life."[32] One lengthy chapter of his *Yaemugura* is devoted to a description of the miracles that the continuous recitation of this forty-two-character chant have performed. The stories are of the familiar *inga monogatari*, or "cause-and-effect-tale" type, and detail visits to hell, and miraculous escapes from the executioner's sword or from the wrath of an irate master. That they still have a currency in Rinzai Zen is illustrated by the fact that at least four different volumes of lectures on Hakuin's account of the miracles performed by this so-called sutra were published in the late 1920's and in the 1930's.[33] What is most surprising is that Hakuin seems to be advocating a practice quite similar to the *nembutsu*, or the concentrated calling of the name of Amida Buddha, of the Pure Land schools.[34] Hakuin was most vociferous in his denuncia-

---

[31] See Translation, "Orategama I," p. 69.

[32] For a discussion of this work, see Translation, "Hebiichigo I," fn. 16.

[33] See Komazawa Daigaku Toshokan, *Shinsan Zenseki mokuroku* (Tokyo, 1962), p. 166.

[34] The Pure Land schools advocated the constant recitation of the phrase *Namu Amida Butsu*, "reverence to Amida Buddha," coupled with a sincere faith in the power of Amida and a fervent desire to be reborn in his Pure Land to the West. Throughout his works Hakuin speaks of the Pure Land methods as

tion of this practice for students seeking enlightenment through Zen. It is clear, however, that the miracles he describes are concerned with benefits accruing in this world and do not involve salvation or enlightenment. The account translated below indicates the kind of story, completely unrelated to the teaching of Zen, that Hakuin found to possess a popular appeal.

Around the beginning of the Gembun era [1736–1740] the mansion of a great family stood to the east of the great bridge in a certain castle town. Among the maids who served in the sitting room of this mansion was a girl by the name of Oyano. Fifteen or sixteen years of age, she possessed a beauty and character so outstanding that others could scarcely be compared with her. The master of the house was greatly impressed and developed a fondness of considerable depth for her. But there was at the time a young man by the name of Satosuke who worked in the living quarters, and the two young people formed an attachment to each other. Unfortunately they became the subject of scandalous gossip by the other maids and servants, and this came to the notice of the master of the house. Enraged and resentful, he had Satosuke brought in for punishment.

Glaring in anger, he shouted: "This is a warrior's household and your conduct has been unspeakable. Prepare yourself to die at once!" Adjusting his garments, he loosened his sword and, approaching Satosuke from the rear, made ready to behead him.

Just at that moment the master's mother, who was close to seventy years of age, came rushing up, having heard of what was happening. In a loud voice she called: "Wait, wait! Are you mad? Today is the seventeenth day of the month; this is the anniversary of the Divine Ruler's death.[35] Don't you know that any warrior who carries out an important decision on this day is bound to be banished and will never be able to be at peace for the rest of his days? Stop what you have planned for today and put it off until tomorrow. If you don't your family will be disinherited for seven generations!"

---

suitable for people of inferior and mediocre talents. Traditional Zen, in which the practitioner must devote his own efforts to his own enlightenment, rejects the concept that it is possible to attain awakening by relying solely on another's (Amida Buddha's) power. See also below, fn. 38.

[35] Tokugawa Ieyasu died on the 17th day of the fourth month, Genna 2 (1616).

Reacting to her tears and scolding, the master scratched his head and responded: "All right then. But only for one day. I will let him live until tomorrow." Then he had Satosuke brought to the bath room where he was placed in the empty tub which was then covered up. He ordered his attendants to bring some fifty straw mats from the various rooms in the house and to pile them on top of the bathtub. Telling them to throw a bit of food in through the drain hole, he warned that if anyone should so much as lay a finger on the pile of fifty straw mats, he would suffer the same fate as Satosuke. Then scolding and screaming in a loud voice, he set out for an appointment at some nearby place.

The old mother had Oyano brought to her in secret and they crept into the bath room together. Peering into the drain hole, the old mother called to Satosuke: "You have only this evening left to live. There is nothing else but for you to die. Yet there is one thing alone that can save your life." Then she taught Oyano this very ten-phrase text [the *Emmei jikku Kannon gyō*], and asking her to recite it too, the three of them intoned it together. Satosuke had learned it some time before so that he was able to join his voice with theirs.

Then the old mother told Satosuke of the powers and virtue of this honored text.[36] She told of how in the past Akushichibyōe Kagekiyo had been able to break out of prison by its powers. She told of how Shume no hōkan Morihisa, already taken a prisoner in Kamakura, spent the night before his scheduled execution in a constant recitation of this text; on the morning of his execution the sword that was to be used to decapitate him broke off at the hilt. She told of Kao-huang who, when he was about to be executed, had swords substituted twice, because each time, as his head was about to be severed, they had broken, and how he was spared the death penalty and allowed to live. She pointed out that the emotions of Morihisa when he awakened from his dream [in which he had been instructed to recite the ten-phrase text] are still celebrated in song. She urged Satosuke that for that night he make each incoming and outgoing breath a recitation of this text. She assured him that if he raised the great vow to enter into Buddhism and recited with complete faith, a miracle was bound to

[36] The following are examples of people whose faith in the power of Kannon helped to spare their lives.

occur and that his life would be spared. And then, together with Oyano, the old mother left the bath room.

Thereupon Satosuke devoted all his efforts throughout the night to reciting this text. Strangely enough, at what he thought must have been toward the end of the hour of the ox, he heard a loud noise as though some one were inside the bath room. Peering through the drain hole, he saw a great huge mountain ascetic (*yamabushi*), some six feet tall, with a bright red face and flashing eyes. The yamabushi peered in at him and called out: "It's almost dawn. Watch out or your life will be lost! Stick your hand through the drain hole and I will pull you out."

While the yamabushi waited Satosuke tried all sorts of ways to figure out how he might push his hand through the hole, but contrive as he might, he could find no way to force it through an opening only one inch square. Thereupon the yamabushi, losing his temper, twisted his right arm, thrust it through the hole, and grasped Satosuke by his thin neck. Grunting mightily he pulled him through. Satosuke's neck and body were crushed and he passed away.

He had been dead for about two hours when, as if in a dream, a particularly cold sensation flooded him about the waist and from the hips down. When Satosuke regained consciousness, started to breathe again, and finally opened his eyes, he found that his body had become perfectly square and that he himself was lying in a long box one foot square, like a batch of seaweed gelatin in the store that has yet to be pushed out of its container. Looking far into the distance, he saw a hole about the size of a bean-curd cake cut in half. Trying to determine where he was, he finally realized that, of all places, he was in the drain box that carried the waste water from the kitchen of his master's mansion. Unconsciously he joined his palms, and while reciting the text, crawled along until unexpectedly he found himself at the opening to the drainage ditch that lay to the rear of the house.

Poking out his head stealthily, he saw to his left a large bridge, on which, strangely enough, stood the huge yamabushi who had peered at him through the drain hole in the bath room. The yamabushi was following after people who were passing by, and while reading petitions to the deities (*saimon*), was offering prayers and receiving in turn contributions of money. Once when the number of passersby had slackened for a moment, he glanced in the direction of the drainage exit, and seeing that someone was there, came running over. Looking at Satosuke, he asked him what he was doing in so strange a place. Satosuke, in tears, joined his palms together and explained what had happened to him. When the yamabushi heard his story, he extended his left arm and grabbing Satosuke by the neck, unceremoniously hauled him out of the drainpipe. Then the yamabushi took off his undergarments to make a rough slip-like gown for Satosuke to wear, put a hood over his head, an abbreviated surplice (*kesa*) about his neck, hung a conch horn at his hips, placed a priest's staff in his hands, and thus transformed Satosuke into an honest-to-goodness small-scale yamabushi priest.

Pushing aside the crowds of people, the yamabushi took Satosuke to the home of his chief, where all that had happened was explained in detail. Satosuke was told that it was all right to remain in hiding for ten or twenty days, but that a person after all had to eat and have clothes to wear, and needed a place to stay in this world. Therefore he was told to solicit alms surreptitiously. So that he might keep himself in food, he was told that he would be instructed in the use of written addresses to the deities. Satosuke bowed his head to the ground and acknowledged that he had incurred an unparalleled obligation and could never think of betraying the instructions of the yamabushi chief. He explained, however, that when his life had been in great peril he had vowed that for the rest of his life with every incoming and outgoing breath he would concentrate on the ten-phrase text. He requested that in place of the written addresses he be allowed to recite this text instead. When he was told that this was indeed a far better idea, without hesitation he shaved his head, changed his name to Chigen, put on the garments of the yamabushi, and set out to solicit alms in the streets.

Then, several days later, he came rushing back, trembling with fear and panting for breath, and threw himself down to hide in the shadows of a large Chinese chest. When asked what was the matter, he replied that as directed he had been soliciting alms stealthily in the alleys when, to his horror, his former master had unexpectedly discovered him. As soon as the master had spotted him, the man had loosened his sword, assumed a position to cut him down, and had stood there glaring in anger. Satosuke—now Chigen—had somehow managed to escape. Under the circumstances Chigen felt that this was scarcely a propitious neighborhood to be wandering about in, and he begged to be allowed, at least for the time being, to conceal himself in some distant province. He was in tears as he vowed to return when the time was right to fulfill his duties and repay his obligations. He swore that he would do so even should his body be ground to dust. He attributed his most recent escape to the power and virtue of the ten-phrase text.

It happened that at that time the director of the mountain ascetics (*Shūgendō*) in Ōshū was a certain teacher-priest. This priest, who received an income of two hundred to three hundred *koku*, had come recently to the capital and was just about to return to Ōshū. The yamabushi chief had for many years maintained a very close relationship with him. Taking along a host of followers, he paid a visit to the lodging-place of the priest. By a stroke of good fortune he had the opportunity, as soon as greetings were exchanged, to tell Chigen's story in detail. He explained that Chigen had at present no place to stay and that if he could accompany the priest back to Ōshū as a servant, it would not only save Chigen's life, but would also represent an action of unparalleled virtue by the priest. He was greatly pleased with the courteous way the story was put, and since four or five days before he had encountered some difficulties with his attendants that had inconvenienced him considerably, he was inclined to accede to the request and thereupon employed Chigen as his personal retainer.

On the journey to Ōshū Chigen recited the text night and day without cease, so impressing the priest that, on their return to his home province, he appointed Chigen to a position as a close retainer. Gradually he acquired a greater and greater affection for him.

The priest had an only daughter of exceptional beauty and superior qualities, who prided herself on her own attractions and took a dislike toward men. She was by now seventeen or eighteen but had yet to agree upon a husband who could be adopted into her family. She did, however, take note of Chigen's handsome appearance. The fact that he seemed to have been born with an exceptional intelligence in regard to everything caused her unexpectedly to develop a deep attachment toward him. Her mother, seeing that the girl neither spoke nor laughed and seemed to have lost her appetite, worried about her daughter and spoke to her husband about it. The priest was delighted and remarked that he too had noticed the same thing, but had been hesitant to speak of it because of his difficulty in assessing his daughter's feelings. The three of them discussed the matter and concluded that by adopting Chigen as his son, not only could the priest save his young servant from almost certain death, but unexpectedly he could ensure the maintenance of the family domains. All this was due to the power and virtue of the ten-phrase text.

Shortly afterwards Chigen came to Kyoto to receive the official post that had been the priest's. By good fortune, his way went by the home of the yamabushi chief who had been so good to him. He was able to present him with gifts of jewels and silks and they delighted in the opportunity to see each other again.

I heard this story some twenty years ago from an old priest who had returned to Edo. He reported that no trace remained of the mansion that belonged to Chigen's first master. I have, however, heard in detail of the home of the yamabushi chief, but being somewhat reticent about the matter, I have not written about it extensively here, but have only covered it in rough outline.[37]

Somewhat different in nature, and having an appeal both to intellectuals and to the populace in general, were the methods of nurturing health and prolonging life that Hakuin advocated. His *Yasen kanna* and certain portions of the *Orategama* are devoted to discussion of these matters. In these works he describes how, suffering from a Zen illness—presumably a nervous breakdown—he went at the age of twenty-nine to visit the hermit Hakuyū at Shirakawa north of Kyoto and there learned the methods for curing his disease. Among the methods advocated are the recitation of a specific formula and a form of inner contemplation, known as *naikan*, that at times seems very close to the practice of meditation in the midst of activity that he constantly champions. Hakuin insists that the best time to practice Zen is when one is ill, because when abed one is relieved of all the usual duties of daily life, and thus can give one's self to meditation practice. The chief reason to nurture one's health, according to Hakuin, is to attain a long life and thus have time to perfect one's Zen practice.

Hakuin was, for the most part, not critical of other forms of Buddhism. He praises men such as Genshin, Hōnen, Myōhen, and others, saying that the ultimate in their teachings is in no way

37 HOZ6, 66–74.

inferior to Zen. Hakuin, however, was highly critical of the Pure Land teaching that held that the world was in an era of degeneration and that man, lacking the capacity to seek enlightenment for himself, must rely on the Buddha Amida for salvation. While acknowledging the degeneracy of the times, Hakuin maintained that it was indeed still possible for man to gain enlightenment by his own efforts. Thus throughout his works he constantly insists that the Pure Land teaching is for men of inferior or mediocre talents, whereas Zen is directed toward those of superior capacities. A passage in the *Orategama zokushū*, the continuation or supplement to his *Orategama*, reveals his attitude.

In Zen it is as though giants were pitted against one another, with victory going to the tallest. In Pure Land it is as though midgets were set to fight, with victory going to the smallest. If the tallness of Zen were despised and Zen done away with, the true style of progress toward the Buddha mind would be swept away and destroyed. If the lowness of the Pure Land teachings were despised and cast aside, stupid, ignorant people would be unable to escape from the evil realms.[38]

Hakuin was violently opposed to methods of Zen other than his own, and throughout his works inveighs against what he describes as heretical Zen practices. The introduction of Pure Land elements into Zen incited him to particular wrath. He concentrated his invective on those of his contemporaries who combined Pure Land and Zen, as well as on the Ming monk Chu-hung, who was instrumental, he felt, in mixing the Pure Land and Zen schools. Of Chu-hung he says:

Then toward the end of the Ming dynasty there appeared a man known as Chu-hung from Yün-ch'i. His talents were not sufficient to tackle the mysteries of Zen, nor had he the eye to see into the Way. As he studied onward he could not gain the delights of Nirvana; as he retrogressed, he suffered from the terrors of the cycle of birth and

---

[38] See Translation, p. 142. It should be noted that Hakuin's comments on the Pure Land teaching did not go unanswered. A work known as *Tōdo yawa*, by a certain Injō and printed most likely in 1762, attacks the *Orategama zokushū*, pointing out various errors and misconceptions about the Pure Land and Hoke school teachings that Hakuin is said to have held.

death. Finally, unable to stand his distress, he was attracted to the memory of Hui-yüan's Lotus Society. He abandoned the "steepness" technique of the founders of Zen, and calling himself "the Great Master of the Lotus Pond," he wrote a commentary on the *Amitayus Sūtra*, advocated strongly the teachings relating to the calling of the Buddha's name, and displayed an incredibly shallow understanding of Zen.[39]

Hakuin on numerous occasions attacks *Mokushō Zen*, or "silent-illumination" Zen. The term is an old one in Zen literature,[40] but by the Sung period it was used to distinguish those schools that, although not rejecting the koan, emphasized a quietistic approach, in contrast to those that championed a systematic and active introspection of the koan (*Kanna Zen*). The Sung Master Ta-hui Tsung-kao used the term in a highly disparaging way to indicate that it represented a heterodox teaching. Hakuin uses *Mokushō Zen* in the same manner. Although he does not specify who these silent-illumination people are, he probably referred to some elements of both the Rinzai and Sōtō schools, to the followers of Bankei, and to anyone who sought to combine Pure Land and Zen. Hakuin does not specifically attack Sōtō Zen by name. Today the Sōtō school openly rejects the organized use of the koan as a teaching method, but this is most probably a fairly recent development, stemming perhaps from the latter half of the nineteenth century. In Hakuin's time Rinzai and Sōtō monks studied freely at temples of each others' schools, and a monk on pilgrimage was always free to visit any teacher he might choose. Hakuin himself practiced at a Sōtō temple and koans were used by both schools, although certainly not in the organized manner that Hakuin and his followers were to develop.

In conclusion, mention must be made of Hakuin's position as a painter and calligrapher. He produced a vast number of works that have largely remained unappreciated until modern times. His was not the refined Zen art of the Muromachi period;

[39] See Translation, p. 147–48.
[40] This term appears in an early eighth-century work, the *Leng-chia shih-tzu chi* (T85, p. 1290c).

it was the work of a simple and virtually untrained artist. He drew caricatures, delightful and amusing pictures—Kannon, for example, with the faces of his parishioners; he wrote out poems, Zen sayings and mottoes. They were the by-product of his activity as a Zen teacher and preacher, not the conscious efforts of a practicing artist. For the most part, Hakuin's drawings and calligraphic works were made at the specific request of parishioners and visitors, or were designed to serve as repayment for gifts that Hakuin or his temple had received.

Hakuin is the major figure in the history of Japanese Rinzai Zen. He revived a moribund school by returning to the Zen of the Sung period that had been established in Japan by Nampo Jōmyō (Daiō Kokushi) and Shūhō Myōchō (Daitō Kokushi). Yet he did not leave this Zen as he found it, but organized it into a course of study based on the koan. At the same time he injected Japanese elements into his teaching to provide for a popular Buddhism of wide appeal to monks and laymen as well, and trained disciples who further organized his teachings and developed them. Such was Hakuin's and his students' influence that his teachings soon dominated the Rinzai temples. As a result, in Japan today all teachers in the great monasteries of Rinzai Zen trace their religious heritage to Hakuin.

❀ ORATEGAMA[1]

I

Letter in reply to Lord Nabeshima,[2]
Governor of Settsu Province, sent in
care of a close retainer

❀ Yesterday I received your letter, delivered to me from afar. It must be a great relief to have successfully brought to a finish your entertainment of the Koreans.[3] Thank you for inquiring about my health: I am well as usual and you need not worry about me. I was most pleased to hear that you are devoting yourself unceasingly to koan meditation[4] in both its active and quietistic aspects. As for the other matters you touch upon in your letter, I find myself in complete agreement. You cannot imagine how delighted I am at your many accomplishments.

If their motivation is bad, virtually all Zen practitioners find themselves blocked in both the active and quietistic approaches to their practice of koan meditation. They fall into a state of severe depression and distraction; the fire mounts to the heart, the metal element[5] in the lungs shrinks painfully, the health generally

---

[1] The exact meaning of this title is unknown, as the postface to *Orategama zokushū* explains (HOZ5, 245). It is the name given to Hakuin's favorite tea kettle.

[2] Presumably this is Nabeshima Naotsune (1701–1749), who served as governor of Settsu (*Settsu no kami*) at the time of the writing of this letter (1748). Riku-kawa (*Kōshō Hakuin oshō shōden*, p. 178), identifies him as Nabeshima Ainao.

[3] A delegation of Koreans arrived in the spring of 1748. They were entertained with displays of horsemanship, military arts, and so forth, so we may assume that Nabeshima participated in the entertainments. See *Tokugawa jikki* (*Kokushi taikei*, 46, 454 ff.) for details of the preparations for this visit.

[4] *Kufū*. This term is used to indicate intensive meditation on a koan. ZD translates it tentatively as "reflective contemplation."

[5] The elements fire and metal are associated with the heart and lungs respectively.

declines, and quite frequently they develop an illness most difficult to cure. Yet if they polish and perfect themselves in the true practice of introspection,[6] they will conform to the secret methods for the ultimate nourishment,[7] their bodies and minds will become strong, their vitality great, and they will readily attain to enlightenment in all things.

Shakamuni Buddha taught this point in detail in the *Āgamas*.[8] Master Chih-i of Mount T'ien-t'ai has culled the import of these teachings and has kindly made them available to us in his *Mo-ho chih-kuan*.[9] The essential point brought out in this book is that, whether reading certain parts of the sacred teachings, whether examining the principles of the Dharma, whether sitting for long periods without lying down or whether engaged in walking practices throughout the six divisions of the day, the vital breath must always be made to fill the space between the navel and the loins.[10] Even though one may be hemmed in by worldly cares or tied down by guests who require elaborate attention, the source of strength two inches below the navel must naturally be filled with the vital breath, and at no time may it be allowed to disperse. This area should be pendulous and well rounded, somewhat like a new ball that has yet to be used. If a person is able to acquire this kind of breath concentration he can sit in meditation all day long without it ever tiring him; he can recite the sutras from morning to night without becoming worn out; he can write all day long without any trouble; he can talk all day without collapsing from

---

[6] *Naikan*. Although this term has a variety of technical meanings, particularly in Tendai Buddhism, Hakuin appears to use it strictly in terms of contemplation or introspection involving therapeutic benefits. Nevertheless, on occasion the term seems to reflect the practice of meditation in the midst of the activities of daily life, a practice that Hakuin strongly advocated.

[7] What the "secret methods for the ultimate nourishment" are is not precisely explained. Hakuin may well be referring to something such as the "soft butter pill" described later in the text (see "Orategama II," below, pp. 84–85).

[8] Hinayana scriptures in general.

[9] Chih-i (Chikai, 538–597) was the founder of the T'ien-t'ai (Tendai) school in China. One of his major works is the *Mo-ho chih-kuan* (T46, pp. 1–140).

[10] Hakuin uses the technical terms *kikai* and *tanden*. The *kikai* is considered to be the center of breathing and is located an inch and a half below the navel. The *tanden*, the center of strength, is two inches below the navel.

fatigue. Even if he practices good works day after day, there will still be no indications of flagging; in fact the capacity of his mind will gradually grow larger and his vitality will always be strong. On the hottest day of summer he will not perspire nor need he use a fan; on the snowiest night of deepest winter he need not wear socks (*tabi*) nor warm himself. Should he live to be a hundred years old his teeth will remain healthy and firm. Provided he does not become lax in his practices, he should attain to a great age. If a man becomes accomplished in this method, what Way cannot be perfected, what precepts cannot be maintained, what *samādhi* cannot be practiced, what virtue cannot be fulfilled!

If, however, you do not become proficient in these ancient techniques, if you have not made the essentials of the true practice your own, if by yourself you recklessly seek for your own brand of awakening, you will engage in excessive study and become entangled in inappropriate thoughts. At this time the chest and breathing mechanism become stopped up, a fire rises in the heart, the legs feel as though they were immersed in ice and snow, the ears are filled with a roaring sound like a torrent sounding in a deep valley. The lungs shrink, the fluids in the body dry up, and in the end you are afflicted with a disease most difficult to cure. Indeed you will hardly be able to keep yourself alive. All this is only because you do not know the correct road of true practice. A most regrettable thing indeed!

The *Mo-ho chih-kuan* speaks of the tentative and the empty tranquilization.[11] The method of introspection that I describe here represents the essentials of this tentative tranquilization.[12] When I was young the content of my koan meditation was poor. I was convinced that absolute tranquility of the source of the mind was the Buddha Way. Thus I despised activity and was fond of quietude. I would always seek out some dark and gloomy place

[11] The *Mo-ho chih-kuan* speaks of three kinds of *chih* (*shi*), or the three tranquilizations. They are set up in opposition to the three *kuan* (*kan*), or views: the empty, tentative, and middle (mean). The two terms are combined to form the *chih-kuan* (*shikan*) in the title of the work.

[12] It is unclear why the introspection described represents the essentials of the tentative tranquilization. Hakuin fails to explain.

and engage in dead sitting.[13] Trivial and mundane matters pressed against my chest and a fire mounted in my heart. I was unable to enter wholeheartedly into the active practice of Zen. My manner became irascible and fears assailed me. Both my mind and body felt continually weak, sweat poured ceaselessly from my armpits, and my eyes constantly filled with tears. My mind was in a continual state of depression and I made not the slightest advance toward gaining the benefits that result from the study of Buddhism.

But later I was most fortunate in receiving the instruction of a good teacher.[14] The secret methods of introspection were handed down to me and for three years I devoted myself to an assiduous practice of them. The serious disease from which I suffered, that up until then I had found so difficult to cure, gradually cleared up like frost and snow melting beneath the rays of the morning sun. The problems with those vile koans— koans difficult to believe, difficult to penetrate, difficult to un- ravel, difficult to enter—koans that up to then had been impossible for me to sink my teeth into, now faded away with the passing of my disease.

Even though I am past seventy now my vitality is ten times as great as it was when I was thirty or forty. My mind and body are strong and I never have the feeling that I absolutely must lie down to rest. Should I want to I find no difficulty in refraining from sleep for two, three, or even seven days, without suffering any decline in my mental powers. I am surrounded by three- to five-hundred demanding students, and even though I lecture on the scriptures or on the collections of the Masters' sayings for thirty to fifty days in a row, it does not exhaust me. I am quite convinced that all this is owing to the power gained from prac- ticing this method of introspection.

Initially emphasis must be placed on the care of the body. Then, during your practice of introspection, without your seeking it and quite unconsciously, you will attain, how many

---

[13] *Shiza.* Sitting in silent meditation. Hakuin, throughout his works, attacks this form of meditation, which he associates with *Mokushō Zen*, silent-illumina- tion Zen.

[14] The hermit Hakuyū. See below, fn. 50.

times I cannot tell, the benefits of enlightenment experiences. It is essential that you neither despise nor grasp for either the realm of activity or that of quietude, and that you continue your practice assiduously.

Frequently you may feel that you are getting nowhere with practice in the midst of activity, whereas the quietistic approach brings unexpected results. Yet rest assured that those who use the quietistic approach can never hope to enter into meditation in the midst of activity. Should by chance a person who uses this approach enter into the dusts and confusions of the world of activity, even the power of ordinary understanding which he had seemingly attained will be entirely lost. Drained of all vitality, he will be inferior to any mediocre, talentless person. The most trivial matters will upset him, an inordinate cowardice will afflict his mind, and he will frequently behave in a mean and base manner. What can you call accomplished about a man like this?

The Zen Master Ta-hui[15] has said that meditation in the midst of activity is immeasurably superior to the quietistic approach. Po-shan[16] has said that if one does not attain to this meditation within activity, one's practice is like trying to cross a mountain ridge as narrow as a sheep's skull with a hundred-and-twenty-pound load on one's back.

I am not trying to tell you to discard completely quietistic meditation and to seek specifically for a place of activity in which to carry out your practice. What is most worthy of respect is a pure koan meditation that neither knows nor is conscious of the two aspects, the quiet and the active. This is why it has been said that the true practicing monk[17] walks but does not know he is walking, sits but does not know he is sitting.

[15] Ta-hui Tsung-kao (Daie Sōkō, 1089–1163). Famous Lin-chi (Rinzai) Master of the Sung period. The following quotation paraphrases a statement in a letter in *Ta-hui shu*, T47, p. 918c.
[16] Po-shan (Hakusan), otherwise known as Wu-i Yüan-lai (Hakusan Genrai, 1575–1630). Ts'ao-t'ung (Sōtō) school Master of the Ming period.
[17] *Shinshō sanzen no nossu.* A monk who is genuinely engaged in Zen study under a teacher. *Sanzen* refers to the koan interview, in which the monk appears before the Master at stated intervals to indicate the state of his understanding of the koan that he is currently studying in meditation.

For penetrating to the depths of one's own true self-nature, and for attaining a vitality valid on all occasions, nothing can surpass meditation in the midst of activity. Supposing that you owned several hundred *ryō* of gold and you wanted to hire someone to guard it. One candidate shuts up the room, seals the door, and just sits there. True, he does not allow the money to be stolen, but the method he adopts does not show him to be a man with much vitality. His practice may best be compared with that of the Hinayana follower, who is intent only on his own personal enlightenment.

Now suppose that there is another candidate. He is ordered to take this money and to deliver it to such and such a place, although the road he must take is infested with thieves and evil men who swarm like bees and ants. Courageously he ties a large sword to his waist, tucks up the hem of his robes, and fastening the gold to the end of a staff, sets out at once and delivers the money to the appointed place, without once having trouble with the thieves. Indeed, such a man must be praised as a noble figure who, without the slightest sign of fear, acts with forthrightness and courage. His attitude may be compared to that of the perfect bodhisattva who, while striving for his own enlightenment, helps to guide all sentient beings.

The several hundred *ryō* of gold spoken of here stand for the great resolve to carry out the true, steadfast, unretrogressing meditation practice. The thieves and evil men, swarming like bees and ants, represent the delusions of the five coverings,[18] the ten bonds,[19] the five desires,[20] and the eight wrong views.[21] The man himself symbolizes the superior man, who has practiced true Zen and has gained perfect attainment. "Such and such a place" refers to the treasure place of the great peaceful Nirvana, endowed with the four virtues of permanence, peace, Self, and

[18] Desire, anger, sleepiness, excitability, doubt.
[19] The ten bonds that tie man, so that he cannot escape from birth and death and attain Nirvana. They are: lack of shame, lack of conscience, envy, stinginess, timidity, sleepiness, busyness, absorption, anger, and secretiveness.
[20] Wealth, sex, food, fame, sleep.
[21] The eight incorrect views of the Madhyamika: birth, death, past, future, sameness, difference, destruction, perpetuity.

purity. For these reasons it is said that the monk who is truly practicing Zen must carry on his activity in the midst of the phenomenal world.

The Hinayanists of old are frequently belittled. People of today, however, can scarcely attain to the power for seeing the Way that they possessed nor achieve to the brilliance of their wisdom and virtue. It was only because the direction of their practice was bad, because they liked only places of solitude and quiet, knew nothing of the dignity of the bodhisattva, and could establish no cause that might enable them to enter a Buddha land, that the Tathāgata[22] compared them to pus-oozing wild foxes and that Vimalakīrti[23] heaped scorn on them as men who would scorch buds and cause seeds to rot.

The Third Patriarch has said: "If one wishes to gain true intimacy with enlightenment, one must not shun the objects of the senses."[24] He does not mean here that one is to delight in the objects of the senses but, just as the wings of a waterfowl do not get wet even when it enters the water, one must establish a mind that will continue a true koan meditation without interruption, neither clinging to nor rejecting the objects of the senses. A person who fanatically avoids the objects of the senses and dreads the eight winds[25] that stimulate the passions, unconsciously falls into the pit of the Hinayana and never will be able to achieve the Buddha Way.

Yung-chia has said: "The power of the wisdom attained by practicing meditation in the world of desire is like the lotus that rises from fire; it can never be destroyed."[26] Here again, Yung-chia does not mean that one should sink into the world of the five desires. What he is saying is that even though one is in the

[22] A title or appellation of a Buddha in his manifestation in this world. The term is variously defined.
[23] A famous lay Buddhist. The *Vimalakīrti Sūtra*, frequently quoted by Hakuin, concerns him.
[24] Quotation from *Hsin-hsin ming* (T51, p. 457b) by the Third Patriarch, Seng-ts'an (Sōzan). Hakuin does not quote accurately.
[25] The eight winds that stir the passions: gain, loss, slander, eulogy, praise, ridicule, pain, pleasure.
[26] Quotation from *Cheng-tao ko* (T51, p. 461a) by Yung-chia Hsüan-chüeh (Yōka Genkaku, 665–713).

midst of the five desires and the objects of the senses, one must be possessed of a mind receptive to purity, as the lotus is unstained by the mud from which it grows.

Moreover, even should you live in the forests or the wilderness, eat one meal a day, and practice the Way both day and night, it is still difficult to devote yourself to purity in your works. How much harder must it be then for one who lives with his wife and relatives amid the dusts and turmoils of this busy life. But if you do not have the eye to see into your own nature, you will not have the slightest chance of being responsive to the teaching. Therefore Bodhidharma has said: "If you wish to attain the Buddha Way, you must first see into your own nature."[27]

If you suddenly awaken to the wisdom of the true reality of all things of the One Vehicle alone,[28] the very objects of the senses will be Zen meditation,[29] and the five desires themselves will be the One Vehicle. Thus words and silence, motion and tranquility are all present in the midst of Zen meditation. When this state is reached, it will be as different from that of a person who quietly practices in forests or mountains, and the state to which he attains, as heaven is from earth. When Yung-chia speaks of the lotus facing the flames, he is not here praising the rare man in this world who is practicing Buddhism. [He is saying that any place whatsoever is the world of Zen meditation.] Yung-chia penetrated to the hidden meaning of the Tendai teaching that "the truths themselves are one." He polished the practice of shikan in infinite detail, and in his biography the four dignities[30] are praised as always containing within them the

---

[27] Bodhidharma, the First Patriarch in China. The passage is found in *Hsüeh-mo lun*, a work attributed to Bodhidharma, but of later origin (*Shōshitsu rokumon*, T48, p. 373c).

[28] Reference to Mahayana Buddhism.

[29] *Zenjō. Zen* is *dhyāna; jō* is *samādhi*. A rather imprecise term that covers the whole area of meditation, but includes by implication the ultimate meditational state.

[30] The four respect-inspiring forms of behavior—dignity when walking, standing, sitting, and reclining—often associated with a bodhisattva. The implication is that the dignity pervades all activities. Frequent references to these dignities occur throughout Hakuin's works.

dhyāna contemplation.[31] His comment is very brief, but it is by no means to be taken lightly. When he says that *dhyāna* contemplation is always contained within the four dignities, he is speaking of the state of understanding in which the two are merged. The four dignities are none other than *dhyāna* contemplation and *dhyāna* contemplation is none other than the four dignities. When [Vimalakīrti][32] says that the bodhisattva without establishing a place for meditation, practices amidst the activities of daily life, he is speaking about the same thing.

Because the lotus that blooms in the water withers when it comes near to fire, fire is the dread enemy of the lotus. Yet the lotus that blooms from the midst of flames becomes all the more beautiful and fragrant the nearer the fire rages.

A man who carries on his practice, shunning from the outset the objects of the five senses, no matter how proficient he may be in the doctrine of the emptiness of self and things and no matter how much insight he may have into the Way, is like a water goblin who has lost his water[33] or a monkey with no tree to climb, when he takes leave of quietude and enters into the midst of activity. Most of his vitality is lost and he is just like the lotus that withers at once when faced with the fire.

But if you dauntlessly persevere in the midst of the ordinary objects of the senses, and devote yourself to pure undistracted meditation and make no error whatsoever, you will be like the man who successfully delivered the several hundred *ryō* of gold, despite the turmoil that surrounded him. Dauntlessly and courageously setting forth, and proceeding without a moment's interruption, you will experience a great joy, as if suddenly you

---

[31] *Zenkan*. To contemplate the true principle while seated in meditation. The term is not commonly used in Zen writing.

[32] The text reads "that bodhisattva." By context this must refer to Vimalakīrti, although the passage that follows is not a direct quotation from the *Vimalakīrti Sūtra*. See Karaki Junzō, ed., *Zenke goroku shū* (*Nihon no shisō*, 10 [Tokyo, 1969] p. 337).

[33] Hakuin uses the term *kenka* [clam and shrimp]. I do not find this as a colloquial term for the *kappa*, or water goblin, although the text indicates that this is what it meant. The *kappa* has a depression filled with water in the top of its head. It loses its power if the water is lost. See Karaki, ed., *Zenke goroku shū*, p. 337.

had made clear the basis of your own mind and had trampled and crushed the root of birth and death. It will be as if the empty sky vanished and the iron mountain crumbled. You will be like the lotus blooming from amidst the flames, whose color and fragrance become more intense the nearer the fire approaches. Why should this be so? It is because the very fire is the lotus and the very lotus is the fire.

I cannot emphasize enough that the true practice of introspection is an absolute essential that must never be neglected. The true practice of introspection (*naikan*) consists of [this contemplation]: "the area below my navel[34] down to my loins and the soles of my feet is all Chao-chou's *Mu*.[35] What principle can this *Mu* possibly have! The area below my navel down to my loins and the soles of my feet is all my own original face.[36] Where can there be nostrils in this original face! The area below my navel down to my loins and the soles of my feet is all the Pure Land of my own mind. With what can this Pure Land be adorned! The area below my navel down to my loins and the soles of my feet is all the Buddha Amida in my own body. What truth can this Amida preach! The area below my navel down to my loins and the soles of my feet is all the village where I was born. What news can there be from this native village!"[37]

If at all times even when coughing, swallowing, waving the arms, when asleep or awake, the practitioner accomplishes everything he decides to do and attains everything that he attempts to attain and, displaying a great, unconquerable determination, he moves forward ceaselessly, he will transcend the emotions and sentiments of ordinary life. His heart will be filled with an extraordinary purity and clarity, as though he were standing on a sheet

[34] Literally, the area below the navel, the *kikai* and the *tanden*.

[35] Reference is to the famous *Mu* koan of Chao-chou Ts'ung-shen (Jōshū Jūshin, 778–897), usually the first to be taken up by the Zen student. See Introduction, fn. 22.

[36] The "original face" refers to the important koan: "Not thinking of good, not thinking of evil, just at this moment, what is your original face before your mother and father were born?" See Philip Yampolsky, *The Platform Sutra of the Sixth Patriarch* (New York, 1967), p. 110.

[37] A similar passage, omitting the statement about Chao-chou's *Mu*, is to be found in the preface to Hakuin's *Yasen kanna* (HOZ5, 343–44).

of ice stretching for thousands of miles. Even if he were to enter the midst of a battlefield or to attend a place of song, dance, and revelry, it would be as though he were where no other person was. His great capacity, like that of Yün-men [38] with his kingly pride, will make its appearance without being sought.

At this time all Buddhas and sentient beings will be like illusions, "birth and death and Nirvana like last night's dreams." [39] This man sees through both heaven and hell; Buddha worlds and demon's palaces melt away. He strikes blind the True Eye of the Buddhas and the Patriarchs. To his own content he expounds the hundred thousand uncountable teachings and the mysterious principle in all its ramifications. He brings benefit to all sentient beings, and passes through innumerable kalpas without becoming wearied. For endless time he spreads the teachings of Buddhism without being once in error. He makes clear all the countless activities [of a bodhisattva] and establishes a teaching of wide influence. Attaching to his arm the supernatural talisman that wrests life from death, [40] he lets reverberate in his mouth the talons and teeth of the Cave of the Dharma, [41] smashes the brains of monks everywhere, and pulls out the nails and knocks out the wedges. [42] Without the least human feeling he produces an unsurpassedly evil, stupid, blind oaf, [43] be it one person or merely half a person, [44] with teeth sharp as the sword-trees of hell, and a gaping mouth like a tray of blood. Thus will he recompense his deep obligation to the Buddhas and the Patriarchs. The status he has achieved is known as the causal conditions for a Buddha-realm

[38] Yün-men Wen-yen (Ummon Ben'en, 864–949). Noted Five Dynasties monk and founder of the Yün-men (Ummon) school.

[39] Quoted from the *Yüan-chüeh ching* (T17, p. 915a).

[40] *Datsumyō no shimpu.* Metaphor for the spiritual power that has been gained. See ZD, pp. 58, 279.

[41] *Hokkutsu no sōge.* The "Cave of the Dharma" is the meditation hall. The "talons and teeth" are the powers he has gained that will aid others in their spiritual quest. See "Orategama zokushū," below, p. 142; ZD, pp. 58, 278.

[42] *Kugi o nuki ketsu o ubau.* Another expression indicating the rendering of assistance to others in their pursuit of enlightenment.

[43] *Donkatsukan.* Here used in a complimentary sense. A splendid disciple.

[44] In other words, if he cannot produce one disciple he will give all his efforts to producing someone, even though his talents are not complete.

or for the dignities of a bodhisattva. He is a great man, far excelling all ordinary people, who has accomplished his cherished desire.

There are some blind, bald idiots who stand in a calm, unperturbed, untouchable place and consider that the state of mind produced in this atmosphere comprises seeing into their own natures. They think that to polish and perfect purity is sufficient, but have never even in a dream achieved the state [of the person described above]. People of this sort spend all day practicing non-action and end up by having practiced action all the while; spend all day practicing non-creating and end up by having practiced creating all the while. Why is this so? It is because their insight into the Way is not clear, because they cannot arrive at the truth of the Dharma-nature.

What a shame it is that they spend in vain this one birth as a human being, a birth so difficult to obtain. They are like blind turtles wandering pointlessly in empty valleys, like demons who guard the wood used for coffins. That they return unreformed in suffering to their old homes in the three evil ways [45] is because their practice was badly guided, and from the outset they had not truly seen their own natures. They have exhausted the strength of their minds in vain and have in the end been able to gain no benefit at all. This is regrettable indeed.

In the past there were men such as Ippen Shōnin [46] of the Ji Sect, who hung a gong around his neck and, while intoning the Buddha's name, cried out: "Once you enter into the three evil ways, you will never be able to return again!" He traveled, spreading his message as far east as Dewa in Ōshū and as far west as the remotest parts of the bay of Hakata in Tsukushi. [47] In the end he went to visit the founder of the temple in Yura, [48] and it was

---

[45] The realms of hell, hungry ghosts, and beasts.

[46] Ippen (1239–1289). Evangelist, whose school is known as the Ji Sect. He was a devotee of Amida Buddha and one of the pioneers of Pure Land Buddhism.

[47] From one end of Japan to the other.

[48] Reference is to Shinchi Kakushin (1207–1298), a Zen monk who studied in China and returned to found the Hattō school. His temple, now known as the Kōkoku-ji, is located at Yura, in present-day Wakayama Prefecture.

from there that he was reborn in the Pure Land.[49] Is this not a splendid example, worthy of respect?

When we consider the human condition as a whole, we see people who lack the merits to be born in heaven but at the same time do not possess the bad karma that will send them to the three evil realms, so that eventually they end up being born into this degenerate world. Among them various emperors, ministers, rich men, and lay Buddhists have in previous lives accumulated considerable good karma; yet, although their deeds were of a superior nature, they were not sufficient to allow them to be born in heaven. Thus, they were born to wealthy families, surrounded themselves with ministers and concubines, piled up wealth and treasures, and exhibiting no discrimination whatsoever, neither showed sympathy for the common people nor were willing to reward their retainers. All that they produced was a heart set on luxury. But today's evil deeds and causations mean murderous deeds and suffering tomorrow. There are so many instances of people who have come into this world with a substantial amount of merit, but have then recklessly sought after pointless glory, produced a heavy burden of crime, and thus doomed themselves to rebirth in the evil ways.

Again I say, do not discard the essentials of introspection but train and nurture them. The true practice of introspection is the most important ingredient in the nourishment of one's own health. This conforms with the basic alchemistic principles of the hermits. These first began with Shakamuni Buddha; later they were described in detail by Chih-i of the Tendai school in his *Mo-ho chih-kuan*. In my middle years I learned them from the Taoist teacher Hakuyū.[50] Hakuyū lived in a cave at Shirakawa in Yamashiro. He is said to have been two-hundred and forty years old and the local inhabitants referred to him as the hermit Hakuyū. It is reported that he was the teacher of the late Ishikawa Jōzan.[51]

[49] The meaning is that he determined here that he would be reborn in the Pure Land. Ippen died elsewhere.
[50] The authenticity of Hakuyū has recently been established, See Itō Kazuo, "Hakuyūshi no hito to sho," *Zen bunka*, no. 6 (November, 1956), pp. 40–48.
[51] Ishikawa Jōzan (1583–1672). Warrior and poet of the early Tokugawa period.

Hakuyū used to say that, for the most part, the technique for nourishing the body is as follows:[52] it is essential always to keep the upper parts of the body cool and the lower parts warm. You must know that to nourish the body, it is imperative that the vital energy be made to fill its lower part. Frequently people say that the divine elixir is the distillation of the five elements, but they are unaware that the five elements, water, fire, wood, metal, and earth are associated with the five sense organs: the eyes, ears, nose, tongue, and body. How does one bring together these five organs in order to distill the divine elixir? For this we have the law of the five non-outflowings: when the eye does not see recklessly, when the ear does not hear recklessly, when the tongue does not taste recklessly, when the body does not feel recklessly, when the consciousness does not think recklessly, then the turgid primal energy accumulates before your very eyes. This is the "vast physical energy" of which Mencius[53] speaks. If you draw this energy and concentrate it in the space below the navel; if you distill it over the years, protect it to the utmost, and nourish it constantly, then before you know it the elixir-oven is overturned and the whole universe becomes a mass of this great circulating elixir. Then you will awaken to the fact that you yourself are a divine sage with true immortality, one who was not born before heaven and earth were formed and who will not die after empty space has vanished.[54] Now you can churn the ocean into curds and change earth into gold. For this reason it is said: "The circulation of one drop of this elixir can change metal into gold."[55] Po Yü-ch'an[56] has said: "The essential thing for nourishing life is to strengthen the physical frame. The secret of strengthening the physical frame lies in concentrating the spirit. When one

---

[52] The passages below summarize the essential points of Hakuin's *Yasen kanna*.

[53] *Mencius*, 2A, 2, 11.

[54] The implication appears to be that you will be one with heaven, earth, and empty space.

[55] Quotation from Tsung-mi's *Yüan-chüeh ching ta-shu* (ZZI, 14, 2, 134b). Hakuin uses the passage quite out of context. The next line reads: "One utterance of the True Principle and the profane changes to become the sacred."

[56] Pseudonym of the Southern Sung Taoist, Ko Ch'ang-keng (flourished 12th–13th centuries). The quotation has not been traced.

concentrates the spirit, the energy accumulates. When the energy accumulates the elixir is formed. When the elixir is formed the physical frame becomes firm. When the physical frame is firm the spirit is perfected."

But above all, one must realize that this elixir is by no means something outside one's own body. For example, there are jewel fields and there are millet fields. The jewel fields produce jewels; the millet fields produce crops. In man there are the *kikai* and the *tanden*. The *kikai* is the treasure house where the vital energy is accumulated and nurtured; the *tanden* is the castle town where the divine elixir is distilled and the life span preserved. A man of old has said: "The reason the great rivers and seas attained to sovereignty over the hundred other streams was that they had the virtue of being lower than the others."[57] The oceans from the outset occupy geographically a position lower than all other waters; thus they receive all these waters but never increase or lessen. The *kikai* is situated in the body at a position lower than that of the five internal organs and ceaselessly stores up the true energy. Eventually the divine elixir is perfected and the status of an immortal is achieved.

The *tanden* is located in three places in the body, but the one to which I refer is the lower *tanden*. The *kikai* and the *tanden* are both located below the navel; they are in actuality one thing although they have two names. The *tanden* is situated two inches below the navel, the *kikai* an inch and a half below it, and it is in this area that the true energy always accumulates. When the body and mind are attuned, they say that even if one is a hundred years old, the hair does not turn white, the teeth remain firm, the eyesight is clearer than ever before, and the skin acquires a luster. This is the efficacy of nurturing the primal energy and bringing the divine elixir to maturity. There is no limit to the age to which one may live; it depends only on the effectiveness with which the energy is nurtured. The inspired doctors of old effected cures even before a disease made its appearance and enabled people to control the mind and nurture the energy. Quack doctors work in just the opposite way. After the disease

[57] *Lao Tzu*, 66.

has appeared they attempt to cure it with acupuncture, moxa treatment, and pills, with the result that many of their patients are lost.

Generally speaking, essence, energy, and spirit are the foundation stones of the human body. The enlightened man guards his energy and does not expend it. The art of nurturing life can be compared to the techniques of governing a country. The spirit represents the prince, the essence the ministers, and the energy the people. When the people are loved and cared for, then the country is perfected; when the energy is guarded, then the body is perfected. When the people are in turmoil, the nation is destroyed; when the energy is exhausted, the body dies. Therefore the wise ruler always turns his efforts to the common people, while the foolish ruler allows the upper classes to have their way. When the upper classes have their own way, the nine ministers demand special privileges, the hundred officers[58] revel in their authority, and no one gives a second thought to the poverty and suffering of the common people. Capricious ministers loot and pillage, tyrannical officials deceive and plunder. Though there is abundant grain in the fields, many in the nation starve to death. The wise and virtuous go into hiding and the people become resentful and enraged. Eventually the commoners are reduced to misery and the continuity of the nation is severed. When attention is directed toward the common people, when their labors are not ignored, then all the people prosper and the nation becomes strong. No one violates its laws and no other country will attempt to attack its borders.

The human body is just like this. The enlightened man allows the vital breath to accumulate fully below. Therefore there is no room for the seven misfortunes[59] to operate, nor can the four evils[60] invade from outside. The circulatory organs work efficiently and the heart and mind brim with health. Thus the physical body need not know the pain of acupuncture and moxa treatment. It will be like the people of a strong country who do not know the sound of war drums.

[58] The entire body of officialdom.
[59] Joy, anger, grief, pleasure, love, hate, desire.
[60] The four elements: earth, water, fire, wind.

A long time ago Ch'i Po[61] answered the questions of the Yellow Emperor: "When the desiring mind is empty, true energy is consonant with it. If the essence and spirit are guarded within, from where can illness come?" But men today do not follow this advice. From the time of their births until the time of their deaths, they do not guard within themselves the mind-as-master (*shushin*). They do not even know what sort of a thing this mind-as-master is, for they are like ignorant dogs and horses that run around all day just because they have legs. A dangerous ignorance indeed! Don't the writers of military works say: "Surprise and distress arise because the mind-as-master is not set firmly."[62] But when the mind-as-master is guarded within, distress and fear are not arbitrarily produced. When a person is at any time without the mind-as-master he is like a dead man, or at the least there is no assurance that he will not descend into recklessness and depravity.

To illustrate the point: supposing there is an old house owned by an aged woman, decrepit, exhausted, impoverished, and starving. Yet no one will recklessly break into this house while it still has a master. But just let the owner of the house disappear and thieves will creep in, beggars will sleep in it, foxes and rabbits will race over the floors, and badgers will crawl in to hide. During the day idle spirits[63] will scream; at night wild demons[64] will sing there. The house will become a gathering place for numberless weird and evil beings. So it is with the body of man.

For the mind that is master of true meditation, the space below the navel is as firm as though a huge rock were settled there, and when this mind functions in its awesome dignity, not one deluded thought may enter, not one discriminating idea can exist. "Heaven and earth are one finger; all things are one horse."[65] This great hero [who has mastered true meditation], dignified as

---

[61] Legendary doctor, minister of the Yellow Emperor and one of the founders of the medicinal arts. The source of the following quotation is not identified.
[62] Source not identified. Reference is to Chinese works on military strategy.
[63] *Kanjin.* Spirits who no longer have people to make sacrifices for them.
[64] *Yaki.* They have no relatives to hold services for them.
[65] *Chuang Tzu,* 2, 4.

a mountain, broad as the seas, practices untiringly all the good works day after day, so that there is no room for even a Buddha or a Patriarch to insinuate his hand and no thing that an evil demon can spy out. Day after day he carries out all good works without tiring. Truly he can be called one who has fulfilled his obligations to the Buddha.

But should this person suddenly be attacked by evil circumstances or be attracted to deluded actions, before he knows it, the mind as master of meditation will be lost. This is referred to in the passage: "When a thought suddenly arises it is known as ignorance."[66] The demons of the passions will swarm like bees; the supernatural beings will race about like ants. [The body composed of] the four elements will be as a dilapidated house seen in a dream; [the mind made up of] the five skandhas[67] like an imaginary hovel. All will suddenly change and become the dwelling place of demons. The form of things changes constantly. Among all things, in one day how many tens of thousands of births and deaths occur!

Although a gentleman may outwardly have the settled appearance of one who has retired from his official duties, inwardly his mind seethes with the abnormalities of a Yaksha.[68] The mind will suffer at all times more agonies than the battle of Yashima[69] produced; the heart will constantly be more troubled than was the world during the wars of the nine kingdoms.[70] It will be just like the burning of the millionaire's house in the parable.[71] This we call constantly sinking into the karmic sea of birth and death. If a person in this condition does not board the

[66] From *Ta-ch'eng ch'i-hsin lun* (T32, p. 577c). When the principle of the equality of True Reality is not penetrated, suddenly discriminating thoughts are activated and ignorance arises.

[67] The five components that make up the universe. They are: form and matter; sensations; perceptions; psychic constructions; consciousness. Each individual is made up of a constantly changing combination of these components.

[68] Violent demons, sometimes described as eating human flesh.

[69] Battle of the 19th day of the second month of 1185, in which the Minamoto defeated the Taira forces at Yashima in Sanuki.

[70] The nine kingdoms of the Warring States period in China, approximately 481–221 B.C.

[71] In the *Lotus Sūtra*.

raft of true meditation nor hoist the sail of indomitable perseverance, he will be drawn into the swift-raging waves of consciousness and emotion. Then how will he be able to transcend the
dark reaches of stench-filled smoke and the poisonous mists, and
reach the other shore of the four virtues?[72]

How truly sad! Man is endowed with the wisdom and form
of the Buddha. There is nothing that he lacks. Each person is
possessed with this treasure jewel that is the Buddha-nature and
for all eternity it radiates a great pure luminescence. But while
dwelling in that true land of the pure dharma-nature of Birushana
(Vairocana) Buddha where this very world is the light of Nirvana,
men, because their eye of wisdom has been blinded, mistake this
realm for the ordinary evil world and err in thinking that it is
peopled by sentient beings. In this one birth as a human being,
one so difficult to obtain, they spend their time wandering about
like ignorant horses and oxen. With no discrimination whatsoever
they extinguish the light and wander through the realms of the
three painful evil existences and suffer the sadness of the six
forms of rebirth.[73] They grasp at the true land of Birushana
Buddha's unchanging eternal calm, and in their fear and delusion,
cry in pain, believing it to be eternal hell. They pride themselves
in their ordinary, pointless, insignificant views, reveling in the
small prejudiced learning that has entered into their mouths and
ears. They do not believe in Buddhism, have not listened to the
True Law, end their days prating nonsense, and have failed to
guard even for a moment the mind that is master of true meditation. More pitiful still is that they revolve for eternal kalpas in
the coils of their evil actions. And even more frightening, they
earn only the bitter fruit of the long nights of birth and
death.

Even the Emperors who ruled from the Engi to the Tenryaku
periods and who are venerated as the three sages, were blackened
by the raging flames of hell. When they saw Nichizō Shōnin of
the Shō cave, they told him that, because as rulers of a small
country they were guilty of extreme arrogance, they had fallen

---

[72] Permanence, peace, Self, and purity as described in the *Nirvāṇa Sūtra*.
[73] The realms of hell, hungry ghosts, beasts, asuras, man, and devas.

to a place such as this.[74] Fujiwara no Toshiyuki was talented in both Chinese and Japanese, was famed for his calligraphy and copied out the *Lotus Sūtra* some two hundred times, but because he was not competent in true meditation, he fell into hell and had to go to Ki no Tomonori to plead for aid.[75] Minamoto no Yoshiie, of whom it is said that there was no warrior his equal in Japan, subdued the numerous enemies of the court, eased the cares of the Emperor, and where the incantations of the high priests of Nara and Kyoto had failed, silenced the troubles of the Emperor merely by twanging his bow. Yet even such a man had to kneel before the court of Emma.[76] Tada no Mitsunaka while ill was taken by a messenger from Emma to see the sights of the dark regions. After he returned to this world he was so terrified that he at once entered the Rokkaku-dō, became a monk, and was so assiduous in his invocation of the Buddha's name that the sweat and tears he shed seeped right through the mat on which he sat.[77]

[74] This story is found in several variant forms: in the biographies of Nichizō in *Genkō shakusho*, 9 and *Honchō kōsō den*, 48 and in the *Jikkinshō* (see Okada Minoru, *Jikkinshō shinshaku* [Tokyo, 1930], pp. 236–38). In the *Jikkinshō* version the story concerns the Emperor Daigo alone. Here Hakuin refers to the three Emperors Daigo, Sujaku, and Murakami. The Engi and Tenryaku eras span the years 901–956. Nichizō (d. 985) is a famous Shingon monk, associated with Mt. Ontake, the Tō-ji in Kyoto, and the Murō-ji in Nara. The Shō cave is located in the recesses of Mt. Ontake. Nichizō is said to have died and gone to hell where he met the Emperor, who was suffering for the arrogance of having exiled Sugawara no Michizane (845–903). The *Genkō shakusho* and *Honchō kōsō den* refer to unidentified high ministers rather than the Emperor. Nichizō is said to have returned to life and to have lived to be over a hundred years old.

[75] This story is found in part in *Uji shūi monogatari* 8 (*Kokushi taikei*, 18, pp. 147–52). Fujiwara no Toshiyuki (d. ca. 905) and Ki no Tomonori (d. 905) were both celebrated poets of the Heian period.

[76] Emma is the Lord of Hell. This story is found in *Zen Taiheiki*, 38 (*Zoku Teikoku bunko*, 10 [Tokyo, 1898], 1030–1033) in somewhat different form. Minamoto no Yoshiie (1041–1108) drives out an evil spirit from Emperor Horikawa by twanging his bow. The priests of Nara and Kyoto had succeeded in curing the Emperor's illness, but he was seized later by an evil spirit. There is no mention here of Yoshiie's excursion to Hell. Hakuin refers to Yoshiie by his popular designation, "Hachiman-dono."

[77] The source of this story has not been traced. Tada no Mitsunaka (or Manjū 912–997) is also known as Minamoto no Mitsunaka. He was a distinguished military leader of the Heian period. The Rokkaku-dō is a temple in Kyoto.

King Chuang-hsiang of the Ch'in,[78] who swallowed up six countries, contained the four seas, and who was feared even beyond the areas where the eight barbarian tribes dwelled, fell into the realm of hungry demons and underwent its sufferings. Emperor Wu of Chou[79] underwent the punishment of the iron bridge. Po Ch'i of Ch'in,[80] who was known throughout the world as an arch-villain, sank into the Hell of Excrement and Filth. Later, at the beginning of the Hung-wu era [1368–1398] of the Ming at a place known as San-mao kuan in Wu-shan, a bolt of lightning struck a white centipede over a foot in length, and it is recorded that on its back the name Po Ch'i was written. From this one may know how difficult it is to escape the force of evil karma.

Do not say that worldly affairs and pressures of business leave you no time to study Zen under a Master, and that the confusions of daily life make it difficult for you to continue your meditation. Everyone must realize that for the true practicing monk there are no worldly cares or worries. Supposing a man accidentally drops two or three gold coins in a crowded street swarming with people. Does he forget about the money because all eyes are upon him? Does he stop looking for it because it will create a disturbance? Most people will push others out of the way, not resting until they get the money back into their own hands. Are not people who neglect the study of Zen because the press of mundane circumstances is too severe, or stop their meditation because they are troubled by worldly affairs, putting more value on two or three pieces of gold than on the unsurpassed mysterious way of the Buddhas? A person who concentrates solely on meditation amid the press and worries of everyday life will be like the man who has dropped the gold coins and devotes himself to seeking them. Who will not rejoice in such a person?

---

[78] Chuang-hsiang (d. 247 B.C.). Title of the reputed father of the founder of the Ch'in dynasty.

[79] Emperor Wu of the Northern Chou dynasty is noted for his persecution of Buddhism.

[80] Po Ch'i (d. 258 B.C.). A famous general of the Ch'in, noted for his cruelty. The source of this story has not been traced.

This is why Myōchō[81] has said:

See the horses competing at the Kamo racegrounds;
Back and forth they run—yet this is sitting in meditation.

The Priest of Shinjū-an[82] has explained it in this way: "Don't read the sutras, practice meditation; don't take up the broom, practice meditation; don't plant the tea seeds, practice meditation; don't ride a horse, practice meditation." This is the attitude of the men of old to true Zen study.

Shōju Rōjin[83] always used to say: "The man who practices meditation without interruption, even though he may be in a street teeming with violence and murder, even though he may enter a room filled with wailing and mourning, even though he attends wrestling matches and the theatre, even though he is present at musical and dance performances, is not distracted or troubled by minutiae, but conscientiously fixes his mind on his koan, proceeds single-mindedly, and does not lose ground. Even if a powerful Asura demon were to seize him by the arm and lead him through innumerable rounds of the great chiliocosm,[84] his true meditation would not be cut off even for an instant. One who continues in this way without interruption can be called a monk who practices the true Zen. At all times maintain an unconcerned expression on your face, steady your eyes, and never for a moment bother yourself with the affairs of man." This statement is truly worthy of respect. Don't we also find in the military laws the instructions: "Fight and cultivate the fields; this is by far the safest method"? Studying Zen is just the same. Meditation is the true practice of fighting; introspection is the ultimate of cultivation. They are what two wings are to a bird; what two wheels are to a cart.

I have already written of the essentials of introspection in my *Yasen kanna*, a book designed for the use of all Zen monks everywhere. I don't know exactly how many have been cured

[81] Shūhō Myōchō (1282–1338). More commonly known by his posthumous title, Daitō Kokushi. He is the founder of the Daitoku-ji in Kyoto.

[82] Ikkyū Sōjun (1396–1481). Famous Rinzai priest, noted for his eccentricities. Shinjū-an is a sub-temple within the grounds of Daitoku-ji.

[83] Dōkyō Etan (1642–1721). Hakuin's teacher. He is known as the "old man of the Shōju hermitage" (Shōju Rōjin).

[84] A billion Buddha worlds in the Tendai cosmology.

of their Zen sickness by reading what I have written there, but I do know of eight or nine, seriously ill and near to death, who were cured by following my instructions. Students, practice the introspective method and pursue your Zen studies, and by this bring to perfection your basic aspirations. Of what use is it to awaken to the essential points of the Five Houses and Seven Schools[85] and then to die young? Even if by the powers of introspection you could live eight hundred years as did P'eng Tsu,[86] if you do not have the eye to see into your own nature, you are no more than an aged demon fit only to guard corpses. What possible good is there in this?

If you think that dead sitting and silent illumination[87] are sufficient then you spend your whole life in error and transgress greatly against the Buddha Way. Not only do you set yourself against the Buddha Way, but you reject the lay world as well. Why is this so? If the various lords and high officials were to neglect their visits to court and to cast aside their governmental duties and practice dead sitting and silent illumination; if the warriors were to neglect their archery and charioteering, forget the martial arts, and practice dead sitting and silent illumination; if the merchants were to lock their shops and smash their abacuses, and practice dead sitting and silent illumination; if the farmers were to throw away their ploughs and hoes, cease their cultivation, and practice dead sitting and silent illumination; if craftsmen were to cast away their measures and discard their axes and adzes, and practice dead sitting and silent illumination, the country would collapse and the people drop with exhaustion. Bandits would arise everywhere and the nation would be in grievous danger. Then the people, in their anger and resentment, would be sure to say that Zen was an evil and an ill-omened thing.

But it should be known that at the time that the ancient monasteries flourished, old sages such as Nan-yüeh, Ma-tsu, Po-chang, Huang-po, Lin-chi, Kuei-tsung, Ma-yü, Hsing-hua, P'an-

---

[85] The divisions of the Zen school in China.

[86] Legendary figure, said to have lived over eight hundred years.

[87] *Koza mokushō.* The term is an old one, descriptive of Zen practice without the use of koans, although the term itself predates the use of koans in Chinese Zen. For a discussion, see Introduction, p. 26.

shan, Chiu-feng, and Ti-tsang,[88] and others heaved stones, moved earth, drew water, cut firewood, and grew vegetables. When the drum for the work period sounded, they tried to make progress in the midst of their activity. That is why Po-chang said: "A day without work, a day without eating." This practice is known as meditation in the midst of activity, the uninterrupted practice of meditation sitting. This style of Zen practice no longer exists today.

I do not mean to say, however, that sitting in meditation should be despised or contemplation damned. Of all the sages, the men of wisdom of the past and of today, there is not one that perfected the Buddha Way who did not depend on Zen meditation. The three essentials, precepts, meditation, and wisdom, have always been the very center of Buddhism. Who would dare to take them lightly? But if anyone should have attempted to approach such men as the great Zen sages mentioned above, men who transcend both sect and rank, while they were engaged in the true, unsurpassed, great Zen meditation, lightning would have flashed and the stars would have leapt about in the sky.

How then can someone with the eye of a sheep or the wisdom of foxes and badgers expect to judge such men? Even should there be such a thing as attaining the status of a Buddha or reaching a state where the great illumination is released by means of dead sitting and silent illumination, the various lords, high stewards, and common people are so involved in the numerous duties of their household affairs that they have scarcely a moment in which to practice concentrated meditation. What they do then is to plead illness and, neglecting their duties and casting aside responsibilities for their family affairs, they shut themselves up in a room for several days, lock the door, arrange several cushions

---

[88] All are Chinese Zen Masters: Nan-yüeh Huai-jang (Nangaku Ejō, 677–744), Ma-tsu Tao-i (Baso Dōitsu, 709–788), Po-chang Huai-hai (Hyakujō Ekai, 720–814), Huang-po Hsi-yün (Ōbaku Kiun, d. ca. 850), Lin-chi I-hsüan (Rinzai Gigen, d. 866), Kuei-tsung Chih-ch'ang (Kisū Chijō, n.d.), Ma-yü Pao-ch'e (Mayoku Hōtetsu, n.d.), Hsing-hua Ts'un-chiang (Kōke Zonshō, 830–888), P'an-shan Pao-chi (Banzan Hōshaku, 720–814), Chiu-feng Tao-ch'ien (Kyūhō Dōken, n.d.), and Ti-tsang (Jizō), another name for Lo-han Kuei-ch'en (Rakan Keishin, 867–928).

in a pile, set up a stick of incense, and proceed to sit. Yet, because they are exhausted by ordinary worldly cares, they sit in meditation for one minute and fall asleep for a hundred, and during the little bit of meditation that they manage to accomplish, their minds are beset by countless delusions. As soon as they set their eyes, grit their teeth, clench their fists, adjust their posture, and start to sit, ten thousand evil circumstances begin to race about in their minds. Thereupon they furrow their brows, draw together their eyebrows, and before one knows it they are crying out: "Our official duties interfere with our practice of the Way; our careers prevent our Zen meditation. It would be better to resign from office, discard our seals, go to some place beside the water or under the trees where all is peaceful and quiet and no one is about, there in our own way to practice *dhyāna* contemplation, and escape from the endless cycle of suffering." How mistaken these people are!

Under ordinary circumstances, service to a master means that you eat the master's food, wear clothes obtained from him, tie a sash he has given you, and wear a sword obtained from him. You do not have to fetch water from a faraway place. The food you eat you do not grow yourself; the clothes you wear you do not weave for yourself. In fact, your whole body in all its parts is dependent on the kindness of your lord. Why is it then that when people mature and reach the age of thirty or forty, when they should be helping their lord to govern, when their talents should exceed those of a minister of state, when they should be seeing to it that their master is another Yao or Shun,[89] and that the people benefit as did those under these ancient kings, when indeed they should be repaying their obligations, that they finger the rosary hidden in their sleeves, stealthily intone the name of the Buddha, appear exhausted for their work and neglect their duties, and have not the slightest intention of repaying their obligations to their lord? Instead they claim to be ill and attempt to retire from all responsibilities. Even if aspirations of this sort are buttressed by painful polishing in some secluded place for several years, and even if a state is achieved where thoughts seem to be stopped and

---

[89] Legendary sage rulers in ancient China.

the passions cut off, such aspirations only result in harming the inner organs and producing so much fear in the mind that the breast will burst open with terror at the sound made by the droppings of a rat.

If such a person were a general or even a foot soldier, how could he fulfill his functions in an emergency? Supposing he were called upon when the country met some serious danger and were asked to strengthen and guard some strategic gate. Seeing the enemy troops pushing forward like the tide, the banners pressing down like clouds, hearing the cannonades resounding like thunder claps, the conches and bells sounding loudly enough to bring down mountains, watching the bared lances and halberds gleaming like ice, his fright would be so great that he could not even swallow his food and drink. He would shake so that he could no longer hold the reins, and clinging to the seat of the saddle, he would tremble and fall from his horse. Then in the end he would be captured by foot soldiers. Why should this be so? It is the result of spending several years practicing dead sitting and silent illumination. Would not even such great heroes as Kumagai and Hirayama[90] have trembled in the same way if they had undertaken this sort of Zen practice?

For this reason the Patriarchs with great compassion were kind enough to point out the correct way of true meditation and uninterrupted meditation sitting. If all possessed this true meditation, the lords in their attendance at court and their conduct of governmental affairs, the warriors in their study of the works on archery and charioteering, the farmers in their cultivation, hoeing, and ploughing, the artisans in their measuring and cutting, women in their spinning and weaving, this then would at once accord with the great Zen meditation of the various Patriarchs. This is why the *Sūtra* says: "The necessities of life and the production of goods do not transgress against True Reality."[91] If you do not have this true meditation it is like sleeping in an empty hole abandoned by some old badger. How regrettable it is that people today "cast aside this Way as if it were a clump of dirt."[92]

[90] Kumagai Naozane (1141–1208) and Hirayama Sueshige (n.d.), warrior heroes of the Kamakura period.
[91] *Lotus Sūtra* (T9, p. 50a), Hakuin does not quote accurately.
[92] Line from Tu Fu's *Song of Poverty*.

Giving recognition to the dark valley where "the self and things are both empty," they take this to be the ultimate Zen. From day to day they knit their eyebrows and furrow their foreheads and are no more than dead silkworms in their cocoons. They are as far removed from the meaning of the Patriarchs as are drifting smoke and clouds. They shun the Buddhist scriptures as a lame rat flees from a cat; they despise the *Records*[93] of the Patriarchs as blind rabbits fear the tiger's roar. They are totally unaware that this is to be sunk in the ancient pit of the Hinayana, that it is a spurious Nirvana. Therefore Shūhō[94] has lamented:

> For three years I lived in a den of foxes;
> That people are bewitched today is only to be expected.

In the past Seng-chao[95] has condemned such people: "The confused fish lies trapped in the weir; the sick bird lives in the reeds. They know a little bit of ease, but of the great peace they know nothing."

For the true hero who has plumbed the mysteries, [understanding] depends only on the degree to which he has entered upon the principle; to the quality of his seeing of the Way. Who tells you to choose between remaining a layman or becoming a monk? Who advocates the virtues of either living in the city or in mountain forests? In the past there were such famous laymen as Prime Minister Kuang-mei,[96] Minister Lu Keng,[97] Presiding Minister Chen Ts'ao,[98] the *tu-wei* Li Tsun-hsü,[99] Yang Ta-

---

[93] The *goroku*, or recorded sayings of the Zen Masters. Usually recorded by disciples, they have from the T'ang period on made up a significant part of Zen literature in both China and Japan.

[94] Shūhō Myōchō (Daitō Kokushi).

[95] Seng-chao (374–414). Famed Master of Madhyamika philosophy. The following quotation is from *Pao-ts'ang lun* (T45, p. 144a) a mid-eighth-century work spuriously attributed to Seng-chao.

[96] P'ei Hsiu (797–870). Famed T'ang official, a disciple of Huang-po. Kuang-mei is his style.

[97] Lu Keng (764–834). Official whose name appears frequently in Zen historical records.

[98] T'ang official who became the heir of Ch'en Tsun-su (Chin Sonshuku, 780–877?). He is mentioned in *Ching-te ch'uan-teng lu*, 12.

[99] Li Tsun-hsü (d. 1038). Prominent official who assisted in the compilation of Zen histories. *Tu-wei* is an official title.

nien,[100] Chang Wu-chin,[101] and others, who saw into their own natures as thoroughly as though they were looking at the palms of their own hands, or as though the mysteries were issuing from their own lungs. They trod the bottom of the sea of Buddhism; they drank from the poisonous waves of the rivers of Zen. So illustrious was their wisdom, so vast their understanding, that the idle spirits ran in fear and the wild demons hid in distress. Each one of these men assisted in the Imperial Government and brought peace to the land. Who can fathom their profundity?

Chang Wu-chin rose to be Prime Minister and the highest official in the government. His talents as a minister of state were superb: princes trusted him, ministers revered him, the military rendered him respect, the people bore him good will. Heaven sent down a plenitude of rain; the Emperor rewarded him with a title. He lived to be almost a hundred years of age and the benefits he gave extended everywhere. The people rejoiced in the autumn harvest as in the days of Yao; men prospered in a world at peace as in the times of Shun. On the one hand he fulfilled his obligations to his prince, on the other he preserved Buddhism. He was indeed one of the great men in the world. Therefore it has been said: "While a layman Chang Wu-chin perfected the Way; while earning a salary Yang Ta-nien studied Zen." Is this not a story that will be told for a thousand years?

Is there any limit to men such as Su Tung-p'o,[102] Huang Lu-chih,[103] Chang Tzu-ch'eng,[104] Chang T'ien-chüeh,[105] Kuo Kung-p'u[106] and many others of whom I have never heard? All of these men were possessed of insight far surpassing that of

---

[100] Yang I (968–1024). Ta-nien is his pen name. A famous literary figure.

[101] Chang Shang-ying (1043–1121). Prime Minister and celebrated layman. Wu-chin is his Buddhist name.

[102] Su Tung-p'o (1037–1101). Famous Sung poet.

[103] Huang Lu-chih (1045–1105). Sung poet, more commonly known as Huang T'ing-chien.

[104] Chang Chiu-ch'eng (1092–1159). Tzu-ch'eng is his style.

[105] T'ien-chüeh is the pen name of Chang Shang-ying (Wu-chin), mentioned above. Hakuin has written "T'ien-lo" in error, and has regarded them as different persons.

[106] Kuo Hsiang-cheng (n.d.). Sung poet and recluse. Kung-p'u is his style.

ordinary monks. Yet they assisted constantly in countless governmental affairs, rubbed shoulders with the elite of many lands,
associated with nobles of the highest rank, participated in music,
the rituals, and military affairs, engaged in ceremonial competi-
tions, but never for a moment did they lose their affinity for the
Way, and in the end awakened to the essentials of the Zen teaching. Isn't this the miracle of true meditation and uninterrupted
sitting? Was this not the deep repayment of their obligations to
the Buddha Way? Isn't this the awesome dignity of Zen? Indeed
they are as different from those fools who starve to death on
mountains, thinking that dead sitting and silent illumination
suffice and that Zen consists of the source of the mind being in
tranquility, as heaven is from earth. Aren't men of this sort like
people who not only fail to catch the hare before their eyes, but
lose the falcon as well?

Why? It is because not only do they fail to see into their
own natures, but they neglect their obligations to their lord as
well. What a regrettable thing this is! It must be understood that
the quality of the accomplishment depends upon the degree of
the perseverance. If in your meditation you have the vitality of a
single man fighting ten thousand, what is there to choose between
being a monk and being a layman? If you say that seeing the
Way can only be accomplished by monks, does this mean that
all hope is lost for parents among the commoners, for those in
service to others, for children? Even if you are a monk, if your
practice of the Way is not intense, if your aspiration is not pure,
how are you any different from a layman? Again, even if you
are a layman, if your aspiration is intense and your conduct
wise, why is this any different from being a monk? Therefore it
has been said:

> If the Way lies deep within the mind,
> It is just as well not to go off to the mountains of Yoshino.[107]

At any rate, there is no kind of sitting more suited to military
leaders than this uninterrupted true meditation. This is an ancient
truth that for the past two hundred years has been discarded.

[107] The source of this verse has not been identified.

What is this true meditation? It is to make everything: coughing, swallowing, waving the arms, motion, stillness, words, action, the evil and the good, prosperity and shame, gain and loss, right and wrong, into one single koan. Making the space below the navel as though a lump of iron were settled there, consider the shogun as the main object of worship, the various ministers and high stewards as the many bodhisattvas that appear in this world, engaged in the same work as you. Consider the various daimyo, both great and small, attending on the lord and living at a distance, as the great Hinayana disciples such as Śāriputra and Maudgalyāyana.[108] Consider the multitude of the common people as sentient beings eligible for salvation, who are to us as children and for whom particular benevolence must be felt.

Make your skirt and upper garments into the seven- or nine-striped monks' robe; make your two-edged sword into your resting board or desk. Make your saddle your sitting cushion; make the mountains, rivers, and great earth the sitting platform; make the whole universe your own personal meditation cave. Consider the workings of Yin and Yang as your two meals of gruel a day; heaven, hell, pure lands, and this impure world as your spleen, stomach, intestines, and gall bladder, the three hundred pieces of ceremonial music as the sutra reading and recitation at morning and night. Think of the countless million Mount Sumerus as fused into your single backbone and all the court ceremonies and military studies as the mysterious operations of the countless good activities of the bodhisattva. Thrusting forth the courageous mind derived from faith, combine it with the true practice of introspection. Then rising or staying, moving or still, "at all times test to see whether you have lost [the true meditation] or have not lost it."[109] This is the true practice of the sages of the past and of today. Tzu Ssu[110] has said: "Do not deviate from the Way even to the smallest degree. What can be

[108] Two of the chief disciples of the Buddha. The former was known for his wisdom, the latter for his supernatural powers.
[109] This quotation appears later (p. 80) and is attributed to Ta-hui Tsung-kao (Daie Sōkō, 1089–1163).
[110] Grandson of Confucius. Hakuin writes "Confucius" in error.

deviated from cannot be called the Way."¹¹¹ In the Li-jen chapter
of the *Analects* we read: "In moments of haste he cleaves to it
[virtue]; in seasons of danger he cleaves to it [virtue]."¹¹² This
teaches that not for a moment must one lose [the true meditation].
This Way may be called the True Way of the *Doctrine of the
Mean*. This True Way is what the *Lotus Sūtra* describes when it
says: "This *Sūtra* is difficult to hold to. Should some one cherish
it even for a short while, I and all the Buddhas will rejoice."¹¹³
Here the *Lotus Sūtra* speaks of the vital importance of true
meditation.

You must become aware that meditation is the thing that
points out your own innate appearance. To carry on the real
practice of seeing into your own nature by transcending the great
matter of birth and death and by closing the True Eye of the
Buddhas and the Patriarchs, is by no means an easy thing to do.
Placing the essential between the two states, the active and the
passive, and being in a position to be able to move in any direction,
with the true principle of pure, undiluted, undistracted meditation
before your eyes, attain a state of mind in which, even though
surrounded by crowds of people, it is as if you were alone in a
field extending tens of thousands of miles. You must from time
to time reach that state of understanding described by old P'ang,
in which you are "with both your ears deaf; with both your
eyes blind."¹¹⁴ This is known as the time when the true great
doubt stands before your very eyes. And if at this time you
struggle forward without losing any ground, it will be as though
a sheet of ice has cracked, as though a tower of jade has fallen,
and you will experience a great feeling of joy that for forty years
you have never seen or felt before.

If anyone should wish to test the authenticity of his seeing into
his own true nature, or to examine the quality of the power he
has attained, let him first with deep respect read the verses of
Fu Ta-shih.¹¹⁵ Why is this so? A man of old has said: "Those who

---

¹¹¹ *Doctrine of the Mean*, 1, 2.   ¹¹² *Analects* 4, 5.   ¹¹³ T9, p. 34b.
¹¹⁴ The layman P'ang. Devout Zen believer of the T'ang dynasty. The quotation has not been located in his sayings: *P'ang chü-shih yü-lu* (ZZ2, 25, 1, 28-41).
¹¹⁵ Fu Ta-shih (497-569). Famed Buddhist layman, known also as Shan-hui
Ta-shih.

have not yet gained understanding should study the meaning
rather than the verses themselves. Those who have gained understanding should study the verses rather than the meaning."

The verses say:

> Empty-handed, but holding a hoe;
> Afoot, yet riding a water buffalo.
> When the man has crossed over the bridge,
> It is the bridge that flows and the water that stands still.[116]

Another verse says:

> The stone lantern dances into the pillar;
> The Buddha Hall runs out the temple gate.[117]

And again:

> When the oxen of Huai-chou eat grain,
> The stomachs of the horses of I-chou are full.[118]

And again:

> When Mr. Chang drinks wine Mr. Li gets drunk.
> If you wish to know the essential meaning,
> Face south and see the Big Dipper.[119]

There is a verse by Han-shan:

> On the green mountain white waves arise;
> At the bottom of the well, red dust dances up.[120]

If a man has seen into his own nature, the meaning of these
verses is as clear as if he were looking at the palm of his own hand.
If you do not understand them, don't say that you have seen into
your own nature. And even if you are able to penetrate these

[116] *Shan-hui ta-shih yü-lu*, ZZ2, 25, 1, 13a.
[117] This verse is given in Hakuin's *Kaian koku go*, 3 (HOZ3, 141). The original
source has not been traced.
[118] This verse, attributed to Tu Shun (557–640) is found in *Shih-shuang Ch'u-
yüan ch'an-shih yü-lu*, ZZ2, 25, 1, 93a.
[119] The first line is to be found in the *Ts'ung-jung lu* (T48, p. 248a), among other
places. The other lines have not been traced.
[120] This verse is not contained in the *Ch'uan T'ang shih*. It is, however, found
in Japanese versions of Han-shan's poems, attributed to Shih-te. See *Kanzan-shi*
(Kyoto, Ogawaraya Hyōe, 1759, 2, 73a). Here the lines are inverted and there
are other slight variations in Hakuin's version.

verses with a detailed understanding, do not think that this is enough. Discard them and take up the koans of Su-shan's Memorial Tower, the Death of Nan-ch'üan, Ch'ien-feng's Three Kinds of Sickness, Wu-tsu's Water Buffalo Passing through a Window, Shūhō's: "In the morning we see each other face to face; in the evening we rub shoulders. What am I?" and Honnu Enjō Kokushi's comment, "The koan of the Cypress Tree in the Garden—herein lies the cleverness of the bandit."[121] If you have mastered these koans without the slightest bit of doubt, then you can be known as one whose ability to see into his own nature is one with the Buddhas and the Patriarchs. You may without the slightest reservation call yourself a hero who has mastered the mysteries.

Why is this so? To study Zen under a Master is to vow to make clear the minds of the Buddhas and the Patriarchs. If this mind has once been made clear, what is there that can be unclear in the words of the Buddhas and the Patriarchs? If these words are not yet understandable to you, then you are one who has yet to awaken to the mind of the Buddhas and the Patriarchs. For this reason the *Sūtra of the Seven Wise Women*[122] says: "The Buddha said: 'My disciples and great arhats are unable to understand this meaning. It is only the group of great bodhisattvas who can understand it.'" What does "this meaning" mean? It is the hidden essential to enlightenment, handed down from India to Japan through the various Patriarchs. To make people awaken to what "this meaning" is, they have left us these koans, so difficult to pass through. Therefore the Priest of Shinjū-an[123] has said:

[121] The first four of the above koans, dealing with celebrated T'ang monks, can be found most conveniently in Fujita Genro, ed., *Kattō-shū* (*Zudokko* [Kyoto, 1957], I, 152, 196, 121–22 respectively). Shūhō's (Myōchō's, Daitō Kokushi's) koan is incorrectly cited in the present version of Hakuin's text. The original is found in *Daitō Kokushi goroku*, T81, p. 244a. Honnu Enjō Kokushi is the posthumous name of Kanzan Egen (1277–1360), the founder of the Myō-shin-ji in Kyoto.

[122] It is difficult to determine to what work Hakuin is referring. The statement is frequently encountered in Mahayana texts. Later on in the text (see "Orategama III," fn. 24) Hakuin repeats the quotation, attributing it presumably to the *Lotus Sūtra*.

[123] Ikkyū Sōjun. He has appeared before.

"The five hundred arhats of Tendai put on their monks' robes and went out among the people. Their supernatural powers and marvelous activities are their own concern. The marvelous Law that even the Buddhas and the Patriarchs cannot transmit is quite beyond their means." Ikkyū was in the seventh generation in Japan after Hsi-keng[124] and his wisdom, as seen here, was brilliant. The Zen style had yet to decline in Ikkyū's time and is much to be respected.

But the idiots of today do not understand. One often hears that band of blind, bald fools, that can't tell a jewel from a stone, say things like: "Our very mind is itself the Buddha. What is there to do after we have finished our koan study? If the mind is pure then the Pure Land is pure. What's the use of studying the *Records* of the Patriarchs?" People of this kind are miserable, moronic heretics who have yet to attain anything, but say that they have attained it, have yet to gain awakening, but say that they are awakened. If you look at what they arbitrarily refer to as the mind, it is the *ālaya*-consciousness,[125] that dark cesspool of stupidity and ignorance. Completely mistaken, they recognize a thief and acknowledge him as a child. They take their errors and pass them along to others, and claim that this is the mysterious Way handed down by the Patriarchs. They see someone earnestly and painfully engaged in the study of Zen under a teacher and say: "So-and-so does not understand the direct pointing to the perfect and sudden wisdom; he has only the capacity of a Hinayana follower; so-and-so does not understand the highest Zen, he is only in the *śrāvaka* class."[126] But if you examine the content of what they call direct pointing to the sudden and perfect wisdom, you will find that it is the basic ignorance so roundly condemned

[124] Hsi-keng (Sokkō) is the pseudonym of Hsü-t'ang Chih-yü (Kidō Chigu, 1185–1269), the teacher of Nampo Jōmyō (Daiō Kokushi, 1235–1309), from whose line Hakuin is descended.

[125] The eighth, or "storing consciousness" of the Consciousness Only (Vijñā-matra) school of Buddhism. While Hakuin accepts the classification of eight kinds of consciousness propounded by this school, he constantly stresses the need to go beyond it.

[126] The *Śrāvaka* is a Hinayana disciple who is working for or who has gained Nirvana. Mahayana takes the position that his Nirvana is incomplete.

in the *Śūraṅgama Sūtra*. Their capacities, when compared to those they call Hinayanists and *śrāvakas*, are as inferior as is earth to heaven. Then they seize upon the learned sages who have gained wisdom of themselves and recklessly make light of their attainments. Really, it is a laughable situation!

Then there are others who say: "Let's make it the *Mu* koan," or "Let's make it the Cypress Tree in the Garden koan." In their delusion they think that this place that is unreachable through their own efforts *is* the Way of Zen, and that they have penetrated to its inner meaning. Such people are an evil lot and suffer from the great Zen sickness, so difficult to cure. This fatal disease, made up of error compounded upon error, all stems from deluded discrimination.

The hero who practices the true study of Zen is not at all like this. Piling study upon more study, he has reached the place that requires no more study. He has exhausted reason, reached the end of words and ingenuity, stretched his hand to the precipice, returned again from the dead, and later been able to attain the peace where the "Ka" is shouted.[127]

It is a frightening thing to see, then, someone with a mind beset by ignorance and delusions about birth and destruction approach these koans, so difficult to pass through and so difficult to understand, as well as this bone-breaking, life-taking Great Matter,[128] and talk about them any which way. My old teacher Shōju used always to knit his brows and say: "The Buddha always sternly warned against preaching about the true form of the Dharma while possessing a mind that concerned itself with birth and destruction." Yet of the monks who move about like clouds and water, eight or nine out of ten will boast loudly that they have not the slightest doubt about the essential meaning of any of the seventeen hundred koans that have been handed down. There are many such people who, though possessing no understanding whatsoever, have not the slightest doubt in their own minds and prattle on in this way. If you test them with one of

[127] *Kaji ichige:* refers to the cry emitted at the moment of enlightenment. "Ka" is said to be the sound made while straining at the oars of a boat. The expression is used frequently by Hakuin.
[128] *Daiji.* The ultimate truth of Buddhism.

these koans, some will raise their fists, others will shout "katsu," but most of them will strike the floor with their hands.[129] If you press them just a little bit, you will find that they have in no way seen into their own natures, have no learning whatsoever, and are only illiterate, boorish, sightless men. From what teacher have they learned this frightening, villainous, outlandish behavior? They wander about shouting their inanities for a few years and then disappear in the end, leaving no traces of themselves whatsoever. Have they gone to India or perhaps to China? Or maybe turned into kites[130] or become rush mats? I can't count the number of people of this type that I have met. Their enlightenment wouldn't even work as medicine to treat a cavity.

It is indeed regrettable that these people, who have the capacities for leadership and are blessed innately with superb talents and who, if they expended their powers to study the mysteries and applied themselves to accumulating virtues, might have been great shade trees to comfort the world, as were Ma-tsu, Shih-t'ou, Lin-chi, and Te-shan,[131] should have learned these pointless deluded views at a time when they were young and still had the motivation to succeed. Now when they see people earnestly expending their energies in the study of Zen, they laugh uproariously and say: "You have not yet stopped the mind that rushes about seeking." This kind of trashy understanding that only goes as far as recognizing the dark cave of the vacuous, neuter *ālaya*-consciousness, could be comprehended by a crow-chasing acolyte, if he spent a few days puzzling over it. It is only natural that what they bring is something that has been learned elsewhere! They have become monks who are beyond the reach of even the Buddhas and the Patriarchs. Although at first they are believed in to a certain extent, these stupid, inane, blind commoners gradually become unacceptable to laymen, and

---

[129] Typical "answers" given in the private interview with the Master, used to indicate the state of understanding of a koan. "Katsu" is the sound of the shout; it is not translatable.

[130] The bird.

[131] Ma-tsu and Lin-chi have appeared before. Shih-t'ou Hsi-ch'ien (Sekitō Kisen, 700–790) and Te-shan Hsüan-chien (Tokusan Senkan, 780 or 782–865) are also famed Zen Masters of the T'ang period.

eventually are despised by both parishioners and patrons. How and where they end up is unknown; this seems to be what the monk's pilgrimage has come to be in these days.

How does one obtain true enlightenment? In the busy round of mundane affairs, in the confusion of worldly problems, amidst the seven upside-downs and the eight upsets,[132] behave as a valiant man would, when surrounded by a host of enemies. Mount your steed, raise your lance, and, with a good showing of your courageous spirit, make up your mind to attack, destroy, and annihilate the enemy. Be a man who always attaches to himself the unsurpassed luster of the true, uninterrupted meditation, one who has no further need to demonstrate his activity, but has attained a state of mind that has extinguished both body and mind and has made all into an empty cave. At such a time, if one allows no fears to arise, and marches forward single-mindedly, one will suddenly be endowed with a great power. At all times in your study of Zen, fight against delusions and worldly thoughts, battle the black demon of sleep, attack concepts of the active and the passive, order and disorder, right and wrong, hate and love, and join battle with all the things of the mundane world. Then in pushing forward with true meditation and struggling fiercely, there unexpectedly will be true enlightenment.

Pradhānaśūra Bodhisattva[133] violated the precepts and found no means for repentance. His mind was tortured with sorrow and grief. Suddenly, of himself, he was inspired to make the great vow[134] and, sitting silently in meditation, he gave battle to his sorrow and grief. And then suddenly he awoke to the realization of non-birth.

The Zen Master Yün-men, when he was at the place of the old monk of Mu-chou,[135] had his left leg broken and thereby

---

[132] Hakuin is probably referring here to the eight upside-down views (*viparyaya*). They are variously defined and include such things as deluded thoughts, views on concepts of pleasure, pain, permanence, the self, and so forth.

[133] Based on a passage in *Cheng-tao ko* (T48, p. 396c).

[134] The great vow is the determination to practice Buddhism.

[135] Reference is to Ch'en Tsun-su (Chin Sonshuku, 780?–877?), who slammed the gate on Yün-men's leg, breaking it, but thereby giving him enlightenment. See ZD, p. 160.

gained a great enlightenment. I Ch'an-shih of Meng-shan[136] constantly suffered from diarrhea day and night until his body was exhausted by the pain and he was on the verge of passing away. Thereupon he gave rise to the great vow and sat in intense meditation, fighting his pain. After a little while his intestines rumbled loudly a few times, and then his disease was cured. Daien [Hōkan] Kokushi[137] went to pay a call on Yōzan Rōshi[138] of the Shōtaku-ji[139] in Hanazono to talk about his understanding of Zen. Yōzan reviled him, struck him, and drove him away. Angered, Gudō went one very hot day to a grove of bamboo and sat in meditation without a stitch of clothing covering his body. At night great swarms of mosquitoes surrounded him and covered his skin with bites. Fighting at this time against the hideous itching, he gritted his teeth, clenched his fists, and simply sat as though mad. Several times he almost lost consciousness, but then unexpectedly he experienced a great enlightenment.

The Buddha underwent painful practice in the Himalaya for six years until he was only skin and bones and the reeds pierced his lap, reaching to his elbows. Hui-k'o[140] cut off his arm at the elbow and penetrated to the depth of his basic origin. Hsüan-sha,[141] while climbing down Mount Hsiang-ku[142] in tears, tripped and broke his left leg and at that moment penetrated to the essence of the teaching. Lin-chi was struck by his teacher Huang-po and suddenly gained awakening.

Described above are examples from the past and present. At no time has there ever been a Buddha, a Patriarch, or a learned sage who has not seen into his own nature. If, as seems to be the custom nowadays, you depend upon a common understanding,

136 Te-i Ch'an-shih (Tokui Zenji, n.d.). Yüan dynasty monk. He is known also as Meng-shan, after the mountain on which he lived.
137 Posthumous title of Gudō Tōshoku (1577–1661), a famous priest in Hakuin's line of descent.
138 Yōzan Keichū (1560–1625).
139 Branch temple, within the compounds of the Myōshin-ji, in the western part of Kyoto.
140 Hui-k'o (Eka). The Second Patriarch of Zen in China.
141 Hsüan-sha Shih-pei (Gensha Shibi, 835–908). Another famed T'ang monk.
142 Another name for Mt. Hsüeh-feng in Fukien.

foolishly generated in the heart, and think that the knowledge
and discrimination of the Great Matter that you have arrived at
for yourself is sufficient, you will never in your life be able to
break the evil net of delusion. A trifling knowledge is a hindrance
to enlightenment, and it is this that these people possess.

In the middle ages when the Zen Sect flourished, samurai and
high officials whose minds were dedicated to the true meditation
would, when they had a day off from their official duties, mount
their horses and, accompanied by seven or eight robust soldiers,
gallop about places crowded with people, as Ryōgoku and
Asakusa[143] are today. Their purpose was to test the quality and
validity of their meditation in the midst of activity.

In the past Ninagawa Shinuemon[144] gained a great awakening
while involved in a fight. Ōta Dōkan[145] composed *waka* poems
while held down by an opponent on the field of battle. My old
teacher Shōju, at a time when his village was beset by an enormous
pack of wolves, sat for seven nights in different graveyards.
Although the wolves were sniffing at his neck and ears, he did this
to test the validity of true meditation, continuous and without
interruption.

Shōkū Shōnin[146] of Mount Shosha used always to lament:
"If worldly thoughts are intense then thoughts of the Way are
shallow; if thoughts of the Way are intense then worldly thoughts
are shallow." I would be the first to admit that these endless
tedious words of mine, hard to read and hard to understand, have
continued on and on as though my "worldly thoughts were
intense." Yet I am in the twilight of my life, near to drawing my
last breath. What is there that has been lacking in my life? Should
I wag my tail and beg for pity? I have no special favors to ask of
any one nor need I fish for fame amidst the waves of the world.
Perhaps I can help somewhat in creating a feeling for the Way,
in fulfilling what is known as the vow to study all the Buddhist

---

[143] Crowded popular sections of the Edo of Hakuin's day.
[144] Ninagawa Chikamasa (d. 1447). A lay disciple of Ikkyū.
[145] Ōta Dōkan (1432–1486). Warrior who first built a castle at Edo.
[146] Shōkū Shōnin (910–1007). Celebrated monk who resided at Mt. Shosha in
Harima.

teachings everywhere,[147] and to assist the group[148] somewhat in the future in their quest for knowledge of Buddhism. There is the saying that it is easy to find a thousand soldiers but that one general is difficult to discover. If in my writing there is even a little bit that you can adopt, if your lord's feeling for the Way be increased and his study of Zen brought to fruition, then that influence will surely be felt by the others around him. If those around him are touched by that influence, then surely it will extend to all the people in his town. And if the whole town is influenced, then surely it will extend to the whole province. Why is this so? It is because the mind of one man is the mind of all men. Then eventually that influence will extend all over the nation; at the top it will assist in the moral example set by the ruler, and below the common people will be benefited. Should this then happen, what could be better than for this influence to extend throughout the entire universe?

[To assist in] this has been my humble aspiration throughout my life. If it were not so, what vanity has led me to write the whole night through by the light of a single lantern, rubbing my tired old eyes, writing again and again this endless, unasked-for scribbling so that I might send it to you? If you think that what I have written has some value, do not throw it away but read it thoroughly. If you come into accord with the techniques of introspection as a means of nourishing life, the body and the mind will both be healthy and you will soon obtain the rewards of Zen meditation and the joy of reaching to the state where the "Ka" is shouted.

Another wish I have is that by the efficacy of this introspection you will gain a life as long as that of Takenouchi no Sukune or Urashima.[149] I hope that you will render service in the administration of government and will cherish with compassion

---

[147] Third of the Four Great Vows used throughout Buddhism. The others are: to save all sentient beings everywhere, to cut off all the passions everywhere, the vow as seen in the text above, and the vow to achieve the unsurpassed Buddha Way.

[148] Presumably a group of men associated with Lord Nabeshima. The term used is *ango*, the summer retreat for meditation and study.

[149] Both are legendary for the great age to which they attained.

the common people; that you will protect Buddhism; that you will secure the delight of constant joy in the Law and in meditation, and reach the ultimate of the teachings. All this is the small wish that I bear constantly in mind.

In my later years I have come to the conclusion that the advantage in accomplishing true meditation lies distinctly in the favor of the warrior class. A warrior must from the beginning to the end be physically strong. In his attendance on his duties and in his relationships with others, the most rigid punctiliousness and propriety are required. His hair must be properly dressed, his garments in the strictest of order, and his swords must be fastened at his side. With this exact and proper deportment, the true meditation stands forth with an overflowing splendor. Mounted on a sturdy horse, the warrior can ride forth to face an uncountable horde of enemies as though he were riding into a place empty of people. The valiant, undaunted expression on his face reflects his practice of the peerless, true, uninterrupted meditation sitting. Meditating in this way, the warrior can accomplish in one month what it takes the monk a year to do; in three days he can open up for himself benefits that would take the monk a hundred days.

Yet nowadays, because they have not the determination or have not been sufficiently instructed, these people mount great horses fit to bear the names "Ikezumi" or "Surusumi."[150] Piling on their backs tremendous loads of ignorance and delusion, they ride heedlessly past with stern countenances. Isn't this a sad thing? Passing by this vital place, they say: "We hold official positions. While we are engaged in our duties we have no time to sit in meditation." Their mental climate is like that of men who, while in the middle of the ocean, search for water.

The *Ssu-shih-erh chang ching* [*Sūtra of the Forty-two Chapters*] says: "Man faces twenty perils. It is difficult to be wealthy and still to like the Way."[151] How true this is! There are numberless people, both nobles and commoners, who possess wealth and fame, but if you search the whole world over, you will not find

---

[150] Famous horses given by Minamoto no Yoritomo (1147–1199) to his retainers at the battle of Ujigawa in 1184. Ikezumi was given to Sasaki Takatsuna (n.d.) and Surusumi to Kajiwara Kagesue (1162–1200).

[151] I do not find this passage in the *Taishō* text.

one who fears the painful cycle of his next rebirth, or who seeks the way to escape from it. This is the time to fix in oneself the state of mind that conforms to the teaching of the Buddha. What good comes from piling wealth upon wealth, not knowing what is enough; from seeking fame greater than the fame one has, without being sated?

Only you, my lord, see that wealth is like flowers in the air, that fame is nothing but an illusion. You have always wisely devoted your thoughts to the unsurpassed Great Way. You have already called on me in my rude hut three times, just as long ago Liu Pei called three times on Chu-ko Liang in his humble cottage.[152] Liu Pei wanted to unite the Three Kingdoms; you seek to transcend the three worlds. The intention is the same, but how different the aspiration! Long ago Chu-ko Liang cast aside his plow and risked his life to give answer three times. How can I begrudge these feeble words to give in return for your three visits? Wondering what principle of the Law to write you of, I can only wish that you may strengthen and expand your noble spirit, that all at once you may penetrate to the Great Matter of our teaching, and that you may experience the great ecstasy of joy on awakening. For these reasons I have continued writing you these quite inadequate lines.

The Great Matter of our teaching cannot, of course, be expressed in words, yet if you maintain without error the essence of your Zen practice, of your own accord you will awaken to the Great Matter. Your messenger returned in such haste the other day that I did not have the time to answer you then. This was an inexcusable impoliteness on my part. Fortunately Kisen[153] announced yesterday that he was returning to Ihara. Delighted with the opportunity, I had him wait until I might finish my answer. I spent the whole night without sleep, writing from dusk to dawn, and although I have written some five hundred lines, I still have not expressed all I wish to convey. I have gotten so old that my powers of memory are failing me: what I wrote about in

152 Liu Pei (162–223) sought the advice of Chu-ko Liang (181–234), who agreed to enter his service, and rendered him invaluable aid in his efforts to reunite the country.
153 Unidentified.

the beginning I find myself writing again in the end. I have made all sorts of mistakes in my sentences, but there is no time to read it over again, so I shall seal it and give it to Kisen to deliver. It is somewhat like sending you a chicken from Ch'u in a basket and calling it the phoenix from Tan-shan.[154]

After having glanced through this letter, please burn it so the contents are not revealed. If, however, you find in it something that you can use, I should like to make a clean copy to present to you. Otherwise have your scribes make a few copies, and have them distributed among your young and talented retainers, as well as to Wada Kunikata[155] and his group. Then have them read it thoroughly from time to time. When you have the leisure, call together some of your faithful retainers, such as Tsutsumi and Nakazawa,[156] as well as several of the older ministers and physicians. Have them sit about you and listen to what I have written. You yourself, seated on your cushion, sometimes listening, sometimes drowsing off, will serve to nourish the feeling for the Way. If a half-day's idle time can be enjoyed in this way, then of itself an atmosphere of delight in the Law and joy in meditation will manifest itself. There will be no need to envy the pleasures of the Four Deva Kings and the heaven of the thirty-three devas, nor the wondrous realms of the Yāma and Tuṣita heavens.[157] How much less so the filthy and opulent parties, the frivolous and extravagant dissipations, the monstrous and cruel illusory sports of the world of man, where the ears are captivated by the eight sounds[158] and the eyes blinded by the many dances. What use indeed even to consider such things!

Give careful consideration to what I have written and if any of your retainers near at hand or in outlying areas seem to be persons suited for instruction, then if they are carefully guided along, they will all conform to the bodhisattva vow to seek enlightenment and to bring the teaching to all beings. From amidst the dusts of the world there will arise a wondrous good teacher—

---

[154] To make something worthless appear to have value.
[155] Unidentified.   [156] Unidentified.
[157] Heavens in the world of desire, where the beings are still subject to the cycle of birth and death.
[158] Of the eight musical scales.

whom I do not know—who, mounted on his steed, a sword at his side, will ride all over and constantly turn the unsurpassed wheel of the Law of the many Buddhas.

They say that beneath a strong general there are no weak soldiers. So soldiers as valiant as Kāśyapa, Ānanda, Śāriputra, and Pūrṇa,[159] beginning with Tamura and Nomura,[160] will appear in numbers under your banner. Then, no matter what event should occur in the world, the general and his troops as well, motivated by the one great true vitality, though but a hundred men facing ten thousand, will be unaware of any birth up to now. How then can there be such a thing as death! They will press forward as though piercing through the hardest stone. Their quiet will be as that of a lofty mountain, their speed that of a roaring typhoon. Nothing that they face will not fall before them; nothing that they touch will not collapse into pieces. Even though they were in the midst of the raging turmoils of the Hōgen and Heiji wars, it would be as though they were standing in a vast plain empty of people. This we call the vital spirit and purpose of the truly great man.

When the benevolence of the lord and the benevolence of the Law are together handed down, the soldiers are well cared for. Who would regret giving his life for his lord? If the fear of birth and death is no longer present, what need is there to seek for Nirvana? All the ten directions dissolve before the eyes; in one thought the three periods[161] are penetrated. This is due to the power of true meditation. At such a time the warriors are filled with respect, the commoners feel close, the prince operates with benevolence, the ministers are motivated by truth. The farmers have sufficient grain, the women sufficient cloth; all, both high and low, feel love for the Way. The country is at peace and will continue for ten thousand generations without decaying. This is the best that man and Heaven can do. Is there any difference between the person who becomes ordained while carrying on administrative affairs, and the bodhisattva who carries out

159 Among the great disciples of the Buddha.
160 Unidentified. Presumably samurai in the employ of Lord Nabeshima.
161 Past, present, and future.

his work of salvation in the form of an administrative officer?[162]

> With deepest respect,
> Written by the old heretic
> who sits under the Sāla tree.

Midsummer, the 26th day of the fifth month of the fifth year of Enkyō [= June 20, 1748]

II

Letter to a Sick Monk living far away

✤ It is always good to have news and letters from you and it was with pleasure that I received your fine letter, with its refreshing scent of the fields, through the kindness of Kin Zenjin.[1] I had been talking of paying you a visit, hoping that your practice was continuing unflaggingly and that perhaps you might have gained the joy of the state where the "Ka" is shouted. Then news came that from last summer you had not been feeling at all well, had been obliged to enter the sick room, and were in constant anxiety. But now Kin Zenjin indicates that things are not all that bad and that for the past two or three days you have been able to enter the meditation hall. You can imagine how happy this made me feel.

No matter how sick a monk may be, disease is something that must be left to the lay world. The monk must concern himself solely with the vital matter at hand, the continuation of his true meditation. Persistent practice at the times one is suffering from illness is essential, and there should be no concern for whatever adverse fortune one might meet in the future. No idleness can be tolerated, for you must be convinced that this is

[162] One of the thirty-three forms in which the bodhisattva Kannon appears is as a government official.   [1] Unidentified.

indeed the most vital time, and must never under any circumstances succumb to carelessness.

Thirty years ago my old teacher Shōju Rōjin[2] told an ill monk: "There is nothing in this world so miserable and painful as the illness of those who are sensitive.[3] Insecure as they are, they think continually of events of the past or wonder about the future. They complain about the qualities of those who are caring for them; they resent not hearing from old friends who are far away. They regret not having achieved fame in their own lifetimes and dread the pains of the long night that will follow their deaths. They think of their native villages and are sorry that they have no wings that might bear them there. They pray to the gods and are infuriated that there is no immediate response. When they lie down and close their eyes they may seem comfortably in repose, yet within their breasts a fierce battle rages and within their minds they suffer more severely than the beings in the three evil ways. They imagine a minor illness to be a major disease. If they are so maddened by illness before they have died, one can imagine what they will be like in the afterworld. If recollections served as medicine and helped in recuperation, I would be glad to come and help make it possible for them to indulge in them. But the very recollections are excruciating: the fire in the heart flames upward, the metal in the lungs exhausts itself in pain, the body fluids dry up and chills and fevers rack the body without cease. Gradually sweating increases until it finally becomes difficult to sustain the root of life. These people spend their whole lives in purposeless idleness and their deluded minds turn slight disease into major illnesses. Such people are not killed by sickness but rather are eaten up by deluded thoughts. Deluded thoughts are indeed more terrifying than tigers and wolves. These animals cannot get in through doors and fences, but the wolves of deluded notions can climb through the floor of the meditation platform and wreak havoc among the folds of the monks' garments. Some

[2] The major portion of this letter, except for the concluding pages, is a quotation attributed by Hakuin to his teacher Shōju Rōjin. The text gives "an old monk," but by context this must refer to Shōju.

[3] The term used is *chie no aru hito* [men of wisdom]; here, however, it is used to signify the tendency to nervousness caused by sensitivity to one's lot.

sick people cry piteously, claiming that none is cursed with such shallow fortune as they. They have been born as men, a state so difficult to attain, and have even gained the venerated calling of monks, yet they have neither accumulated the virtues of sitting in meditation nor seen the light of the Buddha. They shed tears of complaint, regretting that everything has been wasted, and although they seek to gain our sympathy, they are nothing but monks who are unenlightened because of their own sloth and carelessness.

"For effective meditation nothing is better than practice while one is ill. The wise men of old hid themselves in cliffs and valleys, concealed their whereabouts in deep mountain fastnesses in order to put the affairs of the world at a distance, separate themselves from mundane duties, and devote themselves to a single-minded practice of the Way. But when you are ill there is no need to go off to valleys and mountains. After all, the sick monk avoids the difficult tasks of going out on begging rounds and performing temple work. He need not wait on other monks or entertain guests; he is spared the noisy bustle of lectures and idle talk. He knows nothing of the difficulties attendant on running a monastery, nor does he see anything of the ever-shifting vagaries of daily life. Whether he lives or dies depends upon the will of heaven; his hunger and cold are the responsibility of the person who cares for him. Like a cat or dog bowing to circumstance, he need not comprehend things nor make decisions. All he must do is sit intently on his cushion and concern himself only with ensuring that his own true meditation is not lost. Seeing that birth and death are but illusions, and casting aside all concepts of heaven and hell, this evil world and the Pure Land, he turns towards that place where an instant of thought of [the distinction between good and bad] has not yet arisen and where the manifold activities do not reach. If from time to time he investigates this principle and makes the continuation of true meditation the most vital matter, suddenly he will transcend the limits of birth and death and leap over the boundaries of enlightenment and delusion.

"Achieving the true body of the Diamond indestructible,[4]

---

[4] Descriptive of the body of the Buddha.

is he not then a true immortal, unaging and undying? Does he not then think fondly of having been born into the world of man? Is this not the dignity of the monk with the shaven head? Is this not the wondrous miracle of the Buddha Way? For a man who has truly practiced Zen, good fortune and bad fortune, success and shame, contrary cause and accordant cause are all fodder for the karma that leads to Buddhahood. For the indolent and weak, trivial worldly affairs, even an illness no more significant than a mustard seed, turn into enormous obstacles, and in the end become the workings of karma. Making all sorts of excuses, such as that they have no affinity for *prajñā*, they draw away from *prajñā*, which is not far off,[5] and plant and nourish basic karmic hindrances. There is nothing so pitiable as placing one's whole life in error for reasons such as these. Since ancient times there have been many occasions when men have smashed the ball of doubt[6] while still suffering from some grievous illness.

"Some time ago a certain old priest developed so serious a tumor that his back swelled up like a lacerated white gourd-melon. There was nothing to do but apply hot poultices to his hideous wound and to urge food upon him. He did not allow people to come near, but lay alone in agony with his eyes shut. One day two or three of his fellow monks paid a call to console him. At this time a surgeon was present who, as he cut away the offending flesh, remarked: 'If I add medicine to the plaster it will probably be much more painful than usual tonight. It is most regrettable that such a thing as a tumor should have made its appearance on your body and have caused you much pain for so many days. But from today new flesh will form and you can expect gradually to find your health returning.' In this way the doctor tried to soothe his patient's pains.

"The priest opened his eyes, looking as though he had just awakened from a deep sleep. 'You have all been so kind to come to see me. I want to tell you of something that I cannot possibly

---

[5] All men are inherently endowed with *prajñā*, or wisdom.
[6] *Gidan*. The term indicates the accumulated tensions and doubts that when shattered lead to awakening. For a discussion see ZD, p. 247.

conceal. All of you, come close. This severe illness of mine has been an honored good teacher. Because of the tumor I have come to know the errors of the past twenty years and now I possess the joy of fulfilling the vow that I made some forty years ago. Before I became ill I thought that nothing was lacking in my enlightenment, that I had reached a stage where my practice wanted for nothing. Discarding this practice, I brazenly accepted offerings and behaved in a rude and haughty manner. Then unexpectedly, I sank into this severe illness. My head, hands, and feet felt as though they were boiling, my bones and sinews as if they were falling apart. I was on the verge of losing consciousness and it seemed as though there were an impediment in my heart. I felt the tortures of hell beginning imperceptibly to take form and enlightenment and understanding had gone I knew not where. I could not summon even a small part of my strength, and only deluded thoughts and pain were left. How terrible it was! Who would envy me, were I to die amidst such suffering and pain?

"'Feeling that my life could in no way be saved, I set about practicing true meditation. Not knowing whether the pain or the meditation would triumph, I resolved to carry my attack to the utmost limits of my capabilities. I worked up a stern and intense determination and dauntlessly pressed forward. Once or twice I faltered under the suffering but soon picked up my resolve again and pressed on unremittingly. Determined that the time would come when I would be victorious in my battle, I forgot about night and day, sleeping and waking. And then finally a great enlightenment shone before me. For the past two weeks my mind has been cleared of the mists and clouds of delusions and pains; I feel nothing but a great peace. I have awakened to the true principles of the non-duality of birth and death; I transcend the distinctions between Buddha and demon. I have penetrated to the hidden principles of the single Diamond indestructible. From today on, no matter what misfortunes and obstacles may befall me, I realize that there is nothing that can block my enlightenment. I would hope that others, when they arrive at a time like this, would not depend on trivial understanding, acting in the way that I did when I was well. I cannot repeat enough how essential it is that the true meditation not be neglected when you are in good

health. Today has its virtue; may everything be as fortunate as
this! All things considered, has not this tumor been unsurpassed
as a good teacher to me? However, when I think about what
offerings I should make or what praises I should sing, I cannot
help but have a feeling of regret at having to part with my
tumor as it gradually heals.' As he finished speaking his face broke
into a smile. This story I heard from the monks who attended
on him at the time.

"There is another story I have heard that concerns a certain
Dharma-master of the Shūgendō school[7] of Shingon. Desperately
ill of typhoid fever, he lay in bed groaning all day and
night. Hearing his moans, one impertinent fellow among his
disciples remarked jokingly: 'The priest is not his ordinary self.
His words don't sound the way they usually do when he is
scolding us. Just listen to him moan and groan!'

"The priest laughed too: 'Watch out, young acolytes! Three
days ago my groans sounded as though I were suffering the
torments of the Hell of Wailing. Today my groans are the mysterious sounds of the Supreme Dharma. If you mock me you will
suffer the punishments of those who slander the True Law.'

"The young monk then asked: 'Can one attain Buddhahood
as quickly as one can turn over one's hand?'

"The priest replied: 'That's why the Buddha spent three
endless kalpas to achieve Nirvana for the sake of indolent sentient
beings and why he preached that for the courageous among
sentient beings, Buddhahood may be attained in one instant of
thought.

"'In the past I suffered pains of illness that were difficult to
bear, and gradually these shadowy afflictions themselves stirred
fears of the pains of my next rebirth, and I wept all night with
regret for my actions in my present life. But then I changed my
outlook, entered into the contemplation of the non-duality [of
myself and] Birushana (Vairocana) Buddha. I shut my eyes and
clamped my teeth and continued my contemplation. A marvelous
thing indeed! My pains disappeared as though they had been
scraped and washed away. My body, which had been prostrate in

---

[7] Mountain ascetics who stressed austerity and discipline.

pain, appeared as the Treasure Seal of the Yoga Mystery.[8] Unknowingly I attained the True Form of the Diamond indestructible. This groaning voice became one with the Great *Dhāraṇī* of the Three Mysteries.[9] The bed on which I lay became the original great ground [of Enlightenment] of Birushana Buddha. The great mandala of the thousand qualities of the hundred worlds[10] shone majestically before my eyes. What joy I experienced! I realized my cherished desire where beings, sentient and non-sentient, achieve the Way simultaneously; where trees, grass, and lands all attain to Buddhahood.'

"This was nothing that the young monks could comprehend by merely hearing of it, but they wept tears of delight, saying that they would speak of the felicity encountered on this propitious day. Later, because of his experiences, the priest was able to achieve unsurpassed accomplishments in Buddhism.

"Even in a foreign country there were comparatively many men of this sort: Chu-hung[11] was severely scalded and Meng-shan[12] contracted dysentery, yet both made progress in the Way by virtue of their sicknesses. Yet you monks complain about some minor ailment and present a sorry spectacle. Why should you be in any way inferior to the men of old? Right this minute, if death were staring you in the face, if you set out to practice true meditation and passed away propitiously, you surely would be included among the true descendants of the Buddha and the Patriarchs. This is not to say that you must wait to become seriously ill before you begin your Zen study and meditation. But even people who are not in the best of health, if day and night they

---

[8] Correspondence in deed, word, and thought. Here and below we find Shingon terms expressive of *samādhi*.

[9] The Yoga Mystery comprises the three mysteries of body, mouth, and mind.

[10] Hakuin is here combining the Shingon Buddhist mandala, which is a pictorial representation of the cosmos, with a Tendai Buddhist term, the "thousand qualities of the hundred worlds." Used together, these terms indicate that the true form of all things appeared before the sick priest's eyes. Later texts, however, change the term to "the Great Mandala of the Fourfold Circle."

[11] Yün-ch'i Chu-hung (Unsei Shukō, 1535–1615). Ming monk who combined Pure Land and Zen teachings. Hakuin attacks him throughout his writings.

[12] Te-i Ch'an-shih. Seen previously.

resist indolence and always use care as did those monks described above, will each and every one of them succeed in his study of the Way. At any rate, there is nothing so vitally essential as true meditation, nothing more worthy of veneration. Those who have yet to attain to enlightenment should present themselves before a true teacher and should, above all, determine [to study and practice]. Once the determination has been achieved, it is essential never to depart from true meditation in whatever you are doing throughout the day.

"The Zen Master Ta-hui has said: 'At all times test to see whether you have lost [the true meditation] or have not lost it.'[13] This is a generous description of the true meditation as it has been practiced by all the sages of the past. This has been the true practice, unchanged from remotest antiquity. It has been called Direct Mind, the Buddha Nature, Bodhi, Nirvana, the True Man without Rank.[14] This True Man has never, since before the kalpa of emptiness or after it, had the least sign of illness or the slightest indication of even a cold. In the *Lotus Sūtra* he is honored as the Ancient Buddha who gained enlightenment in remote kalpas. What Nan-yüeh, in his *Sui-i yüan hsing*,[15] has explained in these words: 'In the past on the Vulture Peak it was named the Lotus; now in the Western Land he is called Amida; in these degenerate times he is known as Kannon,' is in reference to this very True Man. If you make offerings to him, venerate him, draw close to him and do not lose him, what disease cannot be cured, what Way cannot be fulfilled? Under the Law of the Buddha even a diseased old woman or an emaciated old man, if they practice true meditation without cease, can become strong persons, healthy and without infirmities.

"But even if a man has a body seven or eight feet tall, even if he has the wisdom of Śāriputra and the eloquence of Pūrṇa, even if he can lecture on the Three Sūtras and the Five Śāstras,[16]

[13] This quotation has appeared before. See "Orategama I," fn. 109.
[14] *Mui no shinnin*. The term derives from *Lin-chi lu* (T47, p. 496c).
[15] Nan-yüeh Hui-ssu (Nangaku Eshi, 515–577). The Second Patriarch of Tendai and teacher of Chih-i. This particular work has not been identified.
[16] There are several such groups; which ones Hakuin had in mind cannot be determined.

even if he has penetrated to the ultimate meaning of the teachings of the Five Houses and the Seven Schools, even if his strength is sufficient to raise the tripod of the Court of Chou, even if his eyes can penetrate to the remotest corners of the universe, if he does not possess this true meditation, he will be no more than a putrid, bloated corpse. Use caution! Meditation is nothing that can be taken on lightly. The Great Matter of true meditation is really difficult to maintain, really difficult to guard. The most pathetic thing about this degenerate age is that everyone is constantly in search of fame and profit. There are those whose hearts turn toward the Way, but only to make a vulgar show of things. One who has really determined to practice true meditation is difficult to find. Indeed, if you were to look for a person whose determination is set on uninterrupted true meditation, you would have difficulty in finding one among a thousand or even ten thousand persons.

"When I was thirteen I came to believe in the validity of the Zen teachings. When I was sixteen I destroyed the face that I received from my mother. At nineteen I left home to become a monk, and at thirty-five I concealed myself at this temple.[17] Now I am almost sixty-five years of age. For some forty years I have cast aside all mundane affairs, cut off my ties to the world, and devoted myself solely to guarding [my practice]. Finally, five or six years ago, I became aware that I had attained to the state where I could continuously carry on the real, true meditation practice. It is absurd even to attempt to carry on Zen study and meditation at the same time that one is insincerely flattering parishioners and donors and greedily seeking fame and profit. Often Zen Masters, and their students as well, make constant abundance into luxurious living, and the prosperity of the temple gives the style to the teaching. They think that eloquence and a clever tongue make for wisdom, equate fine food and clothing with the Buddha Way, make haughtiness and beauty into moral qualities, and take the faith exhibited by others as an indication that they themselves have attained the Dharma.

"But saddest of all, they make the human body, this thing

[17] The Shōju-an in Iiyama.

so difficult to obtain, a slave to their search for fame, and thus bury the unsurpassed Buddha mind under the dust pile of delusions. For this invitation, for that offering ceremony, they adorn themselves lavishly in inappropriate silken gowns, and preach recklessly about the difficult-to-attain doctrines of Zen and Buddhism, even though they do not understand them themselves. When dealing with the uneducated laymen they give forth with the eloquence of K'ung-ming or Tzu-fang.[18] In deftly acquiring offerings of money that represent much backbreaking toil on the part of the populace, they would appear to have gained the miraculous powers of a Maudgalyayāna or a Śāriputra. Seeking to steal temporary fame and profit, they neither believe in karma nor fear its recompense. When the time to die arrives and the solitary lamp flickers as they lie halfway between life and death, they cry and moan; the seven upside-downs and the eight upsets[19] assail them. Driven mad, with no place to put their hands and feet, they die so agonizing a death that their disciples and followers cannot bear to look at them. Make no mistake about it! With people today disposed in this way, what Zen practitioner, no matter what province he came from and no matter who he was, could possibly achieve the status of a Buddha or a Patriarch! By a strange series of circumstances people have come to this dreary place to spend the summer's meditation session. Is there any reason that I should spread evil teachings among them? I am an old monk who lives in a dilapidated building and knows nothing of the world, but I do not make the Buddhadharma into a sweet and simple thing.

"At any rate, there is no worse thing than for the practitioner to treasure his body, give it value, and pay it favor. One year when a large number of wolves were ravaging the village at the foot of the mountain, I went for seven nights to sit in meditation in the graveyards hereabouts. I did this to test whether or not I could practice true, uninterrupted meditation while surrounded by wolves that were sniffing at my ears and throat. Even if

[18] K'ung-ming is Chu-ko Liang, seen before; Tzu-fang is Chang Liang (d. 187 B.C.), famed advisor, noted for his eloquence.
[19] Unclear. Hakuin is probably referring to the seven or eight false views, mentioned before.

surrounded by snakes and water spirits, a man, once he has determined to do something, must resolve not to leave unfinished what he has started. No matter how cold or hungry he may be, he must bear it; no matter how much wind and rain may come, he must withstand it. Even if he must enter into the heart of fire or plunge to the bottom of icy waters, he must open the eye that the Buddhas and Patriarchs have opened, achieve the status that the Buddhas and the Patriarchs have achieved, penetrate the essential meaning of the teaching, and see through to the ultimate principle. He must smash the brains of Zen monks everywhere, pull out the nails, and knock out the wedges, and thereby recompense his deep obligation to the Buddhas and the Patriarchs.

"If you devote your efforts uninterruptedly and without backsliding to fulfilling the [Four] Great Vows, where is there a place for disease to strike? If you take the practice of the ancient Patriarchs to yourself and are never negligent, even if you experience the hardships of such men as Hsüan-sha and Tz'u-ming,[20] you are greatly to be venerated. But if you are careless you will become a false practitioner of Zen. By false I mean someone who has the mind of a fraud. There is no one who consciously wishes to change his defectless body into a fraud, but if you do not follow well the examples of the ancient Masters, do not deepen the mind that seeks the Way, and talk of Zen and gain the veneration of others, although you possess only a modicum of understanding yourself, you will become a splendid fraud. If you find that being circumspect in conduct and guarding your thoughts is not sufficient, then you would do well to starve to death in some distant field or freeze to death in the depths of the mountains. Gold is still gold, even when wrapped in straw. The gods will praise with palms pressed together, the dragon kings will protect with heads bowed a true descendant of the Buddhas and the Patriarchs. You may stoop to flattery and pile up wealth and possessions, have a thousand priests in attendance at your funeral, display ornaments of the seven treasures, hang banners and canopies that strike the eye, and erect a place for practice that

[20] Hsüan-sha has appeared before. Tz'u-ming (Jimyō) is the posthumous title of Shih-shuang Ch'u-yüan (Sekisō Soen, 986–1039), an important Zen monk of the early Sung period.

startles the mind, yet Emma, his eyes widened in anger, and the ox-headed devils, brandishing whips of iron, will be waiting for you and your lot will be a bitter one indeed."

These and other things were told to two or three attendant monks from eight in the evening until three the next morning, yet so fascinated were they that it seemed as though only a moment had passed. They shed tears of gratitude and his words were engraved on their minds and their skins broke out in a cold sweat. Later, whenever I became ill, I thought of what he had told us and my heart would suddenly be struck with shame and my ills would seem not so serious after all. Perhaps the gist of what I have written will be of some small help to people in the sick room. What I have described is the common cure that old Shōju dispensed, truly an excellent pill of a single ingredient, effective for reducing fevers.

There is still another remedy especially efficacious for debilitated people. Its properties for relieving exhaustion of the vital breath are particularly wondrous. It counteracts a rush of blood to the head, warms the legs, settles the bowels, brightens the eye, augments good wisdom, and is effective in casting aside all evil thoughts. [The recipe for] one dose of the soft butter pill [is as follows]: one part of the "real aspect of all things," one part each of "the self and all things," and the "realization that these are false," three parts of the "immediate realization of Nirvana," two parts of "without desires," two or three parts of the "nonduality of activity and quietude," one and a half parts of sponge-gourd skin, and one part of "the discarding of all delusions." Steep these seven ingredients in the juice of patience for one night, dry in the shade and then mash. Season with a dash of *Prajñā-pāramitā*,[21] then shape everything into a ball the size of a duck's egg and set it securely on your head.[22] Practitioners who are just beginning their study should not concern themselves with the properties of the medicine nor the amount used, but should merely

---

[21] The highest of the six *pāramitās*, or perfections. They are: charity, maintenance of commandments, patience, perseverance, meditation, and wisdom (*prajñā*).

[22] It is not that this soft butter pill actually exists, but the practitioner is asked to imagine that it is resting on his head, and to contemplate this fact.

contemplate the fact that a delicately scented soft butterish object the size of a duck's egg is suddenly on their heads. When a sick person wishes to use this remedy he should spread for himself a thick cushion, hold his back straight, adjust his eyes, and sit in a correct posture. He should then shift gently to position himself properly, and set about meditating.

After repeating three times the words: "Of the essentials of preserving life, nourishing the breath has no peer. When the breath is exhausted the body dies; when the people are downtrodden the nation collapses," one can truly carry out this contemplation. Those[23] who have this duck egg with the consistency of soft butter on their heads feel a strange sensation as the whole head becomes moist. Gradually this feeling flows downward: the shoulders, elbow, chest, diaphragm, lungs, liver, stomach, backbone, and buttocks all gradually become damp. At this time the various accumulations in the chest, and those of lumbago and constipation all drop down at will, as water flowing naturally to a low place. This sensation is felt throughout the body, and it circulates moving downward, warming the legs, until it reaches the soles of the feet, where it stops. The practitioner should then repeat the same contemplation. The overflow that penetrates downward sinks in and accumulates until it steeps the body in warmth, just as a good physician gathers together various aromatic herbs, brews them, and pours the concoction into the bath. The practitioner feels that his body from the navel down is steeped in this moisture. When this contemplation is being practiced, because it is induced only by mental activity, the sense of smell becomes aware of exotic odors, the sense of touch becomes wondrously acute, and the body and mind become attuned. Suddenly the accumulations dissolve, the bowels and stomach are harmonized, the skin becomes radiant, and the energies increase greatly. If this contemplation is conscientiously brought to maturation, what disease cannot be cured, what magical art cannot be performed? This is indeed the secret method for maintaining health, the wondrous art of longevity.

---

[23] The text for the remainder of this paragraph closely follows that of the *Yasen kanna* (HOZ5, 361).

This treatment was first devised by Shakamuni Buddha. In the middle ages it came down to Chih-i of the Tendai school, who used it widely as a treatment for extreme exhaustion. His elder brother Ch'en Ch'in[24] was saved from the brink of death by it, yet seldom in this degenerate age do we hear of this miraculous treatment. How sad that people today seldom gain knowledge of this way. When I was in my middle years I heard of it from the hermit Hakuyū, who maintained that the speed of its efficacy lay only in the degree to which the practitioner endeavored. If one is not laggard one may obtain long life. Don't say that Kokurin[25] has become senile and is teaching old-woman's Zen.[26] Perhaps if you just get to know it, you will clap your hands and laugh out loud. Why? "Unless you have seen disorders, you do not know the virtues of an honest minister; unless you have accumulated wealth, you do not know the determination of an honest man."[27]

III

Letter in Answer to an Old Nun of the Hoke [Nichiren] Sect

❀ This fall when I gave my lectures on the *Lotus Sūtra* I said that outside the mind there was no *Lotus Sūtra* and outside the *Lotus Sūtra* there was no mind. Thinking what you heard to be strange, you have written to ask me to explain to you the principle I expounded and to tell you of any other pertinent matters. In this letter I shall deal largely with the import of what

[24] This story has not been traced.
[25] Name of the forest in which Hakuin's temple, Shōin-ji, was located. Here Hakuin uses it to refer to himself.
[26] *Rōba Zen.* An old woman frequently appears in Zen stories, very frequently in a helpful capacity. It is used also in a derogatory sense, as here.
[27] In other words, unless you have tried this method you cannot know its validity.

I said, and ask you to read and reread what I write, in the hope that it will prove to be to your satisfaction.

I do indeed always say: Outside the mind there is no *Lotus Sūtra* and outside the *Lotus Sūtra* there is no mind. Outside the ten stages of existence[1] there is no mind and outside the ten stages of existence there is no *Lotus Sūtra*. This is the ultimate and absolute principle. It is not limited to me, but all the Tathāgata of the three periods,[2] and all learned sages everywhere, when they have reached the ultimate understanding, have all preached in the same way. The essential purport of the text of the *Lotus Sūtra* speaks gloriously to this effect. There are eighty-four thousand other gates to Buddhism, but they are all provisional teachings and cannot be regarded as other than expediencies. When this ultimate is reached, all sentient beings and all Tathāgata of the three periods, mountains, rivers, the great earth, and the *Lotus Sūtra* itself, all bespeak the Dharma principle that all things are a non-dual unity representing the true appearance of all things. This is the fundamental principle of Buddhism. We have indeed the 5,418 texts of the Tripitaka, that detail the limitless mysterious meaning spoken by Shakamuni Buddha. We have the sudden, gradual, esoteric, and indeterminate methods. But their ultimate principle is reduced to the 8 volumes of the *Lotus Sūtra*. The ultimate meaning of the 64,360-odd written characters of the *Lotus Sūtra* is reduced to the 5 characters in its title: *Myōhō renge kyō*. These 5 characters are reduced to the 2 characters *Myōhō* [Wondrous Law] and the 2 characters *Myōhō* return to the one word *mind*. If one asks to where this one word, *mind*, returns: "The horned rabbit and the furry turtle cross the nowhere mountain."[3] What is the ultimate meaning? "If you wish to know the mind of one who laments in the midst of spring, it is at the time when the needle is stopped and words cannot be spoken."[4]

---

[1] The ten stages, from hell to Buddha.

[2] Past, present, future, as mentioned earlier ("Orategama I," fn. 161).

[3] This phrase is found in Hakuin's *Kaian koku go*, 4 (HOZ3, 158). Its source in Chinese has not been traced.

[4] This sentence derives from *Kaian koku go*, 1 (HOZ3, 57). Everything is spring-like, but the wife does not share in the mood. She worries about her absent husband and pauses, rapt in thought, the needle held immobile.

This One Mind, derived from the two characters *Myōhō* mentioned above, when spread out includes all the Dharma worlds of the ten directions, and when contracted returns to the no-thought and no-mind of the self-nature. Therefore such things as "outside the mind no thing exists," "in the three worlds there is One Mind alone," and "the true appearance of all things," have been preached. Reaching this ultimate place is called the *Lotus Sūtra*, or the Buddha of Infinite Life[5]; in Zen it is called the Original Face, in Shingon the Sun Disc of the Inherent Nature of the Letter *A*,[6] in Ritsu[7] the Basic, Intangible Form of the Precepts. Everyone must realize that these are all different names for the One Mind.

One may ask: "What proof is there that the five characters *Myōhō renge kyō* point to the fountainhead of the one mind?" These five characters, just as they are, immediately serve as proof that can readily be substantiated. Why? *Myōhō renge kyō* is a title that sings the praises of the mysterious virtues of the One Mind. It is composed of words that point to and reveal the inherent character of this One Mind, with which all men are innately endowed.

To be more specific, look at calligraphy and painting. Or better, when someone says that so-and-so has a genius for performing on the biwa or the koto, if we ask just where that genius lies, nobody, no matter how eloquent or gifted of tongue he may be, will ever be able to explain it in words. We cannot teach this uninherited talent to the child that we cherish. But when this mysterious spot is touched upon, it operates unconsciously, emerging from some unknown place. The mysterious nature of the mind with which all people are endowed is like this.

You may laugh or gossip when you read this letter, but is this not a strange thing, endless as the thread from a reel, that reveals its activity without a trace of error in any one you meet? But if you ask what thing is this that acts freely in this way, and

[5] *Muryōju Butsu.* Another name for Amida.

[6] *A-ji fushō.* The Sanskrit letter *A* is the basis of all language, hence, the basis of all things. Since this letter *A* is inherent and not produced, so it follows that one's own body is from the outset not born.

[7] The Vinaya school that emphasized the precepts.

look inward to seek it there, you will find that it has neither voice nor smell. Furthermore, it is empty and without traces, and if you think it is something like wood or stone, being free and unattached, it will change endless times. If you say it is in existence it will not be there; if you say it is in non-existence it will not be there either. This place, where words and speech are cut off, this free and untrammeled place, is provisionally called the Wondrous Law (*Myōhō*). The Lotus (*renge*), while its roots lie in the mud, is in no way soiled by the mud, nor does it lose the wonderful scent and odor with which it is blessed. When the time comes for it to bloom it sets forth beautiful blossoms. The Wondrous Law of the Buddha mind is neither sullied nor does it decrease within sentient beings and it is neither made pure nor does it increase within a Buddha. In the Buddha, in the common man, among all sentient beings it is in no way different. To be sullied by the mud of the five desires is to be just like the lotus root lying covered by the mud.

Later in the Himalaya the Buddha discovered the nature of the mind that is endowed from the outset. He called in his noble voice: "How marvelous! All sentient beings are endowed with the wisdom and the virtuous characteristics of the Tathāgata."[8] He preached the sudden and the gradual teaching and the partial and complete doctrines of the various sutras, and became himself the great teacher of the three worlds. When he is venerated by Brahmā and Śakra,[9] it is as though the lotus had emerged from the mud and opened to its full beauty. Just as the lotus's color and fragrance inhere in it as it lies in the mud, as it emerges, and as it blooms above the surface, so when the Buddha spoke of the Dharma being as numerous as the sands in the Ganges, he referred to nothing that was brought in from the outside. In terms of the common man, he spoke of the appearance of the Buddha-nature itself, with which all are without a doubt endowed; in terms of sentient beings, once the vow to become a Buddha has been made, the Wondrous Law of the One Mind does not increase nor lessen one bit. It is just the same as the lotus: at the time that it lies amidst the mud and after its blossoms are scattered in the summer, it

[8] *Avataṁsaka Sūtra* (T9, p. 624a). For a discussion of the development of this statement, see ZD, pp. 253–55.
[9] Here gods in the world of desire.

does not undergo any fundamental change whatsoever. Thus he provisionally likened the lotus plant to the Wondrous Law of the One Mind. Is this not irrefutable proof that the Buddha mind, with which all people are endowed, was called the *Lotus Sūtra of the Wondrous Law?*

The word *kyō* [sutra] means "constant," in the same sense as the eternal, unchanging Buddha-nature. This *kyō* teaches that eternal, unchanging Buddha-nature does not increase in a Buddha nor decrease in a sentient being. It is of the same root as heaven and earth and is one substance with all things, and has not changed one iota since before the last kalpa began, nor will it change after it has ended. Moreover, *Myōhō* [Wondrous Law] is the substance of the Buddha mind. The *Lotus Sūtra* was composed as a way of praising this Wondrous Law of the Buddha mind, and so it is nothing more than another name for the One Mind. It is one reality with two names, just as *mochi* and *kachin* are two names for the same thing, a rice-cake.

Moreover, the True Reality that is the *Lotus Sūtra* cannot be seized by the hands nor seen by the eye. How then is one to receive and hold to it? What then should one say to the practitioner of the *Lotus Sūtra* who wishes to take it to himself? There are three types of capacity. The practitioner of inferior capacity is captivated by the yellow scroll with its red handles and copies, recites, and makes explanations of it. The practitioner of average capacity illuminates his own mind and so receives and holds to the *Sūtra*. The person of superior capacity penetrates this *Sūtra* with his [Dharma] eye, just as though he were viewing the surface of his own mind. That is why the *Nirvāṇa Sūtra* says: "The Tathāgata sees the Buddha-nature within his eye."[10] The practitioner of the *Lotus Sūtra*, if he is engaged in the true practice of the ultimate of Mahayana, will not find it an easy thing to do. What is simple is very much so; what is difficult is very, very difficult indeed.

We have seen before the passage in the *Lotus Sūtra* that reads: "To hold to this *Sūtra* is difficult. If someone holds to it even for a short while, I will feel great joy and the many Buddhas like-

---

[10] Quotation not identified.

wise."[11] Thus, the practice of holding to this *Sūtra* is of the utmost importance. Chih-i of the Tendai school has said: "Without taking the book in your hands, always recite this *Sūtra*. Without uttering words from your mouth, recite all the texts everywhere. Even when the Buddha does not preach always listen to the sound of the Law. Without engaging the mind in thinking always illumine the Dharmakaya."[12] This describes the true recitation of this *Sūtra*. Should someone ask: "What sort of a sutra is this that one recites without taking the work up in one's hands?" can one not say in return: "Isn't this the Wondrous Law of your own mind?" If someone asks:"What does 'without engaging the mind in thinking, always illumine the Dharmakaya' mean?" can one not say in return, "Isn't this the True Lotus?" This is known as the *Sūtra* without words. If one just grasps the yellow roll with its red handles and holds to the belief that *this* is the *Lotus Sūtra*, one is like someone who licks a piece of paper extolling the virtues of some medicine, expecting that this will serve to cure a disease. What a great mistake this is!

Should a person wish to hold to this *Sūtra*, he must throughout all the hours of the day and without the slightest doubt in his mind, carry on the real practice of true meditation on the total form of all things, thinking neither of good nor of evil. In this respect Han-shan, who was an avatar of Manjuśrī, has said in a verse: "If you wish to attain the road to enlightenment, let no thread hang in your mind."[13] True practice of this sort is the ancient and changeless great center, the place from which all the Tathāgatas of the three periods and all the wise men and great priests attained to great enlightenment. This is the direct road to [experiencing the state in which] "no-thought is produced, before and after are cut off, and with sudden enlightenment you attain to Buddhahood."[14] Although the Tathāgata said, "This *Sūtra* is difficult to hold to," is this not really the ultimate principle?

[11] *Lotus Sūtra* (T9, p. 34b).   [12] Quotation not identified.
[13] In modern versions of the *Orategama* this verse is correctly attributed to Shih-te. The poem is misquoted. The first part reads: "If you wish to understand the principle of non-action."
[14] Source unidentified. These are all phrases frequently encountered in Zen texts.

The true place to which the sages of all three religions[15] have attained is, to a large measure, the same. Although the degree of efficacy is based on the depth and the quality of the perseverance in practice, the content of the first step is the same. The Confucians call this place the Ultimate Good, the Undeveloped Mean. Taoists call it Nothingness or Nature. Among Shintoists it is known as Takamagahara.[16] The Tendai school calls it "the Great Matter of the cessation and meditation on the three thousand worlds in one instant of thought." In Shingon it is called "the contemplation of the Inherent Nature of the Letter *A*."

The Patriarchs of the various schools encourage sitting in meditation and, although they advocate the recitation of the sutras, isn't this recitation merely a device to make us reach the state where the mind is unperturbed, pure, and without distractions? The founder of Eihei-ji[17] has said: "If one practices and holds to it for one day, it is a day worthy of veneration; if one fails to hold to and practice it for a hundred years, these are a hundred years of regret." It is enough to make one shed tears at the regrettable and wretched state of understanding in which, while possessing the difficult-to-obtain body of a man, a person does not cultivate in himself the determination to practice. Instead, like a dog or a cat or some beast that has no understanding at all, he allows his whole life, one so difficult to encounter, to rot carelessly away, and returns to his old abode in the three worlds of suffering, without having learned a thing. To say "a difficult thing is very, very difficult," leaves no doubt on our part. But what does this "an easy thing is very easy indeed" mean? Should a person release his hold on the *Sūtra* and attempt lightly to maintain the dignities of walking, standing, sitting, and reclining, he must make a vow seeking once to verify for himself the True Face of the Lotus. Once a person sees this True Face of the Lotus, then coughing, swallowing, waving the arms, activity and quietude, words and actions, all plants, trees, tiles, stones, the sentient and the non-sentient, all manifest the *Sutra of the Wondrous Law*,

---

[15] Confucianism, Taoism, and Shinto.   [16] The Shinto heaven.
[17] Dōgen (1200–1253), who introduced the Sōtō School of Zen to Japan. The Eihei-ji is the temple he established in present-day Fukui Prefecture.

and throughout all the hours of the day harmonize deeply with the *Sūtra*. What need is there to hold to any other thing? If you try to hold to the *Lotus Sūtra* without seeing once the True Lotus, you will be like a man who holds a bowl of water in his hands and night and day tries to keep from spilling it or letting it move, but still expects to gain sustenance from it. Even if he should succeed in holding it in this way for his whole life, he wouldn't be able to sustain himself or keep himself from dying of thirst. His hopes to benefit himself and others by the practice of the vow will be cut off midway. What possible use does this serve?

For the person who once sees the True Lotus and holds to this *Sūtra*, it is as if he had poured this one bowl of water into rivers and lakes everywhere. At once it merges with the thirty-six thousand riplets and its beneficence joins with the waters, so that if all the creatures that leap, run, fly, or crawl came to drink at the same time, it would never be exhausted.

The person who has not seen the True Lotus is like the man who holds the bowl of water. Not only can he be of no benefit to others, but neither can he bring benefit to himself. The person who once sees the True Lotus is like the man who pours the bowl of water into all the rivers and lakes. Unconsciously he leaps into the great sea of Nirvana of the various Buddhas, harmonizes deeply with the true Dharma body and the precepts, meditation, and wisdom of the many Buddhas, at once shatters the dark cave of the *ālaya*-consciousness, and releases the Illumination of the Great Perfect Mirror.[18] Passing over numberless kalpas, he practices the almsgiving of the Dharma with no limitations whatsoever. The breadth and greatness of the virtue of the one view of the Lotus is quite without bounds. Rather than read all the works in the Tripitaka, see the True Lotus once. Rather than build countless treasure stupas, see the True Lotus once. Rather than make a million statues of the Buddha, see the True Lotus once. Rather than master the mysteries of the three worlds, see the True Lotus once. Rather than adhering to the view that holding the yellow scroll with its red handles is [the practice of] the *Lotus Sūtra*, see

[18] *Daienkyō kō*. The perfect wisdom attained when the *ālaya*-consciousness is inverted. See ZD, pp. 313–14.

the True Lotus once. Rather than recite the *Lotus Sūtra* a billion times, see the True Lotus once with your own Dharma eye. This is truly a lofty statement of complete truth and in-destructibility.

How can one penetrate to the True Face of the Lotus? To do this one must raise the great ball of doubt. What is being pointed out when we speak of the True Face of the Lotus? It is the Wondrous Law of the One Mind, with which you yourself are endowed from the outset. It is nothing more than to see into your own mind. And what is this "own mind?" Don't look for something white or something red, but by all means see it at once. Courageously and firmly establish your aspiration, raise up the great vow, and night and day investigate it to the end. For investigating the mind there are many methods. If you are a practitioner of the *Lotus Sūtra* who ignores the teachings of the other schools, then you must transcend the practice of the Lotus *Samādhi*. The practice of the Lotus *Samādhi* is from today on to determine, despite happiness and pain, sadness and joy, whether asleep or awake, standing or reclining, to intone without interruption the title of the *Sūtra* alone: Reverence to the Lotus of the Wondrous Law (*Namu Myōhō renge kyō*). Whether you use this title as a staff or as a source of strength, you must recite it with the fervent desire to see without fail the True Face of the Lotus. Make each inhalation and exhalation of your breath the title of the *Sūtra*. Recite it without ceasing with intense devotion. If you recite it without flagging, it will not be long before the mind-nature will truly be set as firmly as a large rock. Dimly you will gain an awareness of a state in which the One Mind is without disturbance. At this time, do not discard this awareness, but continue your constant recitation. Then you will awaken to the Great Matter of true meditation, and all the ordinary conscious-nesses and emotions will not operate. It will be as if you had entered into the Diamond Sphere, as if you were seated within a lapis lazuli vase, and, without any discriminating thought at all, suddenly you will be no different from one who has died the Great Death.[19] After you have returned to life, unconsciously the

[19] *Daishi*. The penetration into Absolute Mind. See ZD, p. 309.

pure and uninvolved true principle of undistracted meditation will appear before you. You will see right before you, in the place where you stand, the True Face of the Lotus, and at once your body and mind will drop off. The true, unlimited, eternal, perfected Tathāgata will manifest himself clearly before your eyes and never depart, though you should attempt to drive him away. This is the time that the Tendai school refers to as "plunging into the treasure abode, where the Dharma-nature is undisturbed, yet constantly illuminating." In Shingon it is to be illumined by the Sun Disc of the Inherent Nature of the Letter *A*. In the Ritsu it is to harmonize with the unparalleled Diamond-Treasure Precepts of the Many Buddhas. In the Pure Land School it is to fulfill one's vow for rebirth in Paradise, to see before one's eyes the marvelous birds and trees of Paradise and to keep constantly in mind the wondrous ornamentation of the Buddha, the Dharma, and the Sangha.[20]

Opening the True Eye that sees that this very world is itself the brilliance of Nirvana, one reaches the state where all plants, trees, and lands have without the slightest doubt attained to Buddhahood. What is there among the good fruits of the worlds of men and devas that can be compared to this? This is the basic vow that accounts for the appearance in this world of the many Buddhas of the three periods. One recitation of the title of this *Sūtra* has no less virtue than a single Zen koan. The purport of all this has been uttered by all the learned sages of all the directions of the three periods and the eighty thousand gods of Japan. If what I say were even slightly incorrect, why should I risk committing a crime by writing it all in a long-winded letter? There is absolutely no doubt about it. If in one's practice one is not remiss, the mind-ground known in Zen as "clenching the left hand and biting the middle finger,"[21] will gradually become clear.

Nowadays one occasionally hears people say: "There is no point in studying koans under a teacher. What do you do after finishing your study of the koans? [Once you have reached the stage of the] direct pointing to 'this very mind is Buddha,' you

[20] The text omits the *Sangha*, or community of monks, but it is included in later editions and required by context.
[21] The source of this expression has not been traced.

neither regret when a thought arises nor feel joy when a thought is stopped. The mountain villager's unpainted bowl is best, for it represents the original nature as it was at the time that the bowl was made. If you don't lacquer the bowl, there will be nothing to chip and wear away." People who talk in this way are like blind turtles that pointlessly enter an empty valley every day and are satisfied with this. This is the view of the Indian heretics of the naturalistic school. If things like this were called the pivot of the progress toward the Buddha mind, even the guardian gods of the remotest village would clap their hands and burst out in laughter.

Why is this so? Aren't such people similar to the imbecile who thinks he sees the spirits that Ch'ang-sha[22] talks about? When the *Śūraṅgama Sūtra* cautions against recognizing a robber and making him your son and talks of the eventual inability to know the substance of original purity,[23] it is referring to people of this type. They are totally unaware of the fact that the Tathāgata did not acknowledge proficiency in meditation even for those sages who had gained the four grades of sainthood, had reached the stage of non-retrogression, had penetrated the principles of the self and the dharmas, were endowed with magical gifts, and had gained great fame everywhere. That is why the *Sūtra*[24] says: "Even the great arhats among my disciples cannot understand the meaning. It is only the group of bodhisattvas who are able to comprehend it." It is speaking of those who, without even possessing the accomplishment of seeing into their own natures, recklessly call themselves worthy of veneration. What sort of mental state is this?

At any rate, nothing surpasses the casting aside of all the myriad circumstances and devoting oneself to recitation. But do not adhere to the one-sided view that the title of the *Sūtra* alone will be of benefit. This applies as well to the Shingon and Pure

[22] Ch'ang-sha Ching-ts'en (Chōsha Keijin, n.d.). The remark is found in *Ching-te ch'uan-teng lu*, 10 (T51, p. 274b).
[23] The first part of the quotation is drawn directly from the *Sūtra* (T19, 108c); the second part paraphrases the meaning of the text.
[24] Presumably the *Lotus Sūtra*, but I do not find the specific quotation. See "Orategama I," fn. 122.

Land schools. The followers of the Pure Land, by the power of the concentrated recitation of the Buddha's name, resolving to see once the Pure Land of their own minds and the wondrous form of Amida Buddha in their own bodies, give rise to a valiant great aspiration, and devote themselves ceaselessly to the recitation of the name, as fervently as though they were dousing flames on their own heads. Is there any reason that they should not see the form of the Buddha, who is spoken of as not being far off, the trees of the seven treasures, and the pond of the eight virtues?[25] The followers of Shingon, by the mysterious power of the *dhāraṇī*, resolving to see without fail the great Sun Disc of the Inherent Nature of the Letter *A*, give rise to a great aspiration to persevere, just as in Zen one koan is taken up and concentrated upon. Is there any reason that they should not polish and bring out the true form of the Diamond indestructible that Kōya Daishi[26] has described as "[attaining enlightenment] without being reborn in a new body"?

But should any one of these people, thinking he has saved up merit, talk about waiting until after he dies, he will find that his ignorance and carelessness have resulted in a situation almost without hope. Do not lament about how far away it is. If you say that you must cross the seas to faraway China and India to see and hear it, then you may well lament about how far away it is. Is there anything nearer than to see your own mind with your own mind, to see your own eyeballs with your own eyeballs? Do not be afraid about how deep a thing this is. If you try to see and hear it at the bottom of a deep chasm or in the depths of the sea, then you may well fear how deep a thing it is. Is there anything nearer than to see your own mind with your own mind, to use your own nostrils to smell your own nose? Although the world is in a degenerate age, the Law itself is not degenerate. If you take the world as degenerate and cast it away without looking back, you will be like someone who enters into a treasure mountain, yet suffers from hunger and cold. Do not fear that because this is a degenerate age [enlightenment] cannot be accomplished.

[25] Wonders of Amida's Pure Land.
[26] Kūkai (774–835). Founder of Shingon in Japan.

In the past the Abbot of the Eshin-in,[27] more recently Sokuō of
Akazawa and Engū of Yamashiro,[28] and the sick girl of Ōsaka,[29]
each by the power of the calling of the name, fulfilled the vow
described above.[30] Hōnen Shōnin[31] also had this aspiration deeply,
but because he had no religious guide, he said that the state of his
mind was as though his wings were too short for so long a flight.

Perhaps it is a mark of this degenerate age that recently bad
customs have arisen and monks and laymen are both so accustomed to seeing and hearing of them that they say that to want to
see the Buddha Mind of the Wondrous Law today is like having
the aspirations of an eel that wants to climb a tree. Yet to spend
one's whole life in darkness certainly represents a miserable
state of mind.

Supposing several sons of a farmer have inherited from him a
large amount of land. Among the sons is one who is weak and
unworthy, but whose words are clever and shrewd. He says:
"In these days it is beyond the ability of people of our humble
status to imitate our ancestors of old, to engage in agriculture and
farming, and to attempt to raise a large family. It would be just
like a duck, in imitation of a hawk, positioning its wings as though
it were about to attack and bring down a crane. Or like a lame
turtle, in imitation of a carp, stretching out its neck as though it
were about to ascend a waterfall. Ridiculous! If we continue in
this way, we'll end up having to drink water from a sickle.[32]
This is quite unthinkable! Just figure it out for yourselves!
Worn out people such as we [must tend] this farm, that stretches
like a vast field filled with luxuriantly growing weeds. We cut
the fields and after they are cut, we cultivate. We irrigate, hoe,
sow the seeds, transplant the seedlings, weed the paddies, cut and
dry the plants, remove the rice, and polish off the rice bran. Then

[27] Genshin (942–1017). Tendai priest who lived at the Eshin-in at Yokawa on
Mt. Hiei. He is one of the forerunners of Pure Land Buddhism.
[28] Sokuō and Engū are Pure Land monks about whom Hakuin is the only
source of information. They are also described in "Orategama zokushū,"
below.
[29] Unidentified.   [30] The vow to be reborn in the Pure Land.
[31] Genkū (1133–1212). Founder of the Pure Land school in Japan.
[32] A proverb, presumably indicating much labor to no avail.

we must braid rope and weave matting and make the bales. When we can sit back and look at the results, we are struck by the tremendous difficulties of the work. It is indeed an old story. The results are worth nothing at all. There is a much better way to pass through this world, taking your ease with your hands in your sleeves. Wherever a person's feet take him, he can spend three days here or five days there."

Someone objected, saying: "If we have shoulders, don't we need clothes to hang on them? If we have a mouth, don't we need food to put in it?"

To this he replied: "I have heard that a certain lord of a certain province is a man of great humanity. They say he gives stipends to such as we. This is where we really ought to go. With things as good as that, we would have nothing to lament about. It's all a great mistake to have to move one's hands and feet to earn a living through one's own efforts. There is nothing to worry about. It's best just to put on a humble appearance from the beginning and make no effort to work. Do not look as if you wanted to pile up money."

Throwing away the two or three old garments they have and putting on clothes of straw matting, people like this say: "We are impoverished and inferior beings, lost, with no place to stay and no one to tell our troubles to. Out of pity, please help us." Wandering about crying in this way, because of the compassion that exists in the world, it is not impossible for a person to be fed. People are taught such things and rejoice without a trace of doubt, believing all this to be true. Thus they become poverty stricken, although they were not so from birth, and end up spending their lives in this way.

Such people are known as destroyers and wasters of their own selves. The Master Lin-chi berated them as "spoiled people of inferior capacity."[33] They are like fish in water who lament the fact that because of their natures they are unable to see the water, or like birds flying through the air who regret the fact that to see the air is an unattainable desire. They are unaware that

[33] The source of this quotation has not been traced. I do not find it in the *Lin-chi lu.*

of all the lands everywhere, there is none that does not contain
True Reality, nor is there any human being anywhere who is
not endowed with this Wondrous Law. It is a pity that while
living amidst the Wondrous Law of the One Mind and the Pure
Land of Tranquil Light, they cling to the prejudice that in this
life they are part of the ordinary world and that as sentient beings
they are as such deluded. Mistakenly they believe that after death
they will enter hell, and so they lament the endless torment in
store for them. They discard the Buddha Mind of the Wondrous
Law that wells up before the eyes and the Dharma-nature of
True Reality that is always pure, feeling that these are things to
which they cannot possibly attain, things for which they cannot
possibly hope. Thus they cast aside their desires as unobtainable,
and look for the pointless concepts of deluded consciousness, and
end up spending their lives in vain. What is most regrettable is
that, although we have this *Lotus of the Wondrous Law*, incomparable in all the three worlds, a scripture of the most exquisite
quality, yet, because there is no one who practices its teachings
properly, it is stuffed away on library shelves along with a lot of
ordinary books, and rots away from disuse. Thus people mistake
the impure world for the Pure Land and concern themselves with
the three evil paths and the six modes of existence. Is there anything more lamentable?

Someone has asked: "What specifically does this teaching
point to? Is it the four peaceful contentments?[34] Is it the conduct
of the five types of Master of the Law?"[35]

In answer I say: "Not at all. It is the 'eye' of the *Sūtra*, that
is described in the text of the chapter on Expediencies in these
words: 'the reason the Buddha appeared in this world was [to
show] the way to open up the wisdom of the Buddha.'"[36]

Although the numerous Tathāgatas who have appeared
successively in the world have expounded Laws as numerous as
the sands in the Ganges, they have all appeared solely for the

[34] Peaceful contentment is reached by proper use of deeds, words, thoughts,
and will to teach the doctrines of the *Lotus*.
[35] Five types of disseminators of the Law as described in the *Lotus Sūtra*. They
are: those who hold to, read, recite, explain, and copy the work.
[36] T9, p. 7a.

purpose of opening up the Buddha's wisdom to all sentient beings. No matter what Law you practice, if you don't seek to open up the Buddha's wisdom, you will never be able to come into accord with the vow of the many Buddhas. The opening up of the Buddha's wisdom is to make clear the Wondrous Law of the One Mind. There is nothing more regrettable in this degenerate world than to discard tidings of this Wondrous Law of the One Mind and to just go along as one pleases. When unexpectedly we meet something that seems to be this Wondrous Law, we find that nowadays everyone has made it into an intellectual teaching, scarcely worth talking about. No one gives heed to the saying in the *Mahā-Vairocana Sūtra*: "Know your own mind as it really is."[37] Not following the teaching of the *Lotus Sūtra* and not knowing where the Wondrous Law is, people rush about madly, saying vague things like: "It's in the West," or "It's in the East," and spend their days declaring that this or that is the Buddha Way. Their behavior can be likened to that of the people in the following story.

Supposing that there were a very rich man, who, after undergoing many hardships, finally managed to bring under cultivation vast tracts of land. Supposing that he were to say to his sons:[38] "You cultivate this land and become rich men like me." He then distributes to his various sons, without regard to the capacities of each, his excess lands. His sons, however, do not follow their father's teaching, but scatter to various provinces. Some stand beside the doors of people's houses and beg their food. Some say: "We are mirror polishers," and walk about polishing tiles.[39] Others scuttle about chasing away the birds that feed on grain. Some say: "We are millionaire's sons," and although looking like beggars and outcasts themselves, they recklessly make light of others. Some turn over the leaves of their account books every day, but do not even know what the fields look like. Others say: "As long as we have our account books we have nothing to fear," and selfishly practice their evil ways. Some say:

[37] T18, p. 1c. Hakuin misquotes the text.

[38] A variation on the parable of the rich man and his son in the *Lotus Sūtra*.

[39] An allusion to the story concerning the polishing of a tile contained in the biography of Nan-yüeh Huai-jang in *Ching-te ch'uan-teng lu*, 5 (T51, p. 240c).

"We know the conduct becoming to a millionaire," but they starve and thirst while practicing the forms of this proper conduct. There are some who do not even know where the fields are, but keep screaming about them day and night. Others are a bit aware of the vast extent of acreage and, becoming greatly boastful, degenerate into a life of sex, wine, and meat-eating. There is not one son among them who carries out the intention of his millionaire father.

The fields stand for the Wondrous Law of the One Mind. The account books are the sacred scriptures. "To stand before people's houses and beg," means to acknowledge the Great Matter of the opening up of the wisdom of the Buddha, the process of learning for oneself whether the water is cold or hot by experiencing in one's own body pain and suffering, and then, because this is a degenerate age, to accept the teachings of others, to hear and learn things that are not the substance, and to consider this to be enlightenment. Is this not like the prodigal son in the *Lotus Sūtra*?

In the Mahayana sutras even the four grades of sainthood of an arhat are condemned as representing ordinary men of the two vehicles. If this [enlightenment] is such an absurd and uncomplicated thing as people say, why then did the Buddha confine himself in the Himalaya for six years until his skin stuck to his bones and he was so emaciated and exhausted that he looked like a tile made to stand by winding string about it? He was unaware that the reeds had pierced his lap and reached to his elbows; so absorbed was he in his painful introspection that he was not conscious of the lightning striking down horses and cattle before his very eyes. Imagine what a thing it was when for the first time he opened up the wisdom of a Buddha!

The Buddha Way from ancient times has been one of vast difficulties. Is it something that should be made easy now? Is it something like radishes, potatoes, or chestnuts that are hard at first but get soft when cooked? If what is easy today is good, then what was difficult in the past must be bad. If what was difficult in the past was good, then what is easy today is bad. What was difficult in the past was the painful introspection, and this was a very painful introspection indeed. With the smallest bit of development and progress, suddenly the state of sage, Buddha, or Patriarch was reached. When that place, when this time was transcended and [understanding] touched upon even to the slightest degree, then lightning flashed and the stars leapt in the sky. The surpassing easiness of today is surpassing indeed, yet when you look into it, it is no more than a painting of a wise monk. With the smallest bit of development and progress, you are still as before, like a fish stuck in a trap, like a lame turtle fallen into an earthen jar. This time and that place are not transcended, and, as you press on, you are like a blind ass walking on ice.

Which will it be, the easiness of the present-day practice or the difficulty of that of the past? No matter how much you insist that this is after all a degenerate age, to speak in such terms is useless. Even the men of old knew that later the teaching of Zen and the true form [of the Lotus] were destined to perish. Let it be known that to seek the Wondrous Mind on soiled paper or to assign the True Law to verbal discussions is indeed a pathetic thing. If everything could be accomplished through the use of written words and talk, then Shen-kuang[40] would not have had to cut off his arm, Hsüan-sha would not have injured his foot, Hosshin's[41] head would not have swollen, and Hattō[42] would not have shed tears. No matter what other people do, you must determine that, "come what may, I will without fail intone the title [of the *Lotus Sūtra*] day and night and see for myself the true form of the Lotus." Then, if you intone it faithfully, without having to enter the Himalaya or to bear the suffering of having your head swell, the real essential Lotus of the Wondrous Law of your own nature will open in all its beauty. The essential point is to resolve not to give in while you have yet to see the Wondrous Lotus of your own mind. Then there will be nothing so venerable

---

[40] Hui-k'o (Eka), the Second Chinese Patriarch, mentioned before. Shen-kuang was his name before he became a monk.

[41] Shōsai Hosshin (d. 1273). One of the first Zen monks to study in China. He founded the Empuku-ji in Matsushima, and later lived in retirement in Kyoto. During the course of his studies his head swelled, but this did not deter him from persevering. The story appears in Shiban, *Honchō kōsō den*, 19.

[42] Presumably this is Hattō Kokushi, the posthumous name of Shinchi Kakushin, seen before. The identification, however, is not certain.

as this thing to which you have devoted all your hopes. When
the Tathāgata, the World-honored One, had still to see the
Wondrous Law of his own mind, he was no different from any
ordinary mortal, endlessly sunk in the rounds of birth and death,
and he himself was constantly dying and being reborn. Later in
the Himalaya he awoke to the Wondrous Law of his own mind
and for the first time achieved True Enlightenment.

The polishing of a tile is to think that as long as one recognizes the non-differentiation of the *ālaya*-consciousness and is not
deluded into thinking that this represents the original face, then
what is left is a Buddha mind that is like a mirror. People are
taught merely that everything is reflected in the mirror just as it
is; the crow is black, the crane white, the willow green, and
flowers red, and they are told to strive constantly to polish [the
mirror] so that not a speck of dust can collect.[43] This wiping away
of deluded thoughts night and day is the same as polishing a tile
or chasing away the birds that feed on millet. This is known as
seeking for the spirit. It permits no chance for the luminescence
to be produced that makes clear the mountains, rivers, and the
great earth. Practice of this sort was fairly frequent even during
the T'ang dynasty. Nan-yüeh's polishing of a tile before Ma-tsu's
hut was for the purpose of conveying this meaning to Ma-tsu.[44]

Thus Ch'ang-sha has said in a verse:[45]

The failure of the student to understand the truth,
Comes from his prior acceptance of spirits.
The basis of birth and death from endless kalpas in the past;
This the fool thinks of as the original man.

It is for this reason that Patriarchs such as Tz'u-ming, Chen-
ching, Hsi-keng, and Ta-hui[46] were indescribably kind in gritting
their teeth and attempting to drive out such concepts. There is

---

[43] Passage from a verse attributed to Shen-hsiu in the *Liu-tsu t'an-ching*. See
Philip Yampolsky, *Platform Sutra of the Sixth Patriarch* (New York, 1967), p. 130.
[44] See fn. 39.
[45] Hakuin has previously quoted from this verse. See fn. 22.
[46] Tz'u-ming is a pseudonym for Shih-shuang Ch'u-yüan; Chen-ching is
Chen-ching K'o-wen (Shinjō Kokumon, 1025–1102); Hsi-keng is a pseudonym
of Hsü-t'ang Chih-yü; Ta-hui is Ta-hui Tsung-kao. All except Chen-ching
have appeared earlier.

no point in bringing up the views of all the other Masters on this subject. There is no Buddha or Patriarch in the three periods and ten directions who has not seen into his own nature. There is no learned sage who has not seen into his own nature. This is the eternal, unchanging center of the teaching. To see into your own nature is to see for yourself the True Face of the Lotus. If you do not have this desire, but think that all varieties of things are the Buddhadharma, you will be like a band of children that rushes to board a large boat that has no captain. They do not know where they wish to go nor what the harbor of their destination is. Crying, "Let's row over here," or "Let's row over there," they pull the oars any which way—yesterday they drifted following the tide to the east, today they drift following the tide to the west—and in the end they are hopelessly lost at sea. Then suddenly a captain who knows the way appears in the boat and, setting his compass, takes the rudder, and within the day reaches the harbor of his destination.

The captain is the great aspiration to see into one's own nature. The compass is the teaching of the True Law. The rudder is the determination and conduct throughout one's life. How is one to row into the harbor of the Wondrous Law? Ordinary practitioners seek the Buddha, seek the Patriarchs, seek Nirvana, or seek the Pure Land. They are accustomed always to rowing to the outside. Therefore, the more they seek the further away from their goal they are.

The practitioner of the true Wondrous Law is not like this. Pursuing the investigation of what sort of thing his own innate Wondrous Law is, he seeks neither the Buddha nor the Patriarchs. He does not say that the Wondrous Law is inside or that it is outside. No matter where it is, no matter what color it is, he will not let things be until he has finally seen it once. All day long, everywhere, without interruption, strenuously, bravely, he forces his spirit on. Refusing to leave what he has determined to achieve undone, to leave what he has resolved to accomplish unfinished, asleep, awake, while standing, while reclining, he does not cast it aside. Night and day he examines things; at times he goes over things again. Constantly he proceeds, asking, "What is this thing, what is this thing? Who am I?" This is called the way of "the lion that bites the man." To proceed asking only, "What is the Wondrous Law of the Mind?" is called the way of "a fine dog chasing a clod of dirt."[47] Just under all circumstances cast aside all things, become without thought and without mind and intone: "*Namu Myōhō renge kyō, Namu Myōhō renge kyō*, Reverence to the Lotus of the Wondrous Law." If you think that this old monk has any Dharma principle better than this to write of, you are terribly mistaken. *Namu Myōhō renge kyō*, "Reverence to the Lotus of the Wondrous Law."

> Written by the old monk
> under the Sāla tree.

25th day of the eleventh month of Enkyō 4 [= Dec. 26, 1747]

Although this long, tedious letter may be difficult to read, please show it to others at your hermitage. I have written it in the hope that it will also serve as the almsgiving of the Dharma. I wish that you will without fail see the Ultimate Principle, the Wondrous Law of your own mind. With the wish that you will continue to intone ceaselessly the title: *Namu Myōhō renge kyō*, "Reverence to the Lotus of the Wondrous Law."

SUPPLEMENT: Kambun *text appended to letter III*

After I had written the draft of this letter[1] I read it over carefully. At that time a monk who had long been a friend of mine was sitting beside me. He read what I had written and when he came to the part about the True Face of the Lotus, he let out a long sigh and said: "Master, are you handing out a yellow leaf to keep the child from crying?"[2]

---

[47] These two expressions are found in *Hsü-t'ang ho-shang yü-lu*, 2 (T47, p. 998a). The former expression describes a man of great capacity and strength; the latter indicates someone who still seeks understanding in words.

[1] The previous letter to the nun of the Hoke Sect.

[2] This expression is usually taken to mean: to give a yellow leaf to a child, pretending it is gold, and thus to keep him from crying. Hakuin, however, is not consistent, and, throughout this section, at some times makes the leaf red, and at other times makes it yellow.

The color drained from my face and I replied: "What are you talking about? Are you saying that what I have written is only worth a red leaf? This is real gold, not a red leaf. I wrote it to bring out the basic meaning of the *Lotus Sūtra*. By calling it a red leaf aren't you slandering the *Sūtra*? Crimes that slander the True Law are beyond the bounds of repentance. What part of what I have written makes you call it a red leaf?"

The monk bowed his head and answered: "Recently the various students from far and near who live at the temple have embraced a heroic resolution. They blithely sit, forgetting their own emaciated condition, and carry on their practice at the risk of their own bodies. Renting an old house or sneaking into an abandoned shrine, for fifteen years they have found sweet the bitter milk of the Master's poison, and are loath to disperse. But this year a tidal wave has swept over the fields and gardens and the rice grains have not formed. The farmers, to support their wives and children, wish in secret that they might move to some other areas. I am deeply distressed and have lost all hope. There will not be a monk's staff left hanging at the Kokurin Monastery. The garden of Zen could not be any more desolate.

"Recently a monk said to me: 'Apart from those common, unstable men who seek fine food and clothing and long for noise and bustle, not one of the superior men who have been studying earnestly for so long a time, seeking understanding and a break-through to enlightenment, has left. Their perseverance and excellence is ten times what it was last month. In groups of five or ten they stay, some by the shore, some under the trees, without eating and without sleeping for five or ten days on end. All of them say: "This is like the association for the Buddhadharma held in olden days in evil years of famine."

"'They are as thin as men in mourning for their deceased mothers, as weak as persons afflicted with a dread disease. Their cold and hunger, the suffering that besets them, would cause spirits to shed tears, and demons to join their palms together in respect.

"'Today monasteries everywhere are equipped with lofty temple buildings and sumptuous quarters for the monks. The two wheels[3] turn at the same time and the four offerings[4] are piled up. What sort of mind is it then that does not pay attention to such things? Living in a place where hunger, cold, and poverty abound, all that enters their ears are the evil words and abuse of the Master; all that passes their mouths is the chaff of millet and wheat, and there is not one thing that in their hearts they feel is good. Yet these monks are not here because they have no other place to go. They are all superior monks, fully qualified to be in monasteries, but each of them devotes himself assiduously to the search for his own enlightenment, and pays no attention to anything else.' When I hear things like this I am greatly impressed and feel that it is fortunate indeed that this is a time when many people will gain the Buddhadharma.

"You must proclaim the need to take up the forging irons of progress toward enlightenment and look for superior monks who have really studied and gained a true awakening. If you approach people with the secondary meaning and use methods with a different import, you will be doing people great harm. They will be blocked by the other gates to enlightenment, and in the end you will not be able to produce even the least significant kind of person. Thirty years ago I suffered the painful polishing accorded by my Master, and after undergoing numerous hardships, attained understanding of the innate Buddha-nature, penetrated the True Face of the Lotus, gained the true understanding without the slightest doubt of the mysterious principles of the three thousand worlds in one instant of thought and the innermost meaning of the perfect unity of the three truths.[5] My Master himself acknowledged that I had gained an understanding of the True Face of the Lotus, and I thought in private to myself that as far as I was concerned, everything in the world had been determined.

"When recently I listened to your lectures on the *Pi-yen lu*,[6]

[3] Of the Law and of donations from laymen.
[4] Shelter, clothes, food, incense.
[5] In Tendai teaching, the three truths (tentative, empty, and middle) are essentially one.
[6] Famous Zen work, first published in 1128. It is widely used in Japan. (T48, pp. 139–225). See Introduction, fn. 15.

however, it was just as if I were a farmer standing far away down the steps, listening to lectures being delivered by various gentlemen of high rank at the Secretariat. I was like a man with bad vision who strains his eyes to see the scenery of Hsiao-shui,[7] like a deaf man who cocks his ears to hear the music emanating from Tung-t'ing Lake.[8] With this, my strength drained away; the sweat of remorse poured from my armpits, and tears of pain filled my breast. It was as though all the painful practice I had been through had not done the slightest bit of good. In the beginning I thought that the powers I had attained were on the same level with yours. But now I realize that to hold doubts about you is like a sheep pointing at a fine steed and saying: 'this is my father,' or like a lame turtle indicating a heavenly dragon and saying: 'This is my Master.'

"I was depressed and irritated because I felt privately that you were making me the butt of a deception. Just now I read what you had written about the True Face of the Lotus, and I was aroused to envy and so said: 'This is a yellow leaf for a crying child.' You can understand my reaction, I hope. The various monks in the temples all lament in the same way, saying that you point to the place to which they have attained by arduous labors, and call it 'the Zen of a corpse in a coffin.'"

I replied: "This is quite true. Ah! Keep going with your practice! Do you see that old pine tree towering above the hills and valleys? Its branches pierce the highest heaven; its roots reach through to the bowels of the earth. Above, the hanging moss reaches for a hundred feet; below, the fungus that grows only after the tree has lived a thousand years clings to the roots. Its strength is that of the flood-dragon that grasps the mists and seeks to rise to the heights of the sky. Below is a pine tree one inch high just putting forth a shoot of needles. One can pluck it out with the fingers, snap it off with the nails.

"If I point to these two trees and ask someone what they are, the answer will invariably be: 'They are both pine trees. It all depends on the amount of time that they have been growing.' But don't say: 'It's a matter of the passage of time.' If you guard

[7] Reference is probably to the eight views of Hsiao-hsiang.
[8] Largest fresh water lake in China.

the materials used for making a coffin and end up by living in a demon's home, even if you pile them up to the year X,[9] of what possible use will they ever be?"[10]

Once there were two children of Mr. Chang. The elder brother was named Chang Wu and the younger Chang Lu. One day they bundled up some provisions and set out on a long journey. While on the way they happened each to find a bar of gold, and they danced for joy at their discovery. But later their ways parted and some thirty years passed in which each of the brothers did not know whether the other was dead or alive. Lu, wondering about his brother, sought him in all directions, and finally having discovered his brother's whereabouts, journeyed there from afar to pay him a visit. When Lu came finally to his brother's place, he was amazed at its opulence: the water wheels groaned as they turned and carts piled with grain came rumbling past. Oxen and horses filled the stables, flocks of geese crowded the ditches. The sound of bamboo flutes and pipes floated from the house and voices were raised in song. Elegant guests came in and out.

Lu, shaking with fear, was unable to cross the threshold. Bowing to the ground with terror and trembling, he offered his name card. Two boys handsome in appearance and elegant in bearing came out to greet him. Chang Lu followed them in, walking with extreme diffidence. The magnificence of the walls and the beauty of the buildings were such that K'ang I and Shih Nu[11] would have felt at home in them. Chang Lu's spirits faltered and his legs trembled and he did not know where to sit down. After a short while Chang Wu, attended by his concubines and female servants, appeared from beneath an embroidered canopy. The resplendent costuming of the women who attended on his brother astounded Chang Lu; the embroidered damasks overwhelmed his eyes. A golden incense burner poured forth the fragrance of a thousand flowers; jade ornaments gave off hundreds of delicate sounds. A crimson embroidered cap adorned Chang

[9] Literally, "the year of the ass," which does not exist.

[10] The text of the above sections contains many passages subject to various interpretations. The translation hence must be considered tentative.

[11] K'ang I is not identified. Shih Nu is probably Shih Ch'ung (d. 300), known for his great wealth and luxurious tastes.

Wu's head; from his shoulders a purple gown hung. He seated himself on a luxurious green cushion and leaned his arm on a sandalwood table. He glared with the haughty eyes of a tiger; he held his shoulders arrogantly in the pose of a kite.

Chang Lu took one look and could not help but lower his eyes to the ground. His body seemed to shrink and his tears flowed without cease. He was quite unable to raise his head and look his brother straight in the face.

Deliberately Chang Wu began to speak: "My brother, why were you so long in coming? How is it that you appear in such distressed circumstances?"

Chang Lu, wiping away his tears, asked then timidly: "My brother, to what lord are you indebted? From whom have you received patronage that you are so great and wealthy now?"

Chang Wu answered: "I am not the minister to any man, nor have I received the largess of a patron. I am just someone who a long time ago found some money."

Chang Lu said: "How many boxes of gold did you find? Was it as much as can be piled into a large wagon or loaded onto a giant ship? Was it money that fell from heaven or a treasure buried beneath the earth? Who was the person who forgot about all this wealth?"

"Not at all. It was the money that thirty years ago you and I found together upon the highway," replied his brother.

Chang Lu responded: "How strange! With only one bar of gold you were able to attain all these riches?" Then suddenly Chang Lu became greatly troubled. "Are you perhaps a member of an evil gang, a partner in crime with the thieves Tao Chih and Chuang Ch'iao?[12] If so, I'd better leave in a hurry so that I'll be able to escape the fate that is sure to fall on the nine families of relatives. If I stay here, I'll just be inviting my own death."

Chang Wu laughed heartily: "What happened to the money you picked up thirty years ago? Did you gamble it away? Squander it on wine and women?"

Chang Lu replied: "I see, I see. My disreputable appearance must seem very strange to you. Please ask the others to leave the

[12] Tao Chih was a famous brigand contemporaneous with Confucius. Chuang Ch'iao was a notorious thief of the Ch'u. Later texts give only Tao Chih.

room. I have something I want to say to you in private." Chang
Wu glanced up and then asked all his women to leave. Chang Lu
cautiously drew nearer: "Do I look like someone who loses his
money gambling or concerns himself with the women of the gay
quarters? I am not poor because I lost the money, but rather
trying to protect it has worn me out. Didn't you tell me long ago:
'Guard your money well. Don't squander it recklessly'? I am
not one who would go against the instructions of his brother."

As soon as Chang Lu had found the money, he wrapped it
in a tenfold cloth and guarded it with the utmost care, as though
he were protecting the jewel of Pien Ho or the precious Night-
illumining Jewel.[13] He carried it with him wherever he went. For
thirty years he had not relaxed, and had remained sleepless,
fearing that he was constantly under the threat of death from
thieves and assassins. He dreaded it if people inquired of his health,
turned away from all his friends, and avoided association with
anyone. He became a man of abject poverty, wearing on his
shoulders a disreputable gown, patched in a hundred places, and
on his head a tattered cap. People paid him absolutely no attention,
never giving him a second thought, and this, in turn, he found a
blessing. Fearing that he might exhaust his money, he took no
wife, remaining always single. He hid himself in places where he
need have nothing to do with other men, seeking out abandoned
houses and dilapidated mausoleums to sleep in. He never stayed
at an inn and was content with the most miserable of food. He
begged beside the gates of people's houses, and if he was forced to
stand for an appreciable length of time, he might on occasion
sing for his food.

Then saying: "The gold is right here," he looked about several
times to make sure that no one else was there to see him, and then
he loosened his filthy, torn gown and fishing about in the folds
finally drew out a packet wrapped around ten times in cloth. He
undid it, and looking all around again, he took out the gold and
showed it to his brother. "Where is the money that you picked
up?" he asked. "Bring it out and let's see it for old time's sake."

Chang Wu laughingly replied: "Not long after you and I
parted some thirty years ago I lost the gold."

[13] Both are jewels of fabulous worth.

Chang Lu paled and stared intently at his brother's face. Reflecting pensively he remarked: "You lost the money while I guarded it, Yet, though you lost it, you have become wealthy, and I who guarded mine am miserably poor." He opened his eyes wide and struck his forehead and gnashed his teeth and gnawed on his lips and could not help feeling deeply depressed. After a while he said: "If it is bad to guard something and starve from poverty and good to discard something and revel in riches, then, even though I am late about it, shouldn't I also throw the gold away? Please tell me how to discard it."

Chang Wu laughed uproariously and said: "The gold that you picked up was worth less than a yellow leaf. Not only did it fail to benefit you, but on the contrary, it impoverished you and did harm to your heart and entrails. Had you wrapped up a red leaf, it would have weighed nothing as you went on your rounds, nor would you have been afflicted by poverty; instead you might have spent your time in a simple cottage, caring for a wife and children, and might have slept comfortably, with your head high on a pillow. What you guarded was the way that led away from these things; what I threw away was the road that led to them.

"After I left you those thirty years ago, I went to Yang-chou. To me my gold was lighter than a yellow leaf, and I bought with it a great amount of salt. As soon as I sold the salt, with the profit I bought silk floss. As soon as I sold the silk floss, with the profit I bought hemp. As soon as I sold the hemp, with the profit I bought grain, fruit, fish, and meat. I sent people throughout the country to gather the treasures of mountain and sea, the beauties of land and water. Bringing all these things together, I opened several large stores with some three hundred employees. People stormed my doors with money in their hands and there was no variety of food that I did not sell. My possessions and wealth became enormous; T'ao Chu-kung's riches were small by comparison, I Tun's[14] possessions would amount to nothing beside mine. My storehouses and granaries stand eave-to-eave in rows. I possess fifteen thousand acres of fertile land. I have purchased

---

[14] T'ao Chu-kung is the pseudonym of Fan Li (5th century B.C.). I Tun was a native of the state of Lu. Both were famous for their enormous wealth.

several score of mountains clothed with cypress and pine and groves of catalpa and cedar, and have set myself up in this establishment. This is the road I trod by casting away the gold, that I regarded as lightly as one does a red leaf."

Chang Lu stood up, bowed, and said: "Blessings on you, my brother. I hope that you continue in the best of health. Your casting away, while only seeming like casting away, actually turned out to be devoting your efforts to guarding. My guarding, which only seemed like guarding, was actually devoting my efforts to throwing away. Guarding and throwing away bring different results indeed. One knows for a certainty that when it comes into the hands of a wise man, a yellow leaf is true gold; when it falls into the hands of a stupid person, true gold is only a yellow leaf. Oh, how I regret the thirty years of pain I have caused myself, the energies I have exhausted without a particle of gain!" His voice was choked with painful sobs.

Studying Zen under a teacher is just like this story. What you obtain at first is the nature with which man is innately endowed. It is the true face of the unique One Vehicle of the Lotus. What I have obtained is this very same nature, innate from the outset, this one and only true face of the One Vehicle of the Lotus. This is called seeing into one's own nature. This nature does not change in the slightest degree from the time one first starts in the Way until complete intuitive wisdom is perfected. It is like the metal refined by the Great Metal-maker.[15] Therefore it has been said: "At the time that one first conceives the desire to study Buddhism, enlightenment has already been attained."[16] In the teaching schools this is the first of the ten stages.[17] But even more so, it is also the very last barrier. Who can tell how far in the distance the garden of the Patriarchs lies?

At times one hears people, from the vantage of a one-sided view, say: "The place that I stand facing now is the mysterious, unproduced pre-beginning where the Buddhas and the Patriarchs have yet to arise. Here there is absolutely no birth, no death, no Nirvana, no passions, no enlightenment. All the scriptures are but paper fit only to wipe off excrement, the bodhisattvas and the

[15] *Chuang Tzu*, 6, 1. 10.   [16] *Avataṁsaka Sūtra* (T9, p. 449c).
[17] The ten stages in the development of a bodhisattva.

arhats are but corrupted corpses. Studying Zen under a teacher is an empty delusion. The koans are but a film that clouds the eye. Here there is nothing; there there is nothing. I do not seek the Buddhas. I do not seek the Patriarchs. In starvation and sleeplessness what is there lacking?"[18]

Even the Buddhas and the Patriarchs cannot cure an understanding such as this. Every day these people seek a place of peace and quiet; today they end up like dead dogs and tomorrow it will be the same thing. Even if they continue in this way for endless kalpas, they will still be nothing more than dead dogs. Of what possible use are such people! The Tathāgata has compared them to scabrous foxes. Angulimālya has scorned them as having the intelligence of earthworms.[19] Vimalakīrti has placed them in the category of those who would scorch buds and cause seeds to rot.[20] Ch'ang-sha has called them people who cannot move from the top of a hundred-foot pole.[21] Lin-chi has described them as being in a deep, dismal, black pit.[22] These are people who do not escape from the realm of their own understanding, who do not separate from the so-called device and rank, and thus fall into the sea of poison. Sticking to a one-sided view, and spending their time polishing and perfecting purity, they end up having spent their whole lives in error. They are like that Chang Lu who, embracing his bar of gold, spent his whole life exhausted and persecuted. Tz'u-ming, Huang-lung, Chen-ching, Hui-t'ang, Hsi-keng, and Ta-hui[23] devoted all their energies to eradicating this attitude, but they could not save people like these.

When I was seven or eight years old my mother took me to a temple for the first time and we listened to a sermon on the hells

[18] Hakuin is, of course, attacking the proponents of silent-illumination Zen.

[19] There are several works devoted to Angulimālya; the exact reference has not been determined.

[20] *Vimalakīrti Sūtra*, T14, p. 547b.

[21] Reference is to a verse and story from *Ching-te ch'uan-teng lu* 10 (T51, p. 274b) that came to be used as a koan.

[22] This expression is found in *Lin-chi lu* (T47, p. 501a). A frightening place from which there is no escape.

[23] Of the Zen monks mentioned here, only Huang-lung Hui-nan (Ōryō E'nan, 1002–1069) and Hui-t'ang Tsu-hsin (Maidō Soshin, 1025–1100) appear for the first time.

as described in the *Mo-ho chih-kuan*. The priest dwelt eloquently on the torments of the Hells of Wailing, Searing Heat, Incessant Suffering, and the Red Lotus.[24] So vivid was the priest's description that it sent shivers down the spines of both monks and laymen and made their hair stand on end in terror. Returning home, I took stock of the deeds of my short life and felt that there was but little hope for me. I did not know which way to turn and I was gooseflesh all over. In secret I took up the chapter on Kannon from the *Lotus Sūtra* and the *dhāraṇī* on Great Compassion and recited them day and night,

One day when I was taking a bath with my mother, she asked that the water be made hotter and had the maid add wood to the fire. Gradually my skin began to prickle with the heat and the iron bath-cauldron began to rumble. Suddenly I recalled the descriptions of the hells that I had heard and I let out a cry of terror that resounded through the neighborhood.

From this time on I determined to myself that I would leave home to become a monk. To this my parents would not consent, yet I went constantly to the temple to recite the sutras and to study the works of Confucianism. At fifteen I left home to become a monk and at that time I vowed to myself: "Even if I should die I will not cease my efforts to gain the power of one whom fire will not burn and water will not drown." Day and night I recited the sutras and made obeisance to the Buddhas, but I noticed that when I was ill or taking acupuncture or moxa treatment, the pain I felt was just as it had been before. I was greatly depressed and said to myself: "I became a monk against my parents' wishes and have yet to make the slightest progress. I have heard that the *Lotus* is the king of all sutras, venerated even by ghosts and spirits. People who are suffering in the lower worlds, when they rely on others in their efforts to be saved, always ask that the *Lotus Sūtra* be recited for them. When one considers that recitation by others can save a person from suffering, how much more effective must be recitation by oneself! There must indeed be profound and mysterious doctrines in this *Sūtra*."

[24] Listed here are three of the eight hot hells, previously mentioned. The Hell of the Red Lotus, where the victims have sores on their bodies the color of this blossom, is the seventh of the eight cold hells.

Thereupon I picked up the *Lotus Sūtra* and in my study of it found that, other than the passages that explain that there is only One Vehicle and that all phenomena are in the state of Nirvana, the text was concerned with parables relating to cause and effect. If this *Sūtra* had all these virtues, then surely the six Confucian classics and the books of all the other schools must be equally effective. Why should this particular sutra be so highly esteemed? My hopes were completely dashed. At this time I was sixteen years of age.

When I was nineteen I happened to read the [*Wu-chia*] *cheng-tsung tsan*,²⁵ in which the story of how the Master Yen-t'ou²⁶ was killed by bandits and how his cries at the time resounded for over three *li* is described. I wondered why such an enlightened monk was unable to escape the swords of thieves. If such a thing could happen to a man who was like a unicorn or phoenix among monks, a dragon in the sea of Buddhism, how was I to escape the staves of the demons of hell after I died? What use was there in studying Zen? What a fraud Buddhism! How I regretted that I had cast myself into this band of strange and evil men. What was I to do now? So great was my distress that for three days I could not eat and for a long time my faith in Buddhism was completely lost. Statues of the Buddha and the sacred scriptures looked like mud and dirt to me. It seemed much better to read lay works, to amuse myself with poetry and prose, and thus to a small degree to alleviate my distress.

When I was twenty-two I went to the province of Wakasa,²⁷ and while attending lectures on the *Hsü-t'ang lu*,²⁸ I gained an awakening. Later, when I was in the province of Iyo,²⁹ I read the *Fo-tsu san-ching*³⁰ and achieved an intense awakening. I concen-

---

²⁵ A collection of seventy-four biographies of famous monks, with verses in their praise attached. Completed in 1254 (zz2B, 8, 5, 452–98).

²⁶ Yen-t'ou Ch'üan-huo (Gantō Zenkatsu, 828–887).

²⁷ At the Jōkō-ji in Obama, present-day Fukui Prefecture.

²⁸ *Hsü-t'ang ho-shang yü-lu.* The recorded sayings and writings of Hsü-t'ang Chih-yü (T47, pp. 984–1064). The *Sokkō-roku kaien fusetsu* (HOZ2, 365–450) contains Hakuin's lectures and commentary on this work.

²⁹ At the Shōshū-ji in Matsuyama, present-day Ehime Prefecture.

³⁰ This work, as such, does not appear to have been published in Japan. Hakuin, no doubt, saw one of several commentaries.

trated night and day on the *Mu* koan without a moment's rest, but to my great disappointment I was unable to achieve a pure and uninvolved state of undistracted meditation. Equally disappointing to me was the fact that I could not achieve the state where waking and sleeping are the same.

The spring of my twenty-fourth year found me in the monk's quarters of the Eigan-ji[31] in Echigo, pursuing my strenuous studies. Night and day I did not sleep; I forgot both to eat and rest. Suddenly a great doubt manifested itself before me. It was as though I were frozen solid in the midst of an ice sheet extending tens of thousands of miles. A purity filled my breast and I could neither go forward nor retreat. To all intents and purposes I was out of my mind and the *Mu* alone remained. Although I sat in the Lecture Hall and listened to the Master's lecture, it was as though I were hearing a discussion from a distance outside the hall. At times it felt as though I were floating through the air.

This state lasted for several days. Then I chanced to hear the sound of the temple bell and I was suddenly transformed. It was as if a sheet of ice had been smashed or a jade tower had fallen with a crash. Suddenly I returned to my senses. I felt then that I had achieved the status of Yen-t'ou, who through the three periods of time encountered not the slightest loss [although he had been murdered by bandits]. All my former doubts vanished as though ice had melted away. In a loud voice I called: "Wonderful, wonderful. There is no cycle of birth and death through which one must pass. There is no enlightenment one must seek. The seventeen hundred koans handed down from the past have not the slightest value whatsoever." My pride soared up like a majestic mountain, my arrogance surged forward like the tide. Smugly I thought to myself: "In the past two or three hundred years no one could have accomplished such a marvelous breakthrough as this."

Shouldering my glorious enlightenment, I set out at once for Shinano. Calling on Master Shōju,[32] I told of my experience and presented him with a verse. The Master, holding my verse up in his left hand, said to me: "This verse is what you have learned

31 Temple located at Takada in present-day Niigata Prefecture.
32 At the Shōju-an in Iiyama, present-day Nagano Prefecture.

from study. Now show me what your intuition has to say," and he held out his right hand.

I replied: "If there were something intuitive that I could show you, I'd vomit it out," and I made a gagging sound.

The Master said: "How do you understand Chao-chou's *Mu*?"

I replied: "What sort of place does *Mu* have that one can attach arms and legs to it?"

The Master twisted my nose with his fingers and said: "Here's someplace to attach arms and legs." I was nonplussed and the Master gave a hearty laugh. "You poor hole-dwelling devil!" he cried. I paid him no attention and he continued: "Do you think somehow that you have sufficient understanding?"

I answered: "What do you think is missing?"

Then the Master began to discuss the koan that tells of Nan-ch'üan's death.[33] I clapped my hands over my ears and started out of the room. The Master called after me: "Hey, monk!" and when I turned to him he added: "You poor hole-dwelling devil!" From then on, almost every time he saw me, the Master called me a "poor hole-dwelling devil."

One evening the Master sat cooling himself on the veranda. Again I brought him a verse I had written. "Delusions and fancies," the Master said. I shouted his words back at him in a loud voice, whereupon the Master seized me and rained twenty or thirty blows with his fists on me, and then pushed me off the veranda.

This was on the fourth day of the fifth month after a long spell of rain. I lay stretched out in the mud as though dead, scarcely breathing and almost unconscious. I could not move; meanwhile the Master sat on the veranda roaring with laughter. After a short while I regained consciousness, got up, and bowed to the Master. My body was bathed in perspiration. The Master called out to me in a loud voice: "You poor hole-dwelling devil!"

After this I devoted myself to an intensive study of the koan on the death of Nan-ch'üan, not pausing to sleep or eat. One day

[33] This koan has been mentioned before. It is given in abbreviated form at the end of this section of the text.

I had a kind of awakening and went to the Master's room to test my understanding, but he would not approve it. All he did was call me a "poor hole-dwelling devil."

I began to think that I had better leave and go somewhere else. One day when I had gone to town to beg for food I encountered a madman who tried to beat me with a broom. Unexpectedly I found that I had penetrated the koan on the death of Nan-ch'üan. Then the other koans that had puzzled me, Su-shan's Memorial Tower and Ta-hui's verse on the Roundness of the Lotus Leaf,[34] fell into place of themselves and I penetrated them all. After I returned to the temple I spoke of the understanding I had gained. The Master neither approved nor denied what I said, but only laughed pleasantly. But from this time on he stopped calling me a "poor hole-dwelling devil." Later I experienced enlightenment two or three times, accompanied by a great feeling of joy. At times there are words to express such experiences, but to my regret at other times there are none. It was as though I were walking about in the shadow cast by a lantern. I returned then and attended on my old teacher Nyoka,[35] who had fallen ill.

One day I read in the verse given by Hsi-keng to his disciple Nampo as they were parting, the passage: "As we go to part a tall bamboo stands by the gate; its leaves stir the clear breeze for you in farewell."[36] I was overcome with a great joy, as though a dark path had suddenly been illumined. Unconsciously I cried aloud: "Today for the first time I have entered into the *samādhi* of words." I arose and bowed in reverence.

[34] Su-shan's Memorial Tower has appeared before. Ta-hui's verse on the Roundness of the Lotus Leaf is to be found in *Ta-hui P'u-chüeh ch'an-shih yü-lu* (T47, p. 855a). It begins: "The lotus leaf is round, round as a mirror; the arrow-root is pointed, pointed as an awl." It is not found in Chinese koan collections and was apparently first used in Japan. See Akizuki Ryūmin, *Kōan* (Tokyo, 1965), p. 104.

[35] Nyoka is apparently another name of Sokudō (d. 1712) who resided at the Daishō-ji in Numazu. Hakuin had studied with him shortly after he became a monk.

[36] Hsi-keng (Hsü-t'ang Chih-yü) was the teacher of Nampo Jōmyō (Daiō Kokushi). Both have been mentioned before. These lines are found as part of a verse in *Hsü-t'ang ho-shang yü-lu* (T47, p. 1037c). They are, however, not addressed to Nampo, but to three monks who are off on a visit to another temple.

After this I set out on a pilgrimage. One day when I was passing through southern Ise I ran into a downpour and the waters reached to my knees. Suddenly I gained an even deeper understanding of the verse on the Roundness of the Lotus Leaf by Ta-hui. I was unable to contain my joy. I lost all awareness of my body, fell headlong into the waters, and forgot completely to get up again. My bundles and clothing were soaked through. Fortunately a passer-by, seeing my predicament, helped me to get up. I roared with laughter and everyone there thought I was mad. That winter, when I was sitting at night in the monk's hall at Shinoda in Izumi,[37] I gained an enlightenment from the sound of snow falling. The next year, while practicing walking meditation at the monk's hall of the Reishō-in in Mino,[38] I suddenly had an enlightenment experience greater than any I had had before, and was overcome by a great surge of joy.

I came to this dilapidated temple[39] when I was thirty-two. One night in a dream my mother came and presented me with a purple robe made of silk. When I lifted it, both sleeves seemed very heavy, and on examining them I found an old mirror, five or six inches in diameter, in each sleeve. The reflection from the mirror in the right sleeve penetrated to my heart and vital organs. My own mind, mountains and rivers, the great earth seemed serene and bottomless. The mirror in the left sleeve, however, gave off no reflection whatsoever. Its surface was like that of a new pan that had yet to be touched by flames. But suddenly I became aware that the luster of the mirror from the left sleeve was innumerable times brighter than the other. After this, when I looked at all things, it was as though I were seeing my own face. For the first time I understood the meaning of the saying, "The Tathāgata sees the Buddha-nature within his eye."

Later I happened to read the Pi-yen lu again, and my understanding of it differed completely from what it had been before. One night, some time after, I took up the Lotus Sūtra. Suddenly I penetrated to the perfect, true, ultimate meaning of the Lotus. The doubts I had held initially were destroyed and I became aware

37 The Inryō-ji at Shinoda in present-day Osaka Prefecture.
38 The Reishō-in at Iwasaki, Yamagata-gun, in present-day Gifu Prefecture.
39 The Shōin-ji, Hakuin's temple at Hara, in present-day Shizuoka Prefecture.

that the understanding I had obtained up to then was greatly in error. Unconsciously I uttered a great cry and burst into tears.

I wish that everyone would realize that studying Zen under a teacher is not such a simple matter after all. Although I am old and dissipated, and have nothing of which I can be proud, I am aware that at least I have not spent forty years in vain. Was it not for this reason that Chang Wu, when he was in Yang-chou, let go of his gold and engaged in his painful struggles [toward success]? As in the example I gave you, if you shoulder the one-sided understanding you have gained and spend your whole life vainly polishing and purifying it, how are you any different from Chang Lu, who guarded his piece of gold throughout his life, starving himself and bringing only harm to his body?

In India such a person is called a poor son of a rich man, [a follower] of the Two Vehicles.⁴⁰ In China he is spoken of as belonging to the group that practices the heretical silent-illumination Zen. None of these knows the dignity of the bod-hisattva, nor does he reach the understanding that illuminates the cause for entrance to a Buddha land. Nowadays people go about carrying on their shoulders a single empty principle and with it "understand the Buddha, understand the Patriarchs, understand the old koans." Then they all say: "Like the stick, like the *dhāraṇī*, like the *katsu*."⁴¹ How laughable this is! Exert your-selves, students, for the Buddha Way is deep and far. Let every-one know that the farther you enter the sea the deeper it becomes and the higher you climb a mountain the taller it gets.

If you wish to test the validity of your own powers, you must first study the koan on the death of Nan-ch'üan.⁴²

⁴⁰ "The Two Vehicles" refers here to the two kinds of Hinayana practitioners, the *śrāvaka* and the *Pratyeka-buddha*. The *śrāvaka* is working toward or has gained Nirvana in Hinayana terms only. The *Pratyeka-buddha* has gained enlight-enment through his own efforts, but gives no thought to aiding others.

⁴¹ This passage is unclear. Presumably these people, who bear a single empty principle on their shoulders, and claim to understand the Buddha, Patriarchs, and koans, equate the stick with the Buddha, the *dhāraṇī* with the koans, and the shout (*katsu*) with the Patriarchs.

⁴² This koan has been mentioned before. The story appears in *Ching-te ch'uan-teng lu* (T51, p. 275b). Hakuin's version varies from the original and is somewhat abbreviated. Of the people who appear in the story below, we have seen

A long time ago San-sheng had the head monk Hsiu go to the Zen Master Tsen of Ch'ang-sha and ask him: "What happened to Nan-ch'üan after he passed away?"

Ch'ang-sha replied: "When Shih-t'ou became a novice monk he was seen by the Sixth Patriarch."

Hsiu replied: "I didn't ask you about when Shih-t'ou became a novice monk; I asked you what happened to Nan-ch'üan after he passed away."

Ch'ang-sha replied: "If I were you I would let Nan-ch'üan worry about it himself."

Hsiu replied: "Even though you had a thousand-foot winter pine, there is no bamboo shoot to rise above its branches."

Ch'ang-sha had nothing to say. Hsiu returned and told the story of his conversation to San-sheng. San-sheng unconsciously stuck out his tongue [in surprise] and said: "He has surpassed Lin-chi by seven paces."

If you are able to understand and make clear these words, then I will acknowledge that you have a certain degree of responsiveness to the teachings. Why is this so? If you speak to yourself while no one is around, you behave as meanly as a rat. What can anyone possibly prove [about your understanding]?

I may have been hitting a dangerous animal in the teeth three times. I join my palms together and say: "Let's leave it at that for today."

Nan-ch'üan, Ch'ang-sha, Shih-t'ou and Lin-chi before. San-sheng Hui-jan (Sanshō E'nen, n.d.) was a disciple of Lin-chi. The head monk Hsiu is not identified. The Sixth Patriarch is Hui-neng (Enō, d. 713).

❋ ORATEGAMA ZOKUSHŪ

Letter in answer to the question: Which
is superior, the Koan or the Nembutsu?[1]

❋ In your recent letter you ask whether the calling of the Buddha's name is of any help to continuous and uninterrupted true meditation, and whether the calling of the name is one with the meditation on Chao-chou's *Mu*. Your kind letter inquires whether there are any particular deficiencies in either of the two methods.

When you kill a man, is it the same thing if you kill him with a sword or with a spear,[2] or are there any particular drawbacks in the two methods? How does one answer such a question? Certainly the sword and spear are two different weapons, yet can we call the killing itself two things? In the past Tadanobu[3] used a chess board to pursue an enemy, Shinozuka[4] ripped loose a board from a ship's deck and used it to beat someone, the Empress Lü used poisoned wine to kill the [Chao King Liu] Ju-i,[5] Hsüan-wu unfastened a lute string and used it to garrote a lady of pleasure,[6] Kuan Yü brandished the dragon sword, and

---

[1] *Nembutsu* is the calling of the Buddha's name, in this instance the Buddha Amida, as practiced by followers of the Pure Land school. I have translated this term throughout this section as "the calling of the Buddha's name." See Introduction, fn. 34.

[2] Adapted from *Mencius*, 1A, 4, 2.

[3] Satō Tadanobu (1161–1186), retainer of Minamoto no Yoshitsune.

[4] Shinozuka Shigehiro. Also known as governor of Iga (*Iga no kami*). Warrior of the Yoshino period.

[5] Empress Lü (d. 180 B.C.) was consort of the first Han Emperor. The story of the murder of the king of Chao appears in *Shih chi*, 9.

[6] This incident is not identified.

Chang Fei[7] took up the viper club. The sword and the spear are two, but the duality lies only in the skill or clumsiness, the honesty or dishonesty, of the person who wields them.

So it is with the study of the Way. Whether you sit in meditation, recite the sutras, intone the *dhāraṇī*, or call the Buddha's name, if you devote all your efforts to what you are doing and attain to the ultimate, you will kick down the dark cave of ignorance, destroy the evil bandits of the five desires, smash the illumination of the Great Perfect Mirror,[8] penetrate to the true status of the perfect knowledge of the Four Wisdoms,[9] and attain to the understanding of the Great Matter. The content of the practices may vary but what difference is there in the goal that is reached?

Say there are two men whose strength and physical makeup are the same. Each is equipped with strong armor and sharp weapons and they engage each other in battle. Yet one does not possess a strong determination. He doubts and he fears; he does not know whether to fight or to run away. He cannot decide whether to live or to die, whether to advance or to retreat. His eyes waver, his footwork is unsteady; confused, he does not know what to do. The other does not consider danger. It matters not who is strong and who weak. His whole body is concentrated, his eyes fixed, his teeth gritted, and with valiant spirit he presses forward. Which man will win is as obvious as the palm of your hand. It is perfectly clear that no matter what odds he encountered, the second man would win every time. Suppose two armies were facing each other. One army has a hundred thousand troops, all mercenaries paid with gold and silver. The other has but a thousand men, trained in virtue and loyalty, their determination wedded with benevolence. To set these thousand men against the hundred thousand would be like loosing a fierce tiger against a flock of sheep. It all comes down to the worthiness or lack of

---

[7] Kuan Yü (d. 219) and Chang Fei (d. 220) are both great Chinese military heroes.

[8] The wisdom achieved when the *ālaya*-consciousness is inverted.

[9] The Four Wisdoms are: Great Perfect Mirror Wisdom, Universal Nature Wisdom, Wondrous Observation Wisdom, and Perfection of Action Wisdom. See ZD, pp. 313–14.

worth of the generals in command. What can differences in strength or the amount of weapons possibly have to do with it?

The same thing applies to concentrated meditation. Supposing you have one man who is occupied with the koan of Chaochou's *Mu* and another who devotes himself exclusively to the calling of the Buddha's name. If the meditation of the former is not pure, if his determination is not firm, even if he devotes himself to the koan for ten or twenty years, he will gain no benefit whatsoever. The man who calls the Buddha's name, on the other hand, should he call it with complete concentration and undiluted purity, should he neither concern himself with the filthy mundane world nor seek the Pure Land, but proceed determinedly without retrogression, he will, before ten days have passed, gain the benefits of *samādhi*, produce the wisdom of the Buddha, and achieve the Great Matter of salvation in the very place he stands.

What is salvation (*ōjō*)? It all comes down to the one thing— seeing into your own nature. The *Sūtra* states the vow: "Until all those who repeat my name ten times in their desire to be born in my land are born there, I shall not accept true enlightenment."[10] Where is "my land?" Is it not the innate self-nature with which you yourself are endowed, standing bright and clear before your eyes? If you have not seen into your own nature it will not be easy for you to see this land. Yet nowadays those who practice the Pure Land teaching recite the name daily a thousand times, ten thousand times, a million times, but not one of them has determined the Great Matter of salvation. Don't they realize that Amida Buddha refused to accept true enlightenment? Still more, don't they realize that one instant of thought is this very Paradise of Salvation? Why wait then for ten repetitions of the name?

For this reason the Buddha has said that for the valiant man, becoming a Buddha is in an instant of thought; for the indolent man, Nirvana will take three *asaṅkheya* kalpas.[11] It should be known that those who think that the *Mu* koan and the recitation of the Buddha's name are two different things belong to the class of evil heretics. How sad it is that the Pure Land practitioners

[10] An adaptation of Amida's Eighteenth Vow, from the *Wu-liang-shou ching*.
[11] An incalculable period of time.

today are unaware of the basic aspiration of the many Buddhas. They believe only that the Buddha is in the Western Land and are unaware that the Western Land is the basis of their own minds. They are convinced that through the power of the recitation of the Buddha's name they will somehow leap through space and after they are dead be reborn in the Western Land. But although they spend their whole lives in painful struggle, they will not be able to achieve their vow to be reborn there. Know then that "in all the Buddha lands everywhere there is the Law of the One Unique Vehicle."[12] This is why it has been said: "The Buddha body fills the Dharmakaya; it appears before all sentient beings everywhere."[13] If the Buddha were only in the Western Land it would not be possible for him to appear before all sentient beings everywhere. And if he does appear before all sentient beings everywhere, then he cannot be only in the Western Land. How sad indeed that, although it is as obvious as the palms of their hands that the pure, true body of the Tathāgata stands in all its brilliance clearly before their eyes, people are all unable to see him because their eye of wisdom is blinded. Unspeakable indeed!

Isn't it said: "His brilliance illumines the world in all directions"?[14] But do not understand this to mean that the brilliance and the world are two different things. If you are awakened, the worlds in all directions, grass, trees, lands are perfected and at once are the true body of the pure light of the Tathāgata. If you are deluded, the true body of the pure light of the Tathāgata is perfected, but in error is made to be the world in all directions, grass, trees, and lands. That is why the *Sūtra* says: "If you see me as form or seek me as sound, you are practicing the ways of the heretic and will never be able to see the Tathāgata."[15]

The true practitioner of the Pure Land doctrine is not like this. He does not contemplate birth, he does not contemplate death; his mind does not falter or fall into error. Reciting the name of the Buddha constantly, he has reached the state where the mind is undisturbed. The Great Matter appears suddenly

[12] *Lotus Sūtra* (T9, p. 8a).
[13] The exact source of this particular quotation has not been traced.
[14] *Kuan wu-liang-shou ching* (T12, p. 343b).
[15] *Diamond Sūtra* (T8, p. 756b). See "Orategama I," fn. 22.

before him and his salvation is determined. Such a man can be called one who has truly seen into his own nature. His own body is the limitless body of Amida, the treasure trees of seven precious gems, the pond of the eight virtues. His own mind is illumined and radiates before his eyes. He has penetrated to the understanding that mountains, rivers, the great earth, all phenomena are the rare and mysterious Sea of Adornment. The ultimate, in which there is complete concentration in calling the name, in which not an instant of thought is produced, and in which the body and life are cast aside is known as "going" (ō). The place where *samādhi* is perfected and true wisdom makes its appearance is known as "being born" (*jō*). The welling-forth of this absolute principle in all its clarity, the immovable place in which he [the true practitioner] stands, not one fraction of an inch apart [from true understanding], is "the welcoming of Amida" (*raigō*). When the welcoming and the rebirth are then and there not two things— this is the true substance of seeing into one's own nature.

Around the Genroku period [1688–1703] there were two Pure Land practitioners, one named Enjo and the other Engu.[16] Each was possessed of the same aspiration and neither of them relaxed one bit in his concentrated recitation of the Buddha's name. Enjo was a native of Yamashiro. His recitation of the name was pure and he had reached the state where his mind was undisturbed. Suddenly he had perfected his *samādhi* and had determined the Great Matter of Salvation. Having attained this state he went to pay a visit to the old Master Dokutan[17] at Hatsuyama in the province of Tōtomi.

Dokutan asked: "From what province do you come?"
Enjo replied: "From Yamashiro."
Dokutan asked: "To what sect do you belong?"
"The Pure Land," Enjo answered.
Dokutan asked: "How old is Amida Buddha?"

---

[16] Hakuin is the only source of information about these two monks. Engu has been mentioned previously.

[17] The Japanese reading for the Chinese monk Tu-chan Hsing-ying (Dokutan Shōei, 1628–1706) of the Ōbaku school of Zen. His temple, the Hōrin-ji (also called Hatsuyama) was at Nakagawa-mura, Inasa-gun, in present-day Shizuoka Prefecture.

Enjo replied: "The same age as I."

"And how old are you?" Dokutan countered.

"The same as Amida," Enjo replied.

Then Dokutan asked: "Then where are you right at this moment?" Enjo clenched his left hand and raised it a little. Dokutan was startled. "You really are a true practitioner of the Pure Land doctrine," he added.

Engu also, after not so long a time, perfected his *samādhi* and determined for himself the Great Matter.

Around the beginning of the Genroku period there was a monk in Akazawa in Izu Province by the name of Sokuō.[18] He also gained great virtue through the power of the recitation of the Buddha's name. I have mentioned here two or three of these Pure Land practitioners; there are many others like them, but I do not have the time to list them one by one. These men in themselves serve as proof of the virtue gained from concentrated recitation of the Buddha's name.

It must be understood that the koan and the recitation of the Buddha's name are both contributing causes to the path that leads to the opening up of the wisdom of the Buddha. The opening up of the wisdom of the Buddha is the main purpose for the appearance of the various Buddhas in this world. In the past the Buddha established expedients; one was called "rebirth in the Pure Land," another "seeing into one's own nature." How can these be two different things! Zen people who have not penetrated to this understanding look at a Pure Land practitioner and think that he is a stupid and evil common person who knows nothing about the Great Matter of seeing into one's own nature. They feel that he is vainly reciting the Buddha's name in the hope of leaping across countless countries in broad daylight in order to be reborn in the Pure Land, and they liken him to a lame turtle that dresses itself up and then expects to jump over to China. They condemn him particularly for not knowing that as far as these countless countries are concerned, the ten evils and the eight wrong views herald the awakening to the wisdom of the

[18] Nothing is known of this man. He has appeared previously.

Buddha, and that when these evils and heresies are dissipated the very place where one stands is the Pure Land.

The Pure Land practitioner, on the other hand, looks at the Zen man and thinks that here is someone who has no faith in the saving grace of Amida, but pridefully seeks to gain awakening through his own efforts and tries to make the great awakening his escape from birth and death. "Isn't this the most ridiculous of practices? Is this something that we poor mortals of inadequate capacities can accomplish in this degenerate age?" they ask. So they scorn the Zen man and compare him to a duck, that, deciding it will fly to Korea, fits itself with wings, thinking that it can emulate a hawk.

The practitioner of the *Lotus Sūtra* berates others, saying: "Our *Sūtra* is the basic vow because of which all Buddhas appear in the world, the one direct way by which all the Tathāgatas attain to Buddhahood. If you disregard our unsurpassedly wondrous *Sūtra* what possible use can there be in reciting the Buddha's name or in practicing Zen? Anyone who, when he sees a specialist in reciting this *Sūtra*, says that this specialist has not perfected his understanding of the unique One Vehicle, has not opened up the knowledge of the true form of the various dharmas, and is merely screaming incongruous sounds every day, like frogs croaking amidst the paddy fields in spring, is himself a prater of nonsense, a fool who disregards the golden words concerning the Arjaka[19] tree, and a perpetrator of evil heresies."

Aren't these people aware that the *Lotus Sūtra* has leaped over the gradual step-by-step methods of the *Āgamas*, *Vaipulya*, and the rest of the four doctrines[20] and speaks of the essential teaching of the opening up of the Buddha's wisdom? This is why the *Sūtra* says: "[The Buddhas] appear in this world to show the Way

---

[19] *Lotus Sūtra* (T9, p. 596): "He who would attack a preacher after hearing this *Dhāraṇī*, his head will be split into seven parts, like the flower of the Arjaka tree."

[20] The Tendai classification of the Buddhist teachings, likened to the four stages in the clarification of ghee: 1) fresh milk, the *Avataṁsaka*; 2) cream, the *Āgamas*; 3) curdled milk, the *Vaipulya*; 4) butter, the *Prajñāpāramita*. The fifth is ghee, the Lotus teaching.

to the opening up of the Buddha's wisdom."[21] Know then that with the luminescence of perfect understanding, the vow to appear in the world is made. Studying Zen, calling the name, even reading and reciting sutras, are all aids in the path toward seeing the Way. They are like the staves that travelers use to aid them in their journeys.

Among staves there are those made of goosefoot and those made of bamboo. Though the staves are made of different materials they both serve the same purpose—to help the voyager in his travels. Do not say then that the goosefoot staff is good and the one made of bamboo poor. If the voyager loses his perseverance and collapses of fatigue, what use is either staff, no matter of what it is made? It is the same with studying Zen under a teacher. Its essence lies only in the one instant of thought, borne by the fierce perseverance of the practitioner. Don't say: "The koan is good, the calling of the Buddha's name is bad." If the practitioner does not have that valiant will to succeed, neither the calling of the name nor the koan will be of any use whatsoever. They will be of as much value as glasses for a blind man or a comb for a monk.

Supposing there are a hundred people, each fitted out with his own provisions, who wish to go to the capital. But their guide is incompetent and in error leads them to a distant, desolate plain, teeming with wolves and tigers. They spend their days fighting over whose staff is made of the better wood, arguing about whose garments are superior, and worrying about the cost of their travels. All they talk about are the staves, all they shout about are the expenses, until they are unable to move one step further. They have spent their time in vain, years have been added to their lives, and their bodies are wearied and exhausted. Finally they fall prey to the wolves and tigers, and in this far and desolate area become idle spirits and wild demons. Thus in the end they never are able to reach the capital. The wise thing to do is to pay no attention to such things as staves and traveling clothes but single-mindedly to advance without losing ground. In this way you will quickly reach the capital. But if you imitate the customs of today by depending upon the power of the Buddha

21 *Lotus Sūtra* (T9, p. 7a).

while alive, and hoping to go to the Western Land after you have died, then throughout your whole life you will never be able to achieve *samādhi* and will never be able to determine your salvation. How much less so will you be able to achieve the Great Matter of the true seeing into your own nature.

The Priest of Shinjū-an[22] has left a verse:

> More tenuous than figures written on a flowing stream,
> The future of those who depend upon the Buddha.

Even though he has written in this way Ikkyū did not mean that the Pure Land practices are to be despised and the calling of the name to be abjured. But if you are looking for something that will help you attain continuous uninterrupted true meditation and insight into your own nature, then calling the Buddha's name is fine, but you could as well recite the grain-grinding song[23] instead. Do not think you are going to become a Buddha by deliberately discarding the essentials of seeing into your own nature and turning instead to the virtues gained from calling the Buddha's name.

To put it in the form of a parable, suppose you had a great ship that could hold ten thousand bales of rice. The ship is moored, ready for sailing; a favorable wind is blowing, the oarsmen are ready, their voices raised in song. The captain, his crew, and the helmsman are all in accord and they set out over the waves rowing toward far-off waters, proceeding bravely onward day after day. But wait: the hawser has not been loosened. They cannot cross over the rolling waves, and though each day they exhaust all their efforts, they are still in the harbor from which they started out. It is but a small hawser that binds them, yet it is stronger than ten thousand men.

So it is with the study of the Way. A man may be physically well endowed, possessed of an enormous vitality, have superb talents, make Ma-tsu and Po-chang his teachers, Nan-ch'üan and Ch'ang-sha his companions, nourish well his valiant energies, advance in his single-minded practice, train himself in pure undistracted meditation, yet if he has not cut off the root of life, he will never attain to the joy where the "Ka" is shouted.

[22] Ikkyū Sōjun. Hakuin has quoted him before.   [23] A common folk song.

What is this root of life? It is that instant of ignorance that has come down through endless kalpas of time. Evolving through heaven and hell, this evil world and the Pure Land, that the three evil realms and the six evil paths are made to appear is all because of the power of this root of life. Although it is nothing but dreamlike, illusory fancied thoughts, it can block the Great Matter of seeing into one's own nature more effectively than an army of a hundred thousand demons. Sometimes it is called illusory thoughts, sometimes the root of birth and death, sometimes the passions, sometimes a demon. It is one thing with many names, but if you examine it closely you will find that what it comes down to is one concept: that the self is real. Because of this view that the self exists, we have birth and death, Nirvana, the passions, enlightenment. That is why it is said: "If the mind is produced, all things are produced; if the mind is destroyed, all things are destroyed."[24] Elsewhere we read: "[Should a bodhisattva give rise to a notion of] the self, of a man, of a sentient being, this is not a true bodhisattva."[25] The Buddha asked Kāśyapa: "What Law do the sons of good families practice so that they can conform with the Law of the Great Nirvana?"[26] Kāśyapa answered by mentioning one by one such things as the five precepts,[27] the ten good characteristics,[28] the eighteen differentiating qualities[29] the six perfections,[30] all the good actions of a bodhisattva, the eight forms of deliverance,[31] the countless Dharma gates, but the Buddha would accept none of his answers. Finally Kāśyapa asked the Buddha: "What laws are there that conform with Nirvana?" and the Buddha answered: "The only Law that conforms with Nirvana is the Law of non-ego."

But non-ego is of two kinds. Take a man who is weak in body and mind. He is afraid of everybody, destroys his vitality,

---

[24] *Ta-ch'eng ch'i-hsin lun* (T32, p. 577c).

[25] *Diamond Sūtra* (T8, p. 749a). The quotation does not follow the original.

[26] The following passage paraphrases the *Nirvāṇa Sūtra*, chapter on Kāśyapa.

[27] The first five of the ten precepts: against killing, theft, adultery, lying, intoxicating liquors.

[28] The avoidance of the ten evils, the non-violation of the precepts.

[29] That distinguish a Buddha from a bodhisattva.

[30] Charity, maintaining the precepts, patience, will to progress, meditation, and wisdom.   [31] Eight stages of mental concentration leading to final liberation.

and is influenced by all external circumstances. He does not get angry even when reviled; he does not care even if he is rejected but always stupidly plods along getting nowhere. His knowledge advances not one bit and he thinks that the non-ego to which he has attained is sufficient. Such a person is a torn rice bag, bloated from gorging himself on the swill of swine, an ignorant, blind fool. This does not represent the true non-ego. How much less so then for the man who, relying on the power of the calling of the Buddha's name, hopes to "go" to the Pure Land and thus tries to "become" a Buddha! What is this "going"? What is this "becoming"? If it isn't ego, then what is it? Don't say: "This is a view that denies karma." Is this denying or not denying? If you are not a hero who has truly seen into his own nature, don't think it is something that can be known so easily. If you wish accordance with the true, pure non-ego, you must be prepared to let go your hold when hanging from a sheer precipice, to die and return again to life. Only then can you attain to the true ego of the four Nirvana virtues.[32]

What is "to let go your hold when hanging from a sheer precipice"? Supposing a man should find himself in some desolate area where no man has ever walked before. Below him are the perpendicular walls of a bottomless chasm. His feet rest precariously on a patch of slippery moss, and there is no spot of earth on which he can steady himself. He can neither advance nor retreat; he faces only death. The only things he has on which to depend are a vine that he grasps by the left hand and a creeper that he holds with his right. His life hangs as if from a dangling thread. If he were suddenly to let go his dried bones would not even be left.

So it is with the study of the Way. If you take up one koan and investigate it unceasingly your mind will die and your will will be destroyed. It is as though a vast, empty abyss lay before you, with no place to set your hands and feet. You face death and your bosom feels as though it were afire. Then suddenly you are one with the koan, and both body and mind are cast off. This is known as the time when the hands are released over the abyss.

[32] Permanence, peace, Self, purity.

Then when suddenly you return to life, there is the great joy of one who drinks the water and knows for himself whether it is hot or cold. This is known as rebirth in the Pure Land. This is known as seeing into one's own nature. You must push forward relentlessly and with the help of this complete concentration you will penetrate without fail to the basic source of your own nature. Never doubt that without seeing into your own nature you cannot become a Buddha; without seeing into your own nature there is no Pure Land.

Even the world-honored Tathāgata, the incomparable great sage of the three worlds who longed to become the guide to all sentient beings, before he entered the Himalaya and saw once into his own nature, was no different from ordinary people, revolving endlessly in the cycle of transmigration, and he himself passed through some eight thousand rebirths. With the coming of the dawn of the great awakening to one's own nature, then are the eyebrows opened wide to enlightenment. It is an unparalleled ignorance to believe that one can become a Buddha without seeing into one's own nature, or that there is a Pure Land outside of one's own nature.

The Twenty-eighth Patriarch, Bodhidharma, borne by the living body of the bodhisattva Kannon, endured endless stretches of raging waves to come to China, a land that already possessed the sacred scriptures in abundance, to transmit the seal of the Buddha mind that had been handed down from the Tathāgata. Hearing of this, and wondering what Great Matter he had to impart, people wiped their eyes, adjusted their garments, and came longing for instruction. And what he had to teach was only the one thing—seeing into one's own nature and becoming Buddha. Although he set up six gates, including the "Breaking through Form" and the "Awakened Nature,"[33] ultimately they all come down to the one thing—seeing into one's own nature.

But sentient beings are numberless; therefore the gates to the Dharma are numberless. Among them [the Buddha] established

[33] Reference is to the *Shōshitsu rokumon* (T48, pp. 365–76), a collection of six works attributed to Bodhidharma, first published in Japan. The "Breaking through Form" and the "Awakened Nature" are titles of two of these works.

one gate, that of rebirth into the Pure Land, as a temporary expedient to rescue Vaidehī[34] from the prison in which she languished. If rebirth in the Pure Land were the pivotal teaching of Buddhism, then Bodhidharma could just as well have written a note of two or three lines and sent it on to China. Would Bodhidharma have endured the painful agonies of the raging waves and risked his life against monster fish to come all the way to China just to say: "Concentrate on the calling of the Buddha's name and you will be reborn in the Pure Land"?

The same was true of the Buddha. At first he lived in the palace of his father Śuddhodana and spent his time in pleasurable enjoyment with his wives Yaśodharā and Gopikā.[35] His position was that of a ruler;[36] he possessed the wealth of India, and he believed that at death it would be satisfactory to call the name and be reborn in the Pure Land. One can imagine the state of his mind then, when he discarded his position as king, for six years engaged in arduous ascetic practices and suffered the scorn of the hermit Arāḍakālāma.[37] Later he entered deep into the Himalaya and fell into so intense a *samādhi* that he was unaware of the reeds that were piercing his thigh or the lightning that struck down horses and oxen beside him. His whole body was so emaciated that he looked like a tile bound with rope and his bones stuck to his skin.

Then finally, on the eighth day of the twelfth month, he glimpsed the planet Venus, and then for the first time saw into his own nature and gained a great awakening. At this time he exclaimed aloud: "How wonderful! All sentient beings are endowed with the great wisdom and virtuous characteristics of the Tathāgata!"[38] And then he came down from the mountain and expounded in full measure the sudden and the gradual, the intermediate and the complete teachings. At this time he was

[34] The story of Queen Vaidehī appears in the *Kuan-wu-liang-shou ching* (T12, pp. 341a–c).

[35] Yaśodharā and Gopikā are both names of Guatama's wife. Hakuin has made her into two people.

[36] *Kurai jūzen.* Because he had practiced the ten virtues in a past life, his position has risen to that of a ruler in this one.

[37] The hermit to whom Gautama went on first leaving the palace.

[38] *Avataṁsaka Sūtra* (T9, p. 624a).

venerated as the Tathāgata, endowed with the ten titles [39] and possessed of the perfect miraculous enlightenment. Is this not what Shan-hui Ta-shih has described in these words: "Suddenly awakening to the source of the mind, the treasure storehouse is opened"? [40] Even though ours is a degenerate age, is this not a splendid example that Buddhists today should venerate? If you look for the essentials and the basic content of the practice that has been transmitted from the Tathāgata who appeared in this world through the Patriarchs and sages and all wise men and famous monks, it is nothing other than the principle of seeing into one's own nature.

Rennyo Shōnin [41] has spoken about everyday rebirth [42] and rebirth without the welcoming of Amida. [43] When you think about it, is this not the true principle of seeing into your own nature? Even Hōnen Shōnin, who delved deeply into the Tripitaka and read through its five thousand volumes five times, who was worshipped as a living Tathāgata by everyone from lord to commoner, always lamented that it was not solely a matter of making the principle clear within the sacred works. Because he had no predecessor who had investigated the basis of the mind in the teachings outside the scriptures, he likened his own state of mind to a line too short to allow the bucket to scoop up the water in a deep well, or to wings too short to fly over the vast reaches of the sky. What is the basis of the mind in the transmission outside the scriptures? Is it not the teaching of seeing into one's own nature? One is indeed struck with awe and veneration to see that not one word uttered by the Taoist sages violates this teaching to the slightest degree. That people today show contempt and

---

[39] The ten titles or epithets given the Buddha.

[40] Shan-hui Ta-shih is another name for Fu Ta-shih, seen previously. The source of this quotation has not been traced.

[41] Rennyo Shōnin (1415–1499). Eighth Patriarch of the Shin Sect of Pure Land Buddhism.

[42] Hakuin has written *heizei ōjō*, "everyday rebirth," in place of *heizei gōjō*, which refers to doing works leading to rebirth in the Pure Land at ordinary times, not only just before death.

[43] Because the practitioner has already, in ordinary life, determined for himself to be reborn in the Pure Land, there is no need to wait for the welcoming of Amida at his death.

scorn for the Great Matter of seeing into one's own nature—a thing for which even the august Hōnen Shōnin, who was venerated and respected by the gods, longed for deeply—is, in my opinion, a serious crime. Of course, for people who do not know of the principle, this cannot be considered so great a crime.

Eshin Sōzu,[44] at the age of twenty-four, saying that he wanted to polish the Great Perfect Mirror of his own nature, retired to the fastness of Yokawa and during the day practiced the three sutras of the Lotus[45] and at night called the Buddha's name sixty thousand times. At other times of the day he was not idle, yet it was only when he reached the age of sixty-four that he felt that he had understood the True Reality of his own nature. He is indeed worthy of veneration. When one reaches this state of the realization of True Reality in one's own body, the mountains, rivers, the great earth, all phenomena, grass, trees, lands, the sentient and the non-sentient all appear at the same time as the complete body of the unchanging True Reality. This is the appearance of Nirvana, the time of awakening to one's own nature.

Myōhen Sōzu[46] of Mount Kōya, in the fall of a year when he was in his fifties, entered into a deep *samādhi* of calling the Buddha's name. [That evening] Kōya Daishi[47] [appeared before him and] presented him formally with a surplice (*kesa*) of lily-root fibre and a golden leaf of the scriptures [explaining the *samādhi*]. The gist of what he said was: "Pointing only in the one direction of the West is an expedient. If you discard the nine other directions and stop the confused mind and throughout your life call the name of the Buddha, you will gain the great virtue of the opening of the mind's eye." The opening of the mind's eye is of itself seeing into one's own nature.

Even though there are over five thousand rolls of the scriptures spoken by the Buddha, and although he preached on the

---

[44] Another name for Genshin; he has already appeared in "Letter to an Old Nun." See "Orategama III," fn. 27.

[45] The *Lotus Sūtra*, the *Wu-liang-i ching* (T9, pp. 383–89) and the *Kuan P'u-hsien p'u-sa hsing-fa ching* (T9, pp. 389–94).

[46] Myōhen (1142–1224). Shingon priest from Mt. Kōya, famed for his devotion to Amida Buddha. The present story does not appear in *Honchō kōsō den* and *Genkō shakusho*.   [47] Kūkai, the founder of the Shingon Sect in Japan.

wondrous meaning of the sudden, gradual, secret, and indeterminate doctrines, nowhere does the Great Matter of seeing into one's own nature appear. This is why the *Sūtra* says: "There is only this one True Reality. Any other is not the True."[48] In all the three periods from the past to the present,[49] there has not been one Buddha or Patriarch who did not see into his own nature. Those sages and wise men who have not seen into their own natures have not achieved the ultimate.

When I was seven or eight my heart turned toward the principles of Buddhism. When I was fifteen I left home to become a monk. From the age of nineteen I began making pilgrimages and when I was twenty-four for the first time I attained insight into my own nature. After this I wandered from monastery to monastery, crossed the thresholds of many good teachers, investigated in detail all the Buddhist scriptures, studied widely the sacred works of Buddhism, Confucianism, and Taoism, as well as the writings of secular literature. I vowed that if I found one teaching that surpassed that of seeing into one's own nature—and these included the works of Lao Tzu, Chuang Tzu, and Lieh Tzu—I would without fail accept it and do my best to propagate it. But I am now sixty-five years old and I have yet to find any teaching that excels that of seeing into one's own nature. You may well ask then, "Why waste all this paper and ink writing all these stupid things for others to read?" It is only to help people to see into their own natures that I keep on ceaselessly talking about it. For if you reach that point where your mind is not agitated, then your eyebrows will open wide with the great joy of awakening.

If you discard the *Mu* koan and, by intoning the name of the Buddha with the power of concentrated recitation of the Buddha's name you can make clear your own nature and penetrate at once to the bones and marrow of the Buddhas and Patriarchs, then this is fine. Even if you cannot see your own nature clearly, by the power of the calling of the name you will without fail be reborn in Paradise. But if what you are really trying to do is to

[48] *Lotus Sūtra* (T9, p. 8a).
[49] The three periods are conventionally given in the order of past, future, and present.

cleverly accomplish both things at the same time, then by all means discard at once the practice of calling the Buddha's name and take up in purity the *Mu* koan. Why do I say this? It is because some two hundred years ago evil and careless Zen followers decimated the Zen monasteries and corrupted the true style of Zen, spreading vulgar and debased heretical understanding.

In the Zen teaching, though "loftiness" is emphasized, even greater loftiness is demanded; in the Zen monasteries "steepness" is venerated, yet even greater steepness is needed.[50] "The vital harbor is always seized,"[51] and the sacred and the profane are not allowed through. When one word is uttered the spirit of the three stages[52] is destroyed and the eye of the four rewards[53] is beclouded. When a single phrase is spoken the idle spirits rush away in fear and the wild demons wail in despair. The bowels of the wooden man are rent and the marrow of the iron woman is split.[54] When one encounters a superb Zen student endowed with marvelous qualities and brilliant talents, the koans that are difficult to pass, difficult to understand, difficult to have faith in, and difficult to enter into, are presented to him. Then the true Dharma eye is blinded and the wondrous mind of Nirvana stolen away. The student will pass by the village with the poisoned water without drinking a drop and will devote himself solely to his koan. He will smash the dark cave of emotional considerations; he will pierce the snug nest of conceptual thinking; he will exhaust reason and bring an end to words; he will bring death to his mind and wipe out consciousness. Then suddenly this strange,

[50] *Koki, kenshun. Koki* is descriptive of a high mountain, impossible to scale. *Kenshun* indicates steepness. The terms are descriptive of a Master's technique in instructing his disciples.

[51] A passage from the preface to the *Lin-chi lu* (T47, p. 496a). The "vital harbor" represents the most important point, the First Principle. This passage refers to a teaching technique in which the student is denied any room for erroneous views.

[52] The three grades of virtue, composing thirty of the fifty-one stages in the advance toward bodhisattvahood.

[53] The four grades of sainthood in Hinayana, leading to arhatship.

[54] The wooden man and the iron woman appear frequently in Zen literature. They represent things that do not exist, concepts inconceivable to rational thought.

blind fool, standing neither in the sacred nor in the profane, neither Buddha nor demon, will leap free, and with this repay his deep obligations to the Buddhas and the Patriarchs.

Techniques such as these are called the "talons and teeth of the Cave of Dharma" and the "supernatural talisman that wrests life from death."[55] They are of great benefit to people of superior talents. Those of medium or inferior talents leave such things alone and quite disregard them. The people of the Pure Land school, in fact, are opposed to them. But the Pure Land is still a teaching to which veneration is due. Amida Buddha, with the skillful concentrated practice of great compassion, on the basis of his forty-eight vows, was endowed with the three minds[56] and four practices.[57] These techniques were established solely for those of medium and inferior talents and are of benefit to ignorant and stupid beings, enabling them to escape from the ten evils and five deadly sins. Giving primary importance to the golden words "to gather [all sentient] beings and to cast aside none,"[58] they make the low important and require still more lowliness, they make the easiness essential and venerate still more easiness. Therefore they tell you: "Even though you have studied well all the teachings of the Buddha, consider yourself an ignorant, illiterate fool, and just single-mindedly practice the calling of the Buddha's name. For these degenerate later days, filled with evil and turmoil, this is a technique that must not be omitted even for a single day."

In Zen it is as though giants were pitted against one another, with victory going to the tallest. In Pure Land it is as though midgets were set to fight, with victory going to the smallest. If the tallness of Zen were despised and Zen done away with, the true style of progress toward the Buddha mind would be swept away and destroyed. If the lowness of the Pure Land teachings

[55] See "Orategama I," fn. 41.

[56] The three ways of assuring rebirth in the Pure Land: perfect sincerity, deep resolve to be reborn there, and the resolve to turn one's merits to benefiting others.

[57] To have deep respect for the Buddha and all sages; to call Amida's name and to give him praise exclusively; to carry out this practice without interruption; to carry out this practice throughout one's life.

[58] *Kuan wu-liang-shou ching* (T12, p. 343b).

were despised and cast aside, stupid, ignorant people would be unable to escape from the evil realms.

Think of the Buddha as the Great King of Healing. He has set up eighty-four thousand medicines to cure the eighty-four thousand diseases. Zen, the teaching schools, Ritsu, the Pure Land are all methods used to treat a disease. Think of these methods as the four classes of people in the world: warriors, farmers, craftsmen, merchants. The warrior is endowed with both knowledge and benevolence. He perfects his command of the military works, protects the ruler, subdues the rebels, and brings peace to the country. He makes his lord like a lord under Yao and Shun,[59] the people like the people under Yao and Shun. He need not show anger, for the people fear him more than the punishment of the axe and halberd, and venerate the severe austerity of his bearing. Indeed he is a beautiful vessel, worthy of respect.

The merchant opens a large store and his ambition is to see it grow by selling his goods, his silks, cottons, grains, fish, and meat. He complies with the demands of everyone, be he monk or layman, man or woman, be he old, young, respectable or disreputable. If the warrior feels envy at the magnitude of the trader's operations and, coveting the tradesman's goods and profits, should try to become a merchant himself, he will discard his capacity for archery and horsemanship, forget the martial arts, and become a laughing stock to his friends. His lord will become enraged and will drive him away. If the merchant, envying the strict dignity of the samurai, girds a sword to his side, mounts a horse and, pretending to be a military figure, rides recklessly about here and there, everybody will laugh at him, and his family calling will be destroyed.

As I said before, if you cannot attain to Zen, then when you face death, try to be reborn in the Pure Land. Those who try to practice both at the same time will be able to obtain neither the fish nor the bear's paw,[60] but instead will cultivate the karma of

---

[59] Legendary sage rulers, seen before in "Orategama I."
[60] An adaptation of *Mencius* 6A, 10, 1: "I like fish and I also like bear's paws. If I cannot have the two together, I will let the fish go and take the bear's paws."

birth and death, fail to cut off the root of life, and will never be able to attain the joy where the "Ka" is shouted.

When I talk about the similarities of the *Mu* koan and the calling of the Buddha's name, I do not mean that they are not without differences when it comes time to test the quality of the virtue gained and the depth or shallowness with which the Way is seen. In general, for the hero who would seek enlightenment, and would cut off the seepages of emotions and conceptions, and destroy the film of ignorance that covers the eye, nothing surpasses the *Mu* koan.

The Master Fa-yen of Mount Wu-tsu has said in a verse:

> The exposed sword of Chao-chou
> Gleams brilliantly like cold frost.
> If someone tries to ask about it,
> His body will at once be cut in two.[61]

To all intents and purposes, the study of Zen makes as its essential the resolution of the ball of doubt. That is why it is said: "At the bottom of great doubt lies great awakening. If you doubt fully you will awaken fully."[62] Fo-kuo[63] has said: "If you don't doubt the koans you suffer a grave disease." If those who study Zen are able to make the great doubt appear before them, a hundred out of a hundred, a thousand out of a thousand, will without fail attain awakening.

When a person faces the great doubt, before him there is in all directions only a vast and empty land without birth and without death, like a huge plain of ice extending ten thousand miles. As though seated within a vase of lapis lazuli surrounded by absolute purity, without his senses he sits and forgets to stand, stands and forgets to sit. Within his heart there is not the slightest thought or emotion, only the single word *Mu*. It is just as though

---

[61] This verse is found in *Fa-yen ch'an-shih yü-lu* (T47, p. 666c). It concerns, of course, Chao-chou's *Mu* koan. Wu-tsu Fa-yen (Goso Hōen, 1024?–1104) is an important Sung monk.

[62] Source not identified.

[63] Fo-kuo (Bukka) is the posthumous title of Yüan-wu K'o-chin (Engo Kokugon, 1063–1135), a disciple of Wu-tsu Fa-yen. The source of the following quotation has not been traced.

he were standing in complete emptiness. At this time no fears arise, no thoughts creep in, and when he advances single-mindedly without retrogression, suddenly it will be as though a sheet of ice were broken or a jade tower had fallen. He will experience a great joy, one that never in forty years has he seen or heard. At this time "birth, death, and Nirvana will be like yesterday's dream, like the bubbles in the seas of the three thousand worlds, like the enlightened status of all the wise men and sages."[64] This is known as the time of the great penetration of wondrous awakening, the state where the "Ka" is shouted. It cannot be handed down, it cannot be explained; it is just like knowing for yourself by drinking it whether the water is hot or cold. The ten directions melt before the eyes, the three periods are penetrated in an instant of thought, What joy is there in the realms of man and Heaven that can compare with this?

This power can be obtained in the space of three to five days,[65] if the student will advance determinedly. You may ask how one can make this great doubt appear. Do not favor a quiet place, do not shun a busy place, but always set in the area below the navel Chao-chou's *Mu*. Then, asking what principle this *Mu* contains, if you discard all emotions, concepts, and thoughts and investigate single-mindedly, there is no one before whom the great doubt will not appear. When you call forth this great doubt before you in its pure and uninvolved form you may undergo an unpleasant and strange reaction. However, you must accept the fact that the realization of so felicitous a thing as the Great Matter, the trampling of the multi-tiered gate of birth and death that has come down through endless kalpas, the penetration of the inner understanding of the basic enlightenment of all the Tathāgatas of the ten directions, must involve a certain amount of suffering.

When you come to think about it, those who have investigated the *Mu* koan, brought before themselves the great doubt, experienced the Great Death, and attained the great joy, are countless in number. Of those who called the Buddha's name and gained a small measure of benefit from it, I have heard of no more

---

[64] *Yüan-chüeh ching* (T17, p. 915a). Only the first clause is found in the *Sūtra*.
[65] Presumably after the great doubt has appeared before the student.

than two or three. The abbot of Eshin-in has called it the benefits
of wisdom or the power of faith in the mind. If you investigate
the *Mu* or the Three Pounds of Flax or some other koan, to
obtain True Reality in your own body should take from two or
three months to a year or a year and a half. The efficacy gained
from calling the Buddha's name or reciting the sutras will require
forty years of strenuous effort. It is all a matter of raising or failing
to raise this ball of doubt. It must be understood that this ball of
doubt is like a pair of wings that advances you along the way. A
man such as Hōnen Shōnin was virtuous, benevolent, righteous,
persevering, and courageous. As he read the sacred scriptures in the
darkness, if he used to some extent the luminescence of his eye of
wisdom, he must, to the extent that this ball of doubt was formed,
have attained to the Great Matter in the place where he stood,
and have determined for himself his rebirth. What a tragedy it was
that the rope was too short, so that he could not draw the water
from the bottom of the well.

Although there were countless billions of Buddha names and
countless billions of *dhāraṇī*, such great Masters as Yang-ch'i,
Huang-lung, Chen-ching, Hsi-keng, Fo-chien, and Miao-hsi[66]
selected, from the vast number of gates to the teaching available, this *Mu* koan alone for their students to study. Is this
not the strong point of the teaching? Consider then that the
Mu koan easily gives rise to the ball of doubt, while the recitation of the Buddha's name makes it very difficult to bring it to
a head.

Moreover, in the Zen schools of China, the concentrated
recitation of the Buddha's name, with the wish to be reborn in
the Pure Land, did not exist at all at a time when the Zen monasteries had yet to wither, and the true teachings had yet to fall to
the ground. The Twenty-eight Indian Patriarchs, the Six Chinese
Patriarchs, their descendants in the transmission of Zen, Nan-
yüeh, Ch'ing-yüan, Ma-tsu, Shih-t'ou, Po-chang, Huang-po,
Nan-ch'üan, Ch'ang-sha, Lin-chi, Hsing-hua, Nan-yüan, Feng-
hsüeh, Shou-shan, Fen-yang, Tz'u-ming, Huang-lung, Chen-

---

[66] Of the famous Zen Masters mentioned here, all except Yang-chi Fang-hui
(Yōgi Hōe, 992–1049) and Fo-chien Hui-ch'in (Bukkan Egon, 1059–1113)
have appeared before.

ching, Hui-t'ang, Hsi-keng, and Miao-hsi,[67] all the masters of the
Five Houses and Seven Schools, all the monks of the Liang, Ch'en,
Sui, T'ang, Sung, and Yüan dynasties,[68] they all raised up the
teaching style of "steepness," attached to their arms the supernatural talisman that wrests life from death, chewed and made
reverberate in their own mouths the talons and teeth of the Cave
of the Dharma. All they were concerned about was to prevent
the style of the teaching from falling in the dirt. Day and night
they kept in motion relentlessly the wheel of the vow, without
slackening for a moment. They never once, even inadvertently,
spoke of rebirth in the Pure Land.

But sad, sad! Times passed; lives were lived out. The great
teachings withered and vulgar concepts arose; the old songs died
out and banalities flourished.[69] Then toward the end of the Ming
dynasty there appeared a man known as Chu-hung from Yün-
ch'i.[70] His talents were not sufficient to tackle the mysteries of
Zen, nor had he the eye to see into the Way. As he studied onward he could not gain the delights of Nirvana; as he retrogressed,
he suffered from the terrors of the cycle of birth and death. Finally,
unable to stand his distress, he was attracted to the memory of
Hui-yüan's[71] Lotus Society. He abandoned the "steepness"
technique of the founders of Zen, and calling himself "the Great
Master of the Lotus Pond," he wrote a commentary on the
Amitayus Sūtra,[72] advocated strongly the teachings relating to the

[67] Of the famous Zen Masters listed here, the following appear for the first
time in "Orategama": Ch'ing-yüan Hui-ssu (Seigen Gyōshi, d. 740), Nan-
ch'üan P'u-yüan (Nansen Fugan, 748–835. He has appeared previously as a
figure in a koan story), Nan-yüan Hui-yung (Nan'in Egyō, d. 930), Feng-
hsüeh Yen-chao (Fūketsu Enshō, 896–973), Shou-shan Sheng-nien (Shuzan
Shōnen, 926–993), and Fen-yang Shan-chao (Fun'yō Zenshō, 947–1024).

[68] The period from 502 to 1341.

[69] A paraphrase. Hakuin here compares the Zen of the old masters to the old
poems of the *Book of Songs*. As these later were replaced by licentious and vulgar
verses, so the teachings of Zen have declined.

[70] Yün-ch'i Chu-hung (Unsei Shukō, 1535–1615) has been mentioned before.
He is attacked by Hakuin throughout his works as a debaser of Zen, because of
his introduction of Pure Land teachings into Zen. See Introduction, pp. 25–26.

[71] Hui-yüan (334–417) was a renowned monk who in 402 set up a statue of
Amida and together with 123 other monks prayed for rebirth in the Pure Land.

[72] *A-mi-t'o ching shu-ch'ao* (zz1, 33, 2–3).

calling of the Buddha's name, and displayed an incredibly shallow understanding of Zen. Yüan-hsien Yung-chiao[73] of Ku-shan wrote a work known as *Ching-tz'u yao-yü*,[74] in which he concurred with Chu-hung's views and rendered him great assistance. With this these teachings spread throughout China, overflowing even to Japan, and ultimately reached a state where nothing could be done about them. Even if Lin-chi, Te-shan, Fen-yang, Tz'u-ming, Huang-lung, Chen-ching, Hsi-keng, and Miao-hsi were to appear in the world of today, were to raise their arms, gnash their teeth, spit on their hands, and proceed to drive these teachings out, they would not be able to undo this madness.

This is not meant to belittle the basic teachings of the Pure Land nor to make light of the practice of the calling of the Buddha's name. But not to practice Zen meditation while within the Zen Sect, to becloud the eye to see into one's own nature because of laziness in the study of Zen under a teacher and idleness in one's aspirations, only weakens the power to study Zen. People such as these end up by spending their whole lives in vain. Then when the day of their death is close at hand, they begin to fear the endless painful cycle of their births to come, and suddenly decide that they will work to seek rebirth in the Pure Land. Solemnly fingering their rosary beads and reciting the Buddha's name aloud, they tell the ignorant men and women among the laity that this is what is appropriate for untalented people in this degenerate age, and that in this miserable and evil world no superior practice exists. With fallen hair and gap-toothed mouths, they are apt to cry with sincerity, to blink their eyes, and entice men with words that seem to ring with truth. Yet what possible miracle can those expect, who up to now have failed to practice Zen?

People of this sort, while within Zen, slander the Zen teachings. They are like those wood-eating maggots that are produced in beams and pillars and then in turn destroy these very beams and pillars. They must be investigated at once. Indolence when in the prime of life leads to regret and misery in old age. The regret and misery of old age is not worthy of censure. The past need not be blamed, but the idleness and sloth of a young man, this each person must really fear.

[73] Yüan-hsien Yung-chiao (Genken Yōkaku, 1578–1657).   [74] ZZ2, 13, 5.

Since the Ming dynasty gangs of this type have become very large. All of them are mediocre and ineffectual Zen followers. Thirty years ago an old monk expressed his dismay, the tears falling from his eyes: "Ah, how Zen is declining! Three hundred years from now all Zen temples will startle the neighborhood by setting up the metal plate, installing the wooden gong, and holding worship six times a day."75 A fearful prospect indeed! In closing, I have one last word to say. Do not regret losing your eyebrows, but for the sake of your lord raise up the teaching. Do not come to an understanding of the Patriarchs as a *katsu*; do not come to an understanding of the koans as the *dhāraṇī*.76 You're not trying to devour the jujube in one gulp! Why is this a kind phrase? A monk asked Chao-chou: "Does a dog have Buddha-nature?" Chao-chou answered: "*Mu!*"

With respect.

APPENDED: *In answer to a visitor's criticism*1

During the Yüan and Ming periods the Zen schools tended to give emphasis to the calling of the Buddha's name. This was like stirring pearls in with rocks that looked like gems, like mixing worthless stones with the jewel of the Duke of Sui.2 From that time on the monasteries all fell into line and marched along behind this teaching; herein lies the basis for the deterioration of the style of Zen. Unless at this time one fearless voice is raised, a large number of ignorant fools will end up by not having their brains split.

I made the above statement in a letter in reply to questions from Lord Nabeshima, and [he replied] that I had "set forth [the principle] from one end to the other and exhausted it,"3 and that

75 The practice of the Pure Land schools.
76 The translation is tentative here. See "Orategama III," Supplement, fn. 41.
1 This section, in *kambun*, is appended to *Orategama zokushū*. The text is very obscure; the translation must therefore be considered highly tentative. It is based on the text as found in HOZ5, 238–44.
2 Legendary gem of enormous value.   3 *Analects*, 9, 7.

this was like setting a compass in fog-bound seas and the return of the pearls to Ho-p'u.[4]

One day a visitor remarked to me: "The one gate of the Pure Land is a superior expedient of the Tathāgata. Aśvaghoṣa praised it and Nāgārjuna[5] longed for it, and it seemed as though this marvelous land actually existed. But now you deny this. When those of inferior talents hear this they will be sure to lose all their hopes in the Pure Land."

To this I reply:

Ah! To be sure, the Pure Land exists in the mysterious Sea of Adornment of the Tathāgata. But it is no more than a reflection in a mirror, no more than an illusion. And when you break through to an understanding of why the illusion is an illusion, then you no longer have need to regard illusion as illusion. The Pure Land people teach you that because the Dharmakaya is so deep and obscure, and because it is so difficult to attain contact with the embodiment of the Dharma, one must for the time being concentrate on the Buddha, see his form, and render him praise. This is only because ignorant common people have weighty obstructions. For any sentient being possessed of the bodhisattva mind, any place at all is the Pure Land. The place where you attach is the adornment incomplete; the place pointed to by the Master is the land of Nirvana illumination. How right it is that you should have doubts!

The *Avataṁsaka Sūtra* says: "The Pure Land of the Tathāgata is in the jeweled crown, it is in the ear-ring, the jeweled waist-

---

[4] From a story in *Hou Han shu*, Lieh-chüan, 66. Biography of Meng Ch'ang. Meng Ch'ang was governor of Ho-p'u. During the administration of the former governor, who was greedy and evil, the pearls had moved away to neighboring Cochin China. Under Meng Ch'ang they came back. An example of the power of virtuous government.

[5] It is possible that Hakuin's interlocutor derived this statement from a work published in 1695, entitled *Zenso nembutsu shū* (*Dai-Nihon Bukkyō zensho* 70, [Tokyo, 1918], 252–88) by Echū, a disciple of Suzuki Shōsan (1579–1655), a monk who sought to combine Pure Land and Zen teachings. This work quotes Zen monks and believers who spoke in praise of the Pure Land doctrine. It quotes from both Aśvaghoṣa (*Awakening of Faith*) and Nāgārjuna (*Laṅkavatāra Sūtra*). Both of these men are included in the traditional Zen list of twenty-eight Indian Patriarchs.

band, the markings of the garments; it is in the hair holes. This is because the hair hole already contains the entire world."[6]

By this we know clearly that there just is no place, that there just is no limit. But the two honored ones,[7] because of the breadth of their vow of compassion, served in the vanguard for the benefit of all beings. Cannot this be called provisionally donning illusory garments, vowing to be born in an illusory land? Cannot this be called not giving rise to the ground of this world, making a birthless rebirth appear? This is in essence the vow of the Tathāgatas that appeared in this world, the activity of the techniques whereby the Patriarchs approached their disciples. Their traces are without number yet their purport was but one. They wished to bring all sentient beings to an awakening to the wisdom of the Buddha so that no skandhas remained.[8]

The *Lotus Sūtra* says: "The many Buddhas and the World-honored One used the various expedients, parables, and causal conditions for the sake of the One Buddha Vehicle. Thus they preached the many Dharmas for the sake of all sentient beings."[9] When this is so, how can the setting-up of the Pure Land not serve to assist the One Buddha Vehicle? How can the generous instructions and admonitions of our Zen teachers serve otherwise? They have stripped off the adornments and presented things in their true colors. It is just as though they offered real gold to stop [a child] from crying. Were they meanly to make it a yellow leaf, it would be the cause for later regret.

To condemn those people who brought shame on the basis of the teaching during the Yüan and Ming dynasties is like beating the drums for an attack in an isolated room. What right have I to preach to the faithful men and women who desire rebirth in the Pure Land and to claim that my own teaching is more important? When someone by the exclusive calling of the name suddenly attains to *samādhi*, in that he does not consciously seek it, he will without fail gain awakening. This is so because the Buddha Way

[6] I have not located this particular passage in the *Sūtra*.

[7] Shakamuni and Amida.

[8] *Youn.* The body of the bodhisattva when it has left the skandhas of the transmigratory world, but has yet to leave the skandhas of the realms beyond transmigration.   [9] T9, p. 7b. The quotation is not accurate.

is not dual. If you think about this well, you will understand it clearly.

The visitor said: "If the Pure Land is illusory then what is there that is not illusory? Is then Zen illusory too? The Buddha piled up good works over the endless kalpas of the past, cleansing away the residual dusts extending from the beginningless beginning, and by means of good recompense made the ground [of reward] pure. This cannot be called an illusion. Even though the Zen teaching condemns it and makes it inconsequential, since it is praised by the Tathāgata it cannot but be great."

To this I reply:

The realm of reward is indeed an illusion. But for the record let us discuss it. The eternal original essence of Daibirushana (Mahāvairocana), perfect and radiant with the fivefold wisdom, is like that of the pure Maṇi treasure jewel.[10] The jewel manifests various images. When they are pure it manifests them in purity; when they are impure it manifests them in impurity. All of these are manifested things. It does not manifest itself, yet it manifests; it is therefore not non-being. It manifests, yet it does not manifest itself; it is therefore not being. When being is not regarded as being, how can non-being be predicated? There is no room in this place of ultimate mysteriousness for being and non-being. Yet what thing is not manifested? Therefore, even though the ten thousand existences are present in abundance, the reason they come is unknown; even though emptiness is present in all its solitude, the reason that it goes is not known. Because images are dependent upon it, there are no images apart from the Maṇi treasure jewel. Because the manifestation of the Maṇi jewel occurs, there is no Maṇi treasure jewel apart from images. When a person truly in this way realizes the great Maṇi jewel, then an indescribable number of Pure Lands appear, which embrace all other lands. The very place in which this person stands is sublime and quiescent. The understanding of the person who worries about one Buddha land is as different as earth is from heaven.

[10] The Maṇi jewel symbolizes the ultimate value of Buddhist truth. "The fivefold wisdom" is a technical term in Shingon Buddhism. It includes the four wisdoms previously mentioned (see "Orategama zokushū," fn. 9), plus the Wisdom of the Embodied Nature of the Dharmakaya.

Therefore, wherever an accomplished person goes the treasure jewel is always with him. Shining brilliantly, chief and retinue form a harmonious whole.[11] The stupid person is just the opposite: wherever he goes images always accompany him. All things are uncertain; purity and impurity are confused. This owes itself only to a failure to attain awakening. The teaching of the Pure Land school is for people of inferior or mediocre capacity. It gives them a feeling of something of the essence of the jewel, which is unapproachable to them unless provided with provisional and subtle images. In order to furnish them with some kind of hope, the image is used as an intermediary. If they can see the images this is fine, but they cannot see the treasure jewel itself. Because men of the Zen school have superior capacities, they point at once to the perfectly illumined treasure jewel and do not see the supporting images. Thus they take mysterious enlightenment and make it the principle and destroy the treasure jewel as well. What images can there be for them?

Furthermore, the paths of Zen and Pure Land are different. Zen has handed down the seal of the Buddha mind and borne the True Dharma Eye. The Buddha mind is Zen. What other Buddha can there be? The True Dharma is the center of the teaching. What other sutras can there be? This is why the Buddha presented the golden surplice (kesa) to Kāśyapa. The teaching has been handed down in an unbroken line, as water poured from jar to jar. It is in truth the king of the Dharma. It has been likened to the emperor of the world, to the destiny of Heaven ensconced in your own body. If you yourself were charged with the affairs of the world, you would with discernment and reason let your knife run freely through all activities.[12] The principle is always under control; the dignity is never trampled under. Therefore, when there is a master in the world, high and low remain in their proper ranks, and all things are at peace. But let this master be lost even for one day, and there will be nothing so awful as the destruction and disorder of the world. How truly great is the master who gains the people and does not neglect his responsibilities. But the Pure Land School gathers together and shelters

[11] The tenth of the "ten profound theories" of the Kegon (Avataṁsaka) school.
[12] A reference to the butcher in *Chuang Tzu*, 3, 1, 2.

people who take the ego into account and who attach to form. Cleverly it adjusts to a person's talents and presents itself as a teaching that makes use of expedients. When you characterize it on the basis of the essence of the jewel, if this isn't illusion then what is it?

This is why the *Yüan-chüeh ching* says: "The indescribably numerous Buddha worlds are like the rising and destruction of imaginary flowers."[13] It should be known that all the worlds persist in illusion. Therefore, wherever the true teaching is made clear is, since this place is without form, the Pure Land.

The *Avataṁsaka Sūtra* says: "An enlightened person abides in the truth; the land itself is not important."[14] Tao-sheng has also said concerning this: "If the Buddha had been fettered by forms he would have been compelled to abide in a land. The Buddha is the eternal Dharma body. What use has he for lands?"[15] It must be known that the lands possessed by all the Buddhas everywhere are nothing but illusions and have no true reality. Because this is so, if you see these lands then you know without a doubt that the Buddha Way is not within them. Ignorant people decide by themselves that to combine Pure Land with Zen is to fit wings to a tiger. Or else saying things like: "If you don't have Pure Land together with Zen nine out of ten will go astray," they are like the followers of Han Fei Tzu, Mo Tzu, Yang Chu, and Shen Pu-hai.[16] Can such men be called qualified to teach the people for the Emperor? Were they to do so not only could the throne not be maintained, but the nation would without doubt be destroyed. When these people have some misgivings about the obscurity of their way, all that they do is to persistently encourage "proceeding in private perfecting one's own virtue." What is it that they expect to carry on at the same time? The *Hua-yen kuan* says: "If you have faith but do not believe in the Dharma world, then your faith is a heresy."[17]

In all the many scriptural writings two practices are described in detail: one is no thought, the other is having thoughts. Although both of these lead to the perfection of the Buddha Way, there is a

---

[13] T17, p. 915a.   [14] Quotation not identified.   [15] Quotation not traced.
[16] All are Chinese philosophers discredited by the Confucianists.
[17] The work to which Hakuin is referring has not been determined.

vast difference in the quality of the methods. Studying Zen under a teacher is to call the Buddha's name with no thought and no concepts. This is the *samādhi* of True Reality. To seek the Pure Land is to call the Buddha's name with thoughts remaining and calculations of fame still present. This is known as learning and practicing the correct works of the Pure Land school. One who is proficient in non-duality alone is a true follower of the Buddha. Consciously to attempt to carry on Pure Land and Zen at the same time divides the basis into two.

The *Kuan-wu-liang-shou ching* says: "The many Buddhas and Tathāgatas are the Dharma body. This very mind is the thirty-two marks and the eighty notable physical characteristics. This very mind creates the Buddha. This very mind is the Buddha."[18] Elsewhere it says: "The body of the Buddha is infinitely tall; its radiance is that of innumerable worlds."[19] The words of the true teaching of the Tathāgatas reveal the internal realization. Its purport is intensely profound. This is called the "broad, vast, superior, solitary, splendid, established, constant, undecaying, unchanging mysterious land."

This kind of mysterious land must not be adorned with forms, must not be ornamented with gold and jewels. That is why the *Diamond Sūtra* says: "If a bodhisattva should say: 'I must adorn the Buddha land,' he cannot be called a bodhisattva. Why? Because the Tathāgata has taught that the adornment of a Buddha land is not adornment. This is what is meant by adornment."[20]

The *Vimalakīrti Sūtra* says: "In proportion to the purity of the mind the Buddha land is pure."[21] This being so, how can the study of Zen under a teacher possibly be the adornment of a Buddha land? Those Zen people of the Yüan and Ming, wishing to gloss over the shallowness of their accomplishments, yielded to the views of others and thus adorned the Buddha land. The most extreme of these people are no better than those who adopt the way of walking of Han-tan.[22] Outwardly they pretend to long for it, but privately they run counter to it. What are they trying to grasp? When people who study Buddhism in this world

---

[18] T12, p. 343a. The thirty-two marks and eighty notable characteristics that distinguish a Buddha from another being.   [19] T12, p. 343b.
[20] T8, p. 751b.   [21] T14, p. 538c.   [22] *Chuang Tzu*, 17, 10, 10.

vacillate and cannot verify this thing for themselves and repeatedly change the difficult into the easy, then the True Dharma Eye of the Tathāgata is close to extinction. Isn't this something to be seriously concerned about? My teacher devoted himself to casting such concepts aside. He was not one to delight in arguments, but he had no other alternative.

My visitor asked: "Why should I look forward to an illusory teaching? Are there any limitations to what you have been talking about?"

I say in reply to this:

There are not. Although there are no differences in the essence of the Dharma that conveys the purport of the Three Vehicles, there are great minds as well as shallow ones, so that one can, in effect, speak of differences. When you accept an illusion and regard the illusion as illusion, then what you regard as illusion must be an illusion. To regard illusion as illusion is accomplished by means of that which is not illusion. Although it is in fact an illusion, it is nevertheless not an illusion. This is why the *Nirvāṇa Sūtra* says: "Sons of good families, there is form or there is non-form. Understanding that there is non-form is the emancipation of the *śrāvakas* and *pratyeka-buddhas*. Understanding that there is form is the emancipation of the many Buddhas and Tathāgatas. Sons of good families, emancipation is therefore both form and non-form."[23] The bodhisattvas from time immemorial set up the teaching in echoes, practiced the ten thousand virtuous actions as flowers in the air. The various images of which I spoke before are the pure treasure jewel and phenomenon and noumenon, become non-dual.

However, if you don't destroy illusions, the illusions come to the fore and pursue other illusions. In the end you are deluded by them and never can escape from them as long as you live. This is why my Master gave all his efforts to dispelling [these illusions] for the sake of those for whom the jewel of our teaching was beclouded. How can someone deny illusion and then expect to prove True Reality!

Nāgārjuna has said: "You may have the view that things

---

[23] T12, p. 392c.

really exist to a degree as large as Mount Sumeru; you must not have the view that karma and Nirvana are not real to a degree even the size of a mustard seed."[24] An ill-informed monk who held to himself the one thousand scriptures of the Vaipulya, fell [into hell] while still alive.[25] Be it known that apart from illusion there is no Buddha, apart from illusion there is no teaching of the Vehicles. If you destroy the miraculous power of illusion and scorch the seeds that lead to the salvation of sentient beings, even if you reach the rank of *śrāvaka*, it is no more than an erroneous view of the Two Vehicles and is far removed from the Buddha Way. When one comes into accord with the mysterious activities of the many Buddhas, then without fail there is a response. If one comes into accord with the response, the response to this accord then is invariably dependent on the power of illusion. It is just like a man who rules a country, taking as his basis the salvation of the people. Given a name, he is the prince [who leads] the common people. It must be known that illusion is the great treasure jewel of the Buddha world; illusion is the cornerstone of the Buddhist teaching. It is the seed from which the bodhisattvas spring; it is the cause of the many Buddhas. But when one makes it appear, when one casts it aside, this then is the mysterious place. But for those who come bearing only an understanding gained from the essence of the treasure jewel; for those who come bearing an understanding gained from the giving-and-taking-away technique, based on the conscious destruction of illusion, how easy can it be for them? How easy indeed!

If these dubious Zen people and belittling laymen do not study the Way, do not make clear the teaching and with loud bragging imitate their teachers, then they have yet to escape [the cycle of birth and death], and they slander the rare dignity of the Tathāgata, and betray the kind words of their teachers so painfully handed down from the past. This you must consider well.

The visitor abashedly withdrew. For this reason I have written an "answer to a visitor's criticism."

A day in the sixth month, Kan'en 4[1751].

[24] Source not identified. [25] Unidentified.

✿ YABUKŌJI[1]

*In response to a request by an eminent and
esteemed lady attending on the Lord of
Okayama Castle, during his retirement into seclusion.[2]*

✿ Your letter dated the twenty-seventh of the fourth month
reached me at the beginning of the fifth month. I, too, thoroughly
enjoyed the unexpected meeting we had at the Hōun Temple[3]
some time ago and am glad to know that you and your attendants
returned safely to the castle and that you continue in the best of
health. When we met you asked me to write some words on the
Dharma that might encourage sentiments toward the Buddha
Way and might serve to indicate how this Way might be accomplished. I was deeply impressed by your praiseworthy request
and never felt that you made it out of mere politeness. However,
all sorts of things kept getting in the way with the result that I
have been putting off writing it.

It so happens that the twenty-seventh day of the fifth month
coincides with the fiftieth anniversary of my mother's death.
I had been casting around in my mind for some fitting memorial
service to perform for her, but my old age makes reciting and
copying the scriptures or holding Buddhist services such as
bowing and paying respects not quite suitable for me. Then it
occurred to me that the work for which you had asked some time
ago would serve as a way to offer the almsgiving of the Dharma.
What better memorial service than this could there be? And so
from nightfall of the twenty-fifth until past midnight of the
twenty-sixth I gave all my time to writing this letter and on the
next morning placed it in offering before my mother's tablet. I

[1] *Aridisia Japonica.* A small evergreen shrub.
[2] The lady is not identified. The Lord of Okayama Castle is Ikeda Tsugumasa
(1702–1776). He retired in the twelfth month of 1752.   [3] Not identified.

have omitted characters here and there and seem also to have inverted many words, but despite this I present it to you for your
examination. My writing is so tedious that I would be embarrassed to have any one else see it, but if you read it in private to
some of the people who are close to you, it should serve as the
almsgiving of the Dharma. You might read it from time
to time, thinking of it as a means of learning of the bodhisattva
Way.

First I must state that, even if by taking into account scriptural and secular literature I could comply with your request and
write without limit on the various Dharma principles, this would
in no way serve as an aid to ridding yourself of the cycle of birth
and death. As the traditional saying has it: "What enters through
the gate is not the treasure of your own home." There is nothing
that surpasses seeing once clearly into the real aspect of your own
nature. How does one accomplish this? In general, all the Tathāgatas who have appeared successively in this world and all the
sages and wise men of the past and present who have appeared
in the three periods have preached without limit such doctrines
as the sudden, the gradual, the partial, the complete, the exoteric,
the esoteric, the definite, and the indefinite. Yet the essential
thing is to realize nothing more than this: the practitioner must
recognize that, whipping up a fiercely determined aspiration, he
must proceed directly without losing ground and must never
allow any flinching or degradation of mind to occur while he
has yet to attain to the joy where the "Ka" is shouted.

How does one obtain this joy where the "Ka" is shouted?
It is said that beneath great doubt lies great awakening. As you
now read this letter and later laugh about it and discuss it, [you
should ask yourself]: what is this thing that operates according
to all circumstances? Is it mind or is it nature? Is it blue, yellow,
red, or white? Is it inside, outside, or in between? If in this way
you do not let the matter rest until you have once awakened
clearly to it and if throughout the twelve divisions of the day you
exert yourself fiercely in the twelve forms of deportment[4]

---

[4] The implication is that no matter what actions are performed, the practice
of one's quest must be continued.

associated with them and proceed striving unremittingly, then before you know it you will transcend the realm of deluded thoughts and the state where before and after are cut off[5] will manifest itself to you. Then the state of mind in which you are not a man, not a woman; not wise, not stupid; you do not see birth, you do not see death; and in which there is only vast emptiness, where the distinction between night and day is not seen and the body and mind are lost, will many times be present.

If at this time you show no fear but press forward without ceasing, you will naturally see through to the real aspect of your own nature in the very place where you stand. The brilliance of the real form of True Reality will appear before your eyes and a great joy, one that for thirty years you have neither seen nor heard, will burst upon you without your having sought it. It has been called the moment of seeing into one's own nature and attaining awakening; it has also been transmitted as the Great Matter of rebirth (ōjō) in the Pure Land. Outside your own mind there is no Pure Land; outside your own nature there is no Buddha. Reaching the state where not even a single thought is produced and before and after are cut off is "going" (ō). Reaching the state where the true principle of the real aspect of things makes its appearance is "being born" (jō). If you do not achieve the true principle and even if you undertake difficult and painful practices, observe the precepts and maintain the eating regulations, recite and copy the scriptures, and perform the various good actions, as advocated by the countless numbers of those seeking a future life who long for rebirth in the Pure Land and seek to become Buddhas, you will hardly achieve Buddhahood, although you will often attain to the good reward of birth in heaven,[6] or may well be born in the world of man as an emperor, shogun, courtier, noble, feudal lord, or be born into a high and wealthy family. Why is this so? It is because outside the mind there is no Buddha; outside the mind there is no Pure Land.

Furthermore, the good fruit of the realms of heaven and man is not to be envied. The blessing of birth in heaven is like

[5] Zengo saidan. The state in which the duality of birth and death is cut off. The enlightened state, as described below in the text.

[6] In the heavens of the world of form, still within the cycle of birth and death.

shooting an arrow into the air; when its strength fails, the arrow will fall back to the ground. Although those who are born in heaven have gained their birth there through the power of the practice of blessings in their previous lives, when their past recompense is exhausted, the odious indications of the five signs of decay[7] appear, and they are finally obliged to descend to a lower realm, perhaps even falling to one of the three evil regions. How much less to be envied is a person of wealth and freedom in the world of man! He forgets as quickly as vanishing dew the fact that the acquisition of wealth and blessings in this world is in response to the power of the good deeds of the past. He relies on his renown, boasts of his status and impoverishes and afflicts the common people and hurts and kills living beings. Thus he piles up hideous crimes and obstructions and adds to his ineradicable evil karma. Then in the next birth he falls without fail into the evil realms of the three paths and eight perils.[8] The good karma acquired through countless tribulations in former lives leads to wealth, fame, and prosperity in this life. Then the wealth, fame, and prosperity of this life lead to the sufferings of the iron floors and the fiery pits of hell in a future life. This is why it has been said that foolish blessings are the enemy of the three periods. Although there are countless teachings that instruct how to obtain enlightenment in a future life, almost all of them are nothing more than expedients. As the ultimate instruction there is simply no teaching that is superior to the true practice of the awakening to one's own nature.

The *Lotus Sūtra* preaches that the Tathāgata, the Lord of the three periods from past to present,[9] appeared in this world for

[7] When the life of an inhabitant of heaven is about to end, five indications appear. These include sweating armpits, the withering of the garland of flowers on the head, unpleasant odors, and so forth.

[8] "The three paths" are the realms of hell, hungry ghosts, and animals. "The eight perils" refers to the eight circumstances under which it is difficult to hear the Buddhist teaching or to see the Buddha: in hell, as a hungry ghost, as an animal, in the Northern continent in Buddhist cosmology (Uttarakuru) where life is pleasant but no Buddha is born, in the various heavens, as deaf, dumb, or blind, as a philosopher, in the period during which a Buddha has departed and a new one has yet to appear.

[9] The three periods are conventionally given in the order of past, future, and present, as mentioned earlier ("Orategama zokushū," fn. 49).

the purpose of bringing all sentient beings to an opening of the eye to the realization of the Buddha wisdom. Shakamuni Buddha underwent birth and death in this world eight thousand times,[10] at last entered the Himalaya, accomplished his desire to open up the Buddha wisdom and realize the truth, and then for the first time expounded the unsurpassed true enlightenment. It is for this reason that in the three periods from past to present there has been no Buddha or Patriarch or learned sage who has not seen into his own nature. You must become convinced that among the good activities as countless as the sands in the Ganges, there is not one that transcends the one Law of seeing into one's own nature.

When I was fifteen I first left home to become a monk. Between the ages of twenty-two and twenty-three I forged a great ambition and night and day, persevering more and more, I devoted myself solely to the *Mu* koan. In the spring of my twenty-fourth year at the Eigan-ji[11] in Echigo I suddenly had a great awakening at the sound of the temple bell at night. Forty-five[12] years have passed since that time and I have always urged people, paying no attention to whether they were relatives or friends, whether they were old or young, of high or low estate, by all means to once obtain the power to penetrate to the Great Matter. Some I have caused to doubt their "self,"[13] some I have required to study the *Mu* koan. I have used a variety of expedients, including teaching with admonitions and instructions. I should estimate that during this period those who have shown a degree of responsiveness and were able to obtain the great joy of awakening were several tens in number.

Five or six years ago I made up my mind to instruct everyone by saying, "Listen to the Sound of the Single Hand." I have come to realize that this koan is infinitely more effective in instructing people than any of the methods I had used before. It seems to raise the ball of doubt in people much more easily and the readiness with which progress in meditation is made has been as

[10] As described in the *Fan-wang ching* (T24, p. 1003c).
[11] Located at Takada in present-day Niigata Prefecture.
[12] This would make Hakuin sixty-nine years old at the time of the writing of this work.
[13] In other words, the "self" that while alive inherently possesses the Buddha-nature.

different as the clouds are from the earth. Thus I have come to encourage the meditation on the Single Hand exclusively.

What is the Sound of the Single Hand? When you clap together both hands a sharp sound is heard; when you raise the one hand there is neither sound nor smell. Is this the High Heaven of which Confucius[14] speaks? Or is it the essentials of what Yamamba[15] describes in these words: "The echo of the completely empty valley bears tidings heard from the soundless sound?" This is something that can by no means be heard with the ear. If conceptions and discriminations are not mixed within it and it is quite apart from seeing, hearing, perceiving, and knowing, and if, while walking, standing, sitting, and reclining, you proceed straightforwardly without interruption in the study of this koan, then in the place where reason is exhausted and words are ended, you will suddenly pluck out the karmic root of birth and death and break down the cave of ignorance. Thus you will attain to a peace in which the phoenix has left the golden net and the crane has been set free of the basket.[16] At this time the basis of mind, consciousness, and emotion is suddenly shattered; the realm of illusion with its endless sinking in the cycle of birth and death is overturned. The treasure accumulation of the Three Bodies[17] and the Four Wisdoms[18] is taken away, and the miraculous realm of the Six Supernatural Powers[19] and Three Insights[20] is transcended.

[14] Reference is to a passage in the *Book of Songs*. See Arthur Waley, *Book of Songs* (New York, 1960), p. 251: "High Heaven does its business without sound or smell."

[15] The mountain witch in the title of the Nō play. Hakuin does not quote the speech correctly. See *Yōkyoku zenshū*, 6, 386.

[16] This expression is found in Hakuin's *Kaian koku go*, 2 (HOZ3, 127). It is descriptive of dying the Great Death and returning to life again.

[17] The bodies of Law, Bliss, and Transformation.

[18] *Shichi.* Great Perfect Mirror Wisdom, Universal Nature Wisdom, Wondrous Observation Wisdom, and Perfection of Action Wisdom. They have appeared also in "Orategama zokushū" (fn. 9).

[19] The six supernatural powers acquired by a Buddha. They are described below in the text.

[20] *Sammyō.* Insight into previous lives of one's self and others; insight into future lives of one's self and others; insight into present sufferings so as to remove passions and temptations.

How worthy of veneration it is! When the [Sound of the] Single Hand enters the ear to even the slightest degree, the sound of the Buddha, the sound of the gods, the sound of the bodhisattvas, *śrāvakas*, *pratyeka-buddhas*, hungry ghosts, fighting demons, the sound of beasts, of heaven and of hell, all sounds existing in this world, are heard without exception. This is called "the pure supernatural power of hearing any sound anywhere." When the [Sound of the] Single Hand enters the ear to even the slightest degree, it is possible at a glance to see through one's own world, other worlds, Buddha worlds, the demons' palaces, all Pure Lands in the ten directions, and the filthy worlds of the six realms, as if one were looking at the palm of one's hand. This is called "the pure supernatural power of seeing anything anywhere." When the [Sound of the] Single Hand enters the ear even to the slightest degree, all traces rising and falling through the endless cycle of rebirth from the infinite kalpas of the past, all shadows revolving back and forth from the infinite kalpas of the past, appear as clearly and brilliantly as though they were placed before the treasure mirror. This is called "the pure supernatural power of knowing of the former existence of one's self and others." When the [Sound of the] Single Hand enters the ear even to the slightest degree, you penetrate to the fact that eating gruel and rice, motion and action do not lie in practice or study, but are the living *samādhi* with which all men are from the outset endowed. At this time the four Dharma worlds of the Kegon[21] and the One Vehicle of the *Lotus* are [realized in terms of] "Empty-handed, but holding a hoe; afoot, yet riding a water buffalo."[22]

The Great Matter of this foul earth changing to become the Pure Land, this common body changing to become the body of the Buddha, stands brilliantly before the eyes. This is called "the pure supernatural power of going anywhere or doing anything."

[21] The fourfold universe as conceived by the Kegon (Avataṁsaka) school: the phenomenal with differentiation, the noumenal without differentiation, the unity of noumenal and phenomenal, the interpenetration of the phenomenal and the noumenal.

[22] Part of a verse by Fu Ta-shih (*Shan-hui ta-shih yü-lu*, ZZ2, 25, 1, 13a). It is also quoted in "Oategama I."

When the [Sound of the] Single Hand enters the ear even to the slightest degree, your mind, another's mind, relatives' minds, the Buddha mind, the minds of gods, the minds of all sentient beings are at one glance seen through without the slightest doubt. This is called "the pure supernatural power of seeing into the minds of others." When the [Sound of the] Single Hand enters the ear even to the slightest degree, in the mind with which all men are originally endowed, not one bit of ignorance exists, not one bit of birth and death remains. All is vast perfection, all is vast emptiness. This is called "the pure supernatural power of exhausting all outflowings."

At this time the hundred thousand gates to the Dharma, the innumerable mysterious meanings, the accumulation of all the virtues of the world and the treasure adornments as well, are all endowed in one's own mind, with nothing whatsoever lacking. Then for the first time you know that "the six perfections and all practices are perfected within the body."[23] What good fruits of the worlds of Heaven or man excel this! How can the joy of the Three Virtuous Positions and Four Rewards[24] exceed this!

Ah, how difficult to obtain and difficult to receive is the body of a man! How difficult to meet and rarely to be heard is the Buddhadharma! But having received it and having heard of it, men still long after illusory fame and profit, wallow in meaningless greed and love, and spend their whole lives in vain. Then they return to their despised and dangerous former abodes in the three evil realms and receive their endless torments. What a sad and regrettable thing this is! Hated, and deservedly so, is the filth of the mundane world; feared, and rightly so, is the bitter fruit of the six paths and the three evil ways. In Buddhism belief in cause and effect and fear of suffering is considered the great wisdom; those who awaken to their own minds and penetrate to their own natures are the learned sages, Buddhas and Patriarchs. What a sad lot are those great fools who possess some worldly knowledge and conceptions! They read a few volumes of the scriptures, listen to a few lectures, and then call themselves

23 A line from the *Cheng-tao ko*, T51, p. 460a.
24 The three virtuous positions or states of a bodhisattva and the four grades of arhatship.

wise and illustrious. Saying that they have destroyed cause and effect and done away with the three periods, they consider themselves wise and knowledgeable. They look at people who believe in cause and effect, fear the fact of rebirth, recite the sutras, offer ceremonies, and practice compassion and good works, and then clap their hands and roar with laughter at them. What sort of mental state is this?

In general, man among all things is known as the spirit-possessed. The reason he differs from horses, oxen, dogs, pigs, wolves, and deer is that he believes in the existence of the three periods, trusts in a future rebirth, and fears the pains and difficulties to come. If such people surrender themselves to their desires, would they be content to consider all men the same as these animals? There was not one person among all the sages, men of wisdom, wise ministers, and good rulers of the past who did not believe in cause and effect and its painful recompenses. If cause and effect were swept away and the three periods destroyed, "There is no land under Heaven that is not the king's land." What place would there be for Buddhas and gods to stay? "To the farthest boundaries of these lands there is none but is the king's slave."[25] What need would there be for priests and nuns? A long time ago even our teacher Shakamuni, the son of King Śuddhodana, ruler of all India, feared deeply the sufferings of the six paths and the three evil ways. He cast aside the emblem of the throne and his princely rank as well, suffered the scorn of strict anchorites, and later entered the Himalaya and sat in concentrated meditation for six years until he was so thin and exhausted that he looked like a tile bound around with string. Then, for the first time, he opened the True Eye of the Diamond and finally became teacher to the three worlds.

Then there were people like Chūjō hime,[26] whose beauty was unsurpassed both within and without the Imperial Court.

[25] The above two quotations are drawn from a poem in the *Book of Songs*. See Arthur Waley, *Book of Songs*, p. 320.

[26] Legendary figure, said to have been the daughter of Fujiwara Toyonari, who was banished to Kyushu. She is said to have fled the court under the persecution of her enemies and to have gone to Hibariyama in Yamato, where she became a nun. The Taima mandala is said to have been woven by her out of lotus fibers. Celebrated in Nō, kabuki, puppet plays, and similar works.

People were insistent in urging her to serve the Empress but she realized that life amidst the jeweled curtains was nothing but a house afire. One night she stole away from the capital in secret and hid herself in Hibariyama, where she undertook unimaginably difficult practices. However, she gained an unsurpassed awakening.

In addition, there have been numberless young men of high station and people from illustrious and wealthy houses who, fearing the torments of hell in a future life, cast aside their bodies, turned away from love and affection, and left home to become monks or to live in seclusion. How much more should this apply to those who are miserable and of low station! Even though a person should have the life span of an immortal and live for eighty thousand seasons, it will be no more than illusory flowers flickering before the eyes, like wild horses galloping by, glimpsed through a crack in the wall. How much less time is there then for man, whose life is as brief as that of the insect that is born in the morning and dies at dusk; that is less stable even than foam and bubbles. To look for something in this life, which is more transient than a drop of dew, is like entrusting one's progress to a blind ass. Without maintaining the practice of Buddhism even for half a day, men just go along in vain from day to night, wasting this precious time. What do they have to rely on? They hop about as though they had entrusted themselves to the minds of mad monkeys and, growing useless in their senescence, end up by having exhausted their treasured bodies without once giving thought to the good. This is something on which you must arouse yourself to reflect deeply.

In examining well the workings of the rising and sinking of the cycle of birth and death in this world, we see instances where people, lacking the power of blessings that will allow them to be born in heaven, yet not having the evil karma to make them fall into hell, unexpectedly find rebirth in this filthy world. Some are noble, some base, some rich, some poor, some wise, some stupid, some clever, some dull. You must bear in mind that this is a reflection of the quality of their deeds in a former life. Those of noble and elevated station lack the blessings to be born in heaven; those miserable and starving lack the evil karma that will send them to hell. A frightening and sobering prospect indeed! I urge everyone to labor and strive and before this dew-like life is ended and the physical body disintegrates, to stand in fear and trembling and seek to hear for himself the Sound of the Single Hand.

Later, even though you have been able to stop all sounds, since there are left such details as the coarse and the fine, the near and the far, come to visit me, for you must ascertain and determine this matter well. Even though you have proved it and awakened to it, do not think that this suffices and that you can now rest content. There have been wise men and eminent monks in the past, possessed of splendid insight and endowed with both knowledge and practice. Yet, not knowing the cause for entrance to a Buddha land or the dignities of a bodhisattva, even though they had mastered the Great Matter taught by the Five Houses and Seven Schools, unconsciously they have either fallen into the old trap of the Hinayana with its limited rewards, or because they had immediately forgotten [the Great Matter] at each new birth, they were born into an unanticipated existence. I do not refer here to those who have fallen into the deep pit where the mind is like dead ash, where their wisdom is obliterated and destructive emptiness pervades all. This is the case with indifferent Zen practitioners everywhere today who cling to emptiness.

What do I mean by the cause for birth in a Buddha land and the dignity of a bodhisattva? These are the good actions that allow one to leap across the empty valley of the Hinayana and reach the treasure palace of the Mahayana. That is why the *Vimalakīrti Sūtra* says: "To have expedients without wisdom is like having legs but no eyes; to have wisdom without expedients is like having eyes but no legs. If the legs and eyes both work together, then finally one may reach the treasure place." [27] All the wise men everywhere from the past until the present have constantly set in motion the wheel of the vows so that they might achieve the completion of the Dharma. That is why Fugen made seventy vows and Amida forty. [28] Both of them, for the sake of the search for enlightenment, put into practice the great

[27] "To have expedients without wisdom" appears in the *Sūtra* (T14, p. 545b). The remaining portion of the quotation is not in the text.
[28] A slip of the memory. Fugen has ten vows, Amida forty-eight.

almsgiving of the Dharma for the conversion of sentient beings. Know then that Buddhism is like the ocean—the farther you enter it the deeper it gets; Buddhism is like a mountain—the more you climb it the higher it gets.

How sad it is that the teaching in this degenerate age gives indications of the time when the Dharma will be completely destroyed. Monks and teachers of eminent virtue, surrounded by hosts of disciples and eminent worthies, foolishly take the dead teachings of no-thought and no-mind, where the mind is like dead ashes with wisdom obliterated, and make these into the essential doctrines of Zen. They practice silent, dead sitting as though they were incense burners in some old mausoleum and take this to be the treasure place of the true practice of the patriarchs. They make rigid emptiness, indifference, and black stupidity the ultimate essence for accomplishing the Great Matter. If you examine these people you will find they are illiterate, stinking, blind, shaven-headed commoners, with no power whatsoever to guard the fortress of the Dharma, people who are completely unprepared to raise up the basis of the teaching.

Then there are those great fools with a general knowledge of worldly affairs and some discriminatory capacity, who pride themselves on their empty views, and basing themselves on their shallow knowledge, say: "The Buddhas and the Patriarchs are beyond disturbance and without form. The old koans are all empty words and there is nothing that we can get out of them." They swallow up the Buddhas and the Patriarchs and revile against everything everywhere. They are just like mad dogs howling as loudly as they can, and are not worth trying to restrain. All that these one-sided, villainous, miserable fools and pathetic blind men are able to do is to greedily gulp their food in the dining hall. They haven't the least bit of ability. What qualifications do they have to convert high officials of broad discernment and great learning, to teach Buddhism to such powerful parishioners as ministers and rulers?

How sad indeed! The great teachings withered and vulgar concepts arose; the old songs died out and banalities flourished.[29]

[29] This expression appears also in the *Orategama*. Hakuin likens the decline in Zen teachings to the vulgarization of Chinese songs that followed the *Book of Songs*.

A hundred years ago[30] the true style changed and Zen followers adopted an obnoxious teaching. Those who would combine Pure Land with Zen are [as common] as hemp and millet. In olden times outward appearance was the *śrāvaka* practice, the internal mystery was the bodhisattva Way. Nowadays outward appearance is the Zen teaching and the inner mystery is the Pure Land practice. It is just like mixing milk and water in one vessel.

They seat themselves in chairs or on the sitting platform, a crimson silk hat on their heads and a gold-embossed surplice (*kesa*) about their necks. The white fly-whisk describes a graceful dance as it sweeps the smoke about. From the golden incense burner a misty stream rises upward. With their stern appearance and solid dignity they resemble the Buddha endowed with the ten powers or a saint who has attained the four rewards. Those who see them quite naturally bow, join their palms, lower their heads to the floor, and weep tears of admiration. After all, they look like true living Patriarchs of direct descent in the lineage, people whom even a Buddha or a demon would not dare approach. They have the miraculous power of a Maudgalyāyana when it comes to collecting wealth and property; they are as eloquent as Pūrṇa when it comes to deceiving the laymen.[31] But if you examine them well, they do not have the slightest capacity to see into their own natures, nor one bit of the vitality and stamina that it takes to attain awakening.

Therefore, as they press forward they cannot attain the pleasure of Nirvana; as they lose ground they come to fear the cycle of birth and death. There is the story of the man who became a monk [and vowed that] if he did not become proficient in the principle, his body would return to repay the alms he had received. When the householder reached the age of eighty-one fungus no longer grew on his tree.[32]

---

[30] The mention of a hundred years would indicate a direct reference to Yin-yüan Lung-ch'i (Ingen Ryūki, 1592–1673) who brought the Ōbaku school of Zen to Japan in 1654, almost exactly a hundred years before the writing of this work. This school contained many elements of the Pure Land teaching.

[31] Maudgalyāyana and Pūrṇa were both disciples of the Buddha, noted for magical powers and eloquence respectively.

[32] This story is found in *Lin-chi lu* (T47, p. 502a). It concerns a monk whose body turned into a delicious fungus that grew on a tree in the garden of an

In this world these people create a great variety of superior environments and delude those on earth today. They attract a lay following and receive obeisances and offerings, but in the life to come they will without question fall to the lowest hell. How do they feel about the tortures of having their flesh pared off and their bones ground to pieces, of drinking molten copper and swallowing balls of iron? If they give it some thought it will make their hair stand on end.

And so these people put their trust in the Buddha's vow to destroy all the countless crimes. In stealth they finger the rosary hidden in their sleeves and in private call the name of the Buddha, asking to be reborn in a pure realm. How pathetic this is! This is the obvious proof of their lack of capacity to see into their own natures, and the divine indication of their deficiency in the vitality and stamina needed to attain awakening, of which I spoke before. How can such people be called Patriarchs in the historical line of transmission?

Look at the twenty-eight Indian Patriarchs, the six Chinese Patriarchs, the seventeen hundred learned sages mentioned in the *Ching-te ch'uan-teng lu*,[33] Ma-tsu, Lin-chi, Nan-ch'üan, Ch'ang-sha, Huang-po, Fen-yang, Tz'u-ming, Yang-ch'i, Chen-ching, Huang-lung, Hsi-keng, Ta-hui[34] and all the other splendid heroes who truly studied Zen and truly gained awakening. Not one of them even inadvertently talked about rebirth in the Pure Land or sought for it by the concentrated calling of the name. Why was this so? It was because at the very moment that they saw the Way and gained awakening, they penetrated to the understanding that any place in all the ten directions was the Pure Land of the treasure trees, and that anybody at all was possessed of the complete body of the pure, golden Amida Buddha. This is the spiritual evidence of seeing the Way and the

---

aged householder. For details see Yanagida Seizan, *Kunchū Rinzai roku*, (Kyoto, 1961) p. 144.

[33] This work is traditionally said to contain the biographies of 1,700 monks. The actual figure is considerably smaller.

[34] The names of all these famous monks appear also in the *Oategama*. Here Hakuin refers to Ma-tsu as "Chiang-hsi" [West of the river] and Lin-chi as "Chi-pei" [North of the ford].

opening up of the wisdom of the Buddha. What else was there for them to seek? People like Nāgārjuna, in order to save those of inferior capacities, preached that if, by calling the Buddha's name repeatedly, one reached the stage where the mind was not disturbed, then before one knew it one would enter into the Pure Land of the One Mind and determine the Great Matter of salvation. But this teaching was set up only as a temporary expedient, so that I shall not discuss here the purport of this type of concentrated calling of the Buddha's name.

These people have placed their bodies within the gates of Zen. They wear on their shoulders the robes of Zen. They call themselves members of the Zen community. Yet in secret they call the Buddha's name, sully the Zen teaching, and bring confusion to the essentials of our school. What sort of behavior is this? If they really long for the true Pure Land practice and believe in calling the Buddha's name, why don't they openly join the Pure Land school and become Pure Land saints, set up the metal plate, install the wooden gong, convert everyone all about, and night and day invoking the Buddha's name in a loud voice, determine for themselves the Great Matter. Why are they so despicable? Isn't this like putting on a lion's skin and screaming like a wild fox? These people are just like bats; you can't call them birds but neither can you call them rats. They are apt also to imitate Zen Masters: raise up the fly-whisk, grasp the Master's staff, and wield the stick. What's the purpose of all this? Isn't it enough for someone who concentrates on calling the Buddha's name just to set up one wooden gong? Why use the tools of another's trade? It's like a high priest keeping a mistress;[35] like a blind mother being attached to her mirror.

When we think about it well, if the views that exist today can be considered sufficient, then Shakamuni need not have surrendered his position as heir to the throne nor have cast aside his three thousand courtesans, but could merely have accepted as he saw fit the wealth and honor of all India, kept on reciting the Buddha's name, and then have been born in the

[35] This expression is unclear. Hakuin writes a circle in the text. It may also mean that the high priest collects money.

Pure Land. But he underwent the sadness of leaving home when he was nineteen and spent six years of painful practice in the Himalaya. Wasn't this a stupid thing for him to have done? The other five hundred great disciples ate one meal a day and lived under the trees. Pārśva [36] spend forty years without lying down, the Second Patriarch [37] cut off his arm at the elbow, Po-ai [38] spent forty years without crossing a threshold, Hsüan-sha injured his leg, Lin-chi asked a question three times and was beaten three times, Yün-men broke his left leg, Tz'u-ming stabbed his thigh with an awl. [39] Weren't these stupid things for them to have done? Why didn't they just call the Buddha's name and attain rebirth in a Pure Land? Bodhidharma could just as well have written a letter of two or three lines saying: "Call the Buddha's name in complete concentration and be reborn in the Pure Land," and sent it off to China. Why did he have to suffer innumerable dangers, endure the passage over ten thousand miles of raging seas, to hand down the teaching of seeing into one's own nature? Could it be that most of the ancient sages had never known that there was such a place as the Pure Land? Isn't it strange that everything in the past was so difficult and everything at present is so easy? If the difficulty of the past was good then the easiness of today must be bad. If the easiness of today is good then the difficulty of the past must have been bad.

Once someone called Kanjōshi [40] said to me: "The Zen followers of Japan of both the Rinzai and Sōtō Schools have in recent times become like those gangs who practice silent illumination, dead sitting, and concepts of no-thought and no-mind. You will not find a single person among those who are close to seventy, who does not practice the concentrated calling of the Buddha's name. What an impossible thing it must be to be alone in berating this type of Zen follower."

To this I reply: "When one investigates the source of the calling of the Buddha's name in the Zen temples of our country, it lies, in reality, in the waters of Min. When the waters of Min

[36] The tenth of the twenty-eight Indian Patriarchs.
[37] Hui-k'o.   [38] Unidentified.
[39] Other than Po-ai, these Zen Masters are also mentioned in the *Orategama*.
[40] Unidentified. *Kanjōshi* is another name for the writing brush.

are not blocked, the Ch'u River runs deeper still.[41] Don't say, 'Old Kokurin[42] is half dead and about to draw his last breath. What's he after that he suddenly vilifies another school of Zen?' I reach a point where I can no longer stand the distress and misery in my heart, and am apt unconsciously to utter bitter words from an excess of despair. I liken myself to trees and grass that themselves have no voices, yet give off sounds when stirred by the wind."

The other day a certain monk remarked: "All the famous Zen temples and giant monasteries of the T'ang: Ching-shan, T'ien-t'ung, Hsing-sheng, Ching-tz'u, Chiang-hsi, Nan-yüeh, Niu-t'ou, Pao-en[43] as well as the temples of the Vinaya and the teaching schools, have all been destroyed and not one remains. The sacred precincts have been plowed under to make fields for the peasants; the temple bells have been melted down to make ploughs and hoes for the farmers. Not one fragment of the Buddhist statues or the scriptures is left. It is true that traces of Huai-shen's temple at Tz'u-shou[44] still remain, but the walls are crumbling into ruin and the corridors lean crazily. Thorn trees stand in rows and wisteria and vines grow rank throughout the grounds. Idle spirits wail by day; wild demons scream at dawn."

Alas for the time when the Zen teaching flourished! The banners waved on high; the regulations were strictly maintained. The shout terrified the thunder; the stick inspired fear in the rain.[45] The canopies of kings and princes stood arrayed in rows;

---

[41] This passage is untranslatable. Tokiwa Daijō, the editor of the HZS edition (p. 212), suggests that the "Waters of Min" refers to Fukien, the home of Yüan-hsien Yung-chiao (Genken Yōkaku) and the "Ch'u River" to Yün-ch'i Chu-hung (Unsei Shukō), the Ming Masters attacked frequently by Hakuin throughout his works.　　[42] Another name for Hakuin.

[43] Listed are the names of famous Chinese temples. "Chiang-hsi" is, of course, a place name.

[44] A character has been dropped in the text and the identification is tentative. Tz'u-shou Huai-shen (Jishu Eshin, 1077–1132) appears in Chia-t'ai pu-teng lu, 9 (ZZ2B, 10, 1, 73b–74a).

[45] This statement probably derives from an earlier work, but its source has not been traced. It indicates the flourishing state of Zen in the past, when teaching techniques which utilized the stick and the shout were employed to great effect.

monks and laymen followed one after the other. Ah, but time passes! Only two to three hundred years have passed since that time; why should things have come to this? It is not the fault of Heaven nor is it the fault of fate. Zen was vandalized by the heretical gangs who made the mind like dead ash and obliterated wisdom, and by the proponents of the Pure Land doctrines within the Zen teaching. It was overthrown by the evil style of those who advocated the heretical silent-illumination Zen and concepts of no-thought and no-mind. And so we are witness to this devastation.

When we think about this well, these types are the symbol of the deterioration of the teaching, they are the signs foretelling the destruction of the Buddha Way. Indeed they cause more harm than did the persecutions of the three Wu.[46] The three Wu attacked from outside; thus the persecutions did not endure for long and Buddhism soon recovered. The Seven Schools[47] were destroyed from within; thus even the hand of the Buddha was not able to heal them. It may be likened to the difference between having an ordinary cold and suffering from a serious internal ailment.

The deterioration of Buddhism in Japan must not continue for long. Don't tell me that the combination of Zen and Pure Land is like fitting wings to a tiger. This is all wrong. In man, when a serious disease afflicts the area that lies between the lower part of the heart and the diaphragm, the person cannot last for long and will surely die. If Zen is combined with Pure Land, Zen cannot last for long and will surely be destroyed. How I grieve for Zen! The twenty-eight Indian Patriarchs, the six Chinese Patriarchs form an unbroken line in the transmission of the teaching; in actuality they form the framework of the Eight Schools.[48] It is no different from a large mansion; should the eaves and beams collapse and fall, the rest of the building would not be worth bothering about. Are we to think then

[46] The three persecutions of Buddhism in China under the Emperors Wu of the Wei, Chou, and T'ang dynasties.   [47] The Seven Schools of Zen in China.
[48] Presumably Hakuin is referring to the classification of eight schools of Chinese Buddhism in Japan: Kusha, Jōjitsu, Ritsu, Hossō, Sanron, Kegon, Tendai, and Zen. Pure Land, Nichiren, and Shingon are considered to be of Japanese origin.

that the destruction of the Buddhism of the T'ang is so strange?
Let it be known that Zen is really not so easy a thing.

In the past our First Patriarch, Bodhidharma, in the palace
at the age of eight, was able to identify a precious jewel much
to the amazement of all who witnessed him.[49] Later he left home
to become a monk and attended on Prajñātāra[50] for twenty
years, until finally he succeeded in plumbing the deepest mysteries. Zen is surely not an easy thing. This is why the Buddha
said: "Even the great arhats among my disciples cannot understand the meaning. It is only the group of bodhisattvas who are
able to comprehend it." Certainly this thing is difficult to believe
in, difficult to enter, difficult to pass through, and difficult to
understand. Moreover, when a single word is uttered, it is like a
vast conflagration; when a single word is spit out, it is like a
raw iron wedge. Even a splendid hero, should he not devote
himself to exhausting all his efforts for twenty years after he has
seen the Way and attained awakening, will not readily be able to
gauge the distance from the edge of the precipice.

Yet the careless Zen followers of today, with no talent for
probing the mysteries without, and lacking the eye to see into
their own natures within, affect a most superior manner, from
time to time recite the Buddha's name, and say that they are
carrying on Zen and Pure Land teaching at the same time. Such
people are not worth laughing at. I most earnestly wish that all
loyal, distinguished, superior men, heroes whose hearts are inspired by righteousness, without regretting their own lives and
without regard for their own bodies, would vow to destroy the
key to the barrier[51] untransmitted by the Buddhas and Patriarchs, to pluck out the forest of thorn trees,[52] so difficult to enter
and so difficult to pass through, to fasten on to the ultimate
mysteries of Zen, to attach to their arms the miraculous talisman
that snatches life from death, to chew and make reverberate in
their mouths the talons and teeth of the Cave of the Dharma, to

---

[49] The story appears in *Ching-te ch'uan-teng lu*, 2 (T51, p. 216a). Bodhidharma
and his two brothers were shown a jewel. Only Bodhidharma understood
that the jewel of Buddhism surpassed in value the precious gem he was shown.
[50] In Zen tradition, the Twenty-seventh Indian Patriarch, Bodhidharma's
teacher. 	[51] *Kanreisu*. The hidden meaning, not transmitted in words.
[52] The koans.

smash the brains of all monks everywhere,[53] to restore the true style of Zen that has fallen to the ground, and to impart fresh color to the "steepness" technique of the garden of the Patriarchs.

Last night as I was inspired to compose this sermon by the light of a solitary lamp, I suddenly realized what I was writing and it made me clap my hands and burst out laughing. Why? Here I had begun to write instructions for you so that you might attain the power to see into the Way, when, in the quiet of the deep night while I was half asleep and half awake, I discovered that I had unconsciously written quite a number of lines in which I expressed my despair at the manner in which the Way of the Patriarchs had been destroyed. I must confess to the habit of constantly talking about this subject, just as merchants always delight in talking about profits and mountain dwellers always love to chatter about the place where they live. Hearing the other day that the great T'ang temples had all been destroyed so that not one building remained, I was both upset and saddened. In my depression I unconsciously departed from the tenor of my sermon and ended up by writing about the reasons for this destruction. I have been rather like a distressed man talking in his sleep. These idle deluded thoughts [about this destruction] constantly distress and plague me and are a source of deep grief for me. This is why I talk about the subject so persistently.

Yet all of this is a means for supporting Buddhism; please do not acquire a distaste for it as a worthless thing.[54] It is my small wish that I may in this way assist in the fierce determination and zeal of those who are studying and practicing Zen. All I want to emphasize is that you hear once for yourself the Sound of the Single Hand, without fail whip up the wheel of the vow not to retrogress for all time, and devote your energies without interruption to practicing the great practice of the bodhisattva until you have reached the perfection of the Dharma. Whether layman or monk, if you do not hold to the great vow not to retrogress for all time, no matter how many good deeds and good actions you perform, you will never, in the end, escape from

[53] These expressions appear throughout Hakuin's writings as descriptive of a superior Zen practitioner.
[54] Reference is presumably to the contents of this letter by Hakuin.

birth and death. But if somehow you come to a realization of the dignity of the bodhisattva, then you will awaken to the understanding that this very birth and death is enlightenment.

If you become aware that you have heard even to a small extent the Sound of the Single Hand, please let me know about it by letter. I have been writing along as things came to mind without going over it again. Because I have been working throughout the night my sentences are clumsy and my handwriting abominable. I am embarrassed to have anyone else see it.

With respect,

Prayer-riddles for the village head,
that he may live a thousand springs
and ten thousand lives and that
his descendants may prosper.[55]

Why are the plane of a barrel-maker and a village head alike? They both shave away the "*mura.*"[56]

Why are a ripe persimmon deep in the mountains and the family of a village head alike?

They both rot away without anyone knowing about it.[57]

If people who are village heads repeat these riddles three times daily their descendants for all time will have good fortune, even in the life to come. Here end the riddles of the village head.

Written by the old monk
under the Sāla tree.
The day the Buddha attained the Way, Hōreki 2.[58]

[55] These riddles also appear in *Hebiichigo*, the next work translated here. They do not appear in other texts of the present work, and there is no explanation of why Hakuin has inserted them here.

[56] The barrel-maker shaves away unevenness (*mura*) with his plane; the village head (in his greed) shaves away the village (*mura*).

[57] I have omitted here a passage that I find untranslatable. It has been dropped in the version of the riddle that appears in *Hebiichigo*.

[58] The eighth day of the twelfth month (=January 11, 1753).

❋ HEBIICHIGO[1]

I

Draft of a letter written at the behest
of a close retainer of Ikeda, Iyo no Kami,[2]
of Okayama Castle in Bizen

❋ I was delighted to meet you again unexpectedly the other day after not having seen you for so long a time. It is indeed splendid news to know that you arrived safely in Edo. For my own self, I have been experiencing no difficulties.

First I must mention the precious incense that you so kindly gave me. The incense burner also is not of the ordinary type, and it was with deep emotion that I at once heaped some in the burner and lit it. Its unusual scent permeated my hermitage and it seemed that I had entered into a forest of sandalwood trees or had wandered into the land of Hsiang-chi.[3] And then again I had the feeling that I was enjoying an amusing conversation with you. I treasure the incense and when I have an idle moment, I take up a pinch in my fingers and am overcome by a strange feeling of tranquility. To whom can I tell my delight?

[1] Literally, snake-strawberry. *Duchesnea indica*. Small strawberry-like plant with inedible yellow fruit. The present translation is based on the Shōin-ji text, as established in the HZS. Another version, the Hosokawa text, has considerable variations. No attempt has been made here to reconcile these variations, except where they help in an elucidation of the meaning. It should be noted that the editor of the HZS, Tokiwa Daijō, has supplemented the Shōin-ji with the Hosokawa version in establishing his text. About one-third of the present text is found in substantially the same form in the *Sashimogusa*.

[2] Ikeda, governor of Iyo (*Iyo no kami*), is Ikeda Munemasa (1725–1764), the son of Tsugumasa, to whom the *Yabukōji* is indirectly addressed.

[3] Hsiang-chi is the Buddha of Fragrance. His land is described in the *Vimala-kīrti Sūtra*. The inhabitants live on the odor of incense surpassing that of all other lands.

I wanted, therefore, to send with this letter something worthy of your admiration, something that would not be inferior to that precious incense. I rushed about looking here and there for some such thing, but as you know, my isolated hermitage has only eggplants and cowpeas, with some calabashes winding about, and some winter melons dangling from the vines. I was at my wit's end and, desperately trying to find something, I suddenly recalled your having asked recently whether I did not have a suitable sermon written, because unusual sermons in the kana syllabary seemed to be very rare these days. This is certainly not a first-rate piece and I fear you will find the rustic style scarcely acceptable, and my harping constantly on the same subject quite absurd. Yet in the hope that it will serve somehow as an aid to benevolent government, I have written this kana sermon, entitled *Hebiichigo*, and offer it to you for your examination.

The *hebiichigo* plant bears flowers and fruit, but it does not have the fragrance of the spring orchid or the chrysanthemum in fall, nor does it have the medicinal value of the Chinese milk vetch or the dotted bell flower. It isn't a tonic like cinnamon or ginger, nor is it a purgative like the China or the coptis root. Unrecognized by Shen Nung,[4] it was nevertheless recently listed in the herbal compiled by I Ju-shui.[5] Among all the plants given in the various collections it is the least significant. But then, calling this sermon after the *hebiichigo* serves to indicate that, written by a person of inferior attainments, it contains words no less banal than the plant itself. But cannot even such a thing as the *hebiichigo* perhaps be of some insignificant assistance in the conduct of government? In the past the sermon has been used to point out the means of studying Zen under a teacher and of seeing into one's own nature, and works in the kana syllabary have frequently been written for the purpose of encouraging good and condemning evil. In encouraging good there is the fast and the slow; in seeing into one's own nature there is the coarse and the fine.

Those who are masters of a province or a city must first protect the imperial throne. In order to bring ease to the populace,

---

[4] Legendary emperor who taught the arts of agriculture and the properties of medicinal herbs.

[5] The specific herbal to which Hakuin is referring has not been identified.

if they are to maintain the nation, they must first treat the people with affection. If the people are well fed the nation prospers; it is called a strong country. The master of a strong province, if he wants to protect the nation's throne, must first take into account keeping his body in health so that his span of years may be extended. Should he suffer many diseases and have only a short life, what time would he have to protect the imperial throne, govern his province, and treat the people with affection? If he wants to keep his body in health and extend the span of his years, he must be moderate in what he eats and drinks, restrain his physical desires, and seek to nourish his life. The essentials of nourishing life lie in nourishing one's military destiny by equipping one's self with introspection and the power of faith. If someone would be a great general and assume the task of defeating a strong enemy, defending the capital, and bringing ease to the people, he must always be possessed of a firm faith and mind, and should make the nourishment of his military destiny the first principle.

In the past Hachiman-dono,[6] the founder of the Minamoto family, was never remiss in reciting the chapter on Universality in the *Lotus Sūtra*. He always used to say that the warrior who wanted to nourish his military destiny must never recklessly take the life of another being. Not only did he apply this to humans, but he never needlessly destroyed such creatures as worms and insects. Not only was his military destiny at all times strong, but his power and virtue were superb. He eased the cares of the Emperor, and where the incantations of the high priests of Kyoto and Nara had failed, silenced the troubles of the Emperor merely by twanging his bow.[7] One year he was appointed by the Emperor as a general in charge of subjugating the barbarians.[8] He had a golden statue of Kannon, a little less than two inches high, set into his hair when it was dressed. Starting out alone for the region of Ōshū, he easily defeated an enormous enemy force,

---

[6] Minamoto no Yoshiie (1041–1108).

[7] This story, from *Zen Taiheiki*, 38, is also described in "Orategama I." By twanging his bow Yoshiie drove out an evil spirit from Emperor Horikawa.

[8] There is no record of Yoshiie having received this appointment.

killed Sadatō and took prisoner Munetō,[9] putting the latter into his service as virtually a slave. He laid the Emperor's cares to rest, so that his great name has endured through all the years. This all stemmed from the virtue and power of his firm faith and mind.

Sakanoue no Tamuramaro, through the strength gained by fitting the arrow of wisdom to the bow of compassion, destroyed the evil demons of Suzuka Mountain without even lowering his sword.[10] Others who had this firmness of faith and mind were General of the Right Yoritomo,[11] Shume no hōkan Morihisa,[12] Akushichibyōe Kagekiyo,[13] and Kusunoki Hyōe Masashige.[14] Tada no Mitsunaka[15] felt deeply this power of faith. When he became old he entered the Rokkaku-dō and devoted himself so energetically to his incantations that his sweat and tears soaked through the cushion on which he was sitting.

But how can timid, negligent, careless warriors of these degenerate days abjectly borrow the power of Kannon or any other Buddha or bodhisattva? They scream pretentiously that they are endowed at birth with a substantial amount of strength and that there is no need to depend upon being rescued by another's power, yet when an emergency arises they are the first to run and hide and to besmirch and debase the fame of their warrior ancestors. The everyday functions and the special techniques of these grossly negligent people seem to consist in using clever words and making an outward display of strength.

[9] Reference is to the battle of Kurigawa in Northern Japan in 1062, in which Abe no Sadatō (1019–1062) was killed and his brother Munetō (n.d.) was captured, taken to Kyoto, and later banished to Kyushu where he became a monk.

[10] Sakanoue no Tamuramaro (758–811) was a famed warrior, noted for his subjugation of the Ainu. He is said to have been a devotee of the bodhisattva Kannon. The story mentioned here is based on the Nō play *Tamura*, where, aided by the thousand-armed Kannon, the demons are destroyed.

[11] Minamoto no Yoritomo (1147–1199).

[12] Morihisa is a celebrated character in Nō and puppet plays. Arrested and sentenced to death in Kamakura, he is spared by the intercession of Kannon (see *Yōkyoku zenshū*, II, 26).

[13] Taira no Kagekiyo (n.d.). Famed warrior, celebrated in literature.

[14] Kusunoki Masashige (1294–1336). Famed supporter of Emperor Godaigo.

[15] Tada no Mitsunaka (912–997). This story appears also in "Orategama I."

The good general while dwelling in peace gives heed to danger. While the government is stable he fears disorder and thus does not for one moment neglect the military arts. I pray only that you will keep your body in health, will govern your province with good fortune, will alleviate the sorrows of the common people, and that your benevolent influence will endure a thousand years. When we met the other day I had meant to encourage you to take up the *Emmei jikku Kannon gyō*,[16] but our meeting was so brief that I did not have the opportunity. I therefore send it for your inspection along with this letter.

This work has been associated with wondrous miracles that have taken place in both China and Japan. Because it is so brief, I sincerely hope that you, not to speak of your close retainers and the common people as well, will recite it two or three hundred times each day. The reason lies in the testing.[17] Give this work to those who are seriously ill or who have met with some unexpected disaster, and have them examine it for their consolation. If it is recited with sincerity, awe-inspiring miracles will without fail be accomplished. Its first advantage is that the person who recites it will be completely free from disease and will attain to long life. This applies to anyone at all.

The person who takes this work to himself takes the greatest pleasure at all times in uninterrupted recitation, paying no attention to the place or time, whether he is astride a horse or

---

[16] The *Emmei jikku Kannon-gyō* [Ten-Phrase Kannon Sutra for Prolonging Life], a text in forty-two characters and ten phrases, is championed by Hakuin for the virtue it possesses in bringing about miracles. The second chapter of his *Yaemugura* gives an account of the miracles that the recitation of this text has performed. According to Hakuin, the text is an extract from the *Kao-wang Kuan-shih-yin ching*, selected by the Hiei-zan monk Reikū at the behest of Emperor Reigen (see HZS, p. 337). For a discussion see Shimizutani Zenshō, *Kanzeon bosatsu no shinkō* (Tokyo, 1941), pp. 215–30. The *Kao-wang Kuan-shih-yin ching* (T85, p. 1425–26) is a spurious sutra made in China, long banned from Tripitaka collections. Despite Hakuin's explanations of its origin, the forty-two-character text appears as such in the *Fo-tsu t'ung-chih* (T49, p. 345c), from which it doubtless derives, although it may well have been originally selected from the former work.

[17] In other words, if you do not try it out for yourself, you cannot know its true value.

with his head on a pillow, whether he is walking, standing, sitting, or reclining. Then no matter how busy the lord or his attendants may be, they will be able to work in freedom. If the elders in the family are each given a copy, all within the family, of high rank or low, will be able to use it in their prayers, and this in turn will serve as a great virtuous action on the part of the lord. Practicing the numerous good things, as well as avoiding the numerous evils, conforms with the precepts of the many Buddhas. As far as good things are concerned, no matter how trivial a task may be, it should be undertaken without talking about it and without encouraging others to assist, and it should be carried out without setting other things aside. As far as bad things are concerned, no matter how inconsequential they may be, if you find some act improper, it should never be done a second time. Then maintaining practice will be the equivalent of maintaining all the many precepts.

In ancient China a certain Kao-huang,[18] a man of constant faith, was for some reason or other sentenced to be executed. Around midnight of the night before he was to die, as he was devoutly concentrating all his attentions on Kannon, the august form of the bodhisattva appeared before his eyes. He was told that if he were able to recite the *Kannon Sūtra*[19] a thousand times during the night his life would be spared. Kao-huang then asked: "It is already past midnight. How can I possibly recite it a thousand times by morning?" But the bodhisattva told him to recite the sutra nevertheless and gave him personal instruction. The next morning when the executioner lifted the sword to strike off his head, the blade snapped off at the sword guard.

[18] The following story derives from the *Fo-tsu li-tai t'ung-tsai*, 9 (T49, p. 550c). Hakuin tells the same story in the *Yaemugura* (HZS, p. 341), where the version more accurately follows the original, although both here and in the *Yaemugura* the story is greatly enlarged. The man in question is one Sun Ching-te who was falsely accused and sentenced to death. On the night before his death he was reciting the *Lotus Sūtra*, when a man appeared in a dream and told him to recite the *Kao-wang Kuan-shih-yin ching* 1,000 times. He managed it 900 times by morning, and another hundred on a slow walk to the execution grounds.

[19] This does not refer to the chapter on Kannon in the *Lotus Sūtra*, commonly known under this title, but to the *Kao-wang Kuan-shih-yin ching* mentioned below.

Other swords were brought out, but three times the same thing happened. Amazed, the executioner inquired into the reasons for this. After he had been told the story in all its details, Kao-huang was pardoned. From that time on this sutra was known as the *Kao-huang Kuan-yin ching*.[20] Ever since then people, monks or laymen, men or women, who recite this sutra in faith have had their illnesses cured or escaped from perilous disasters. In addition, those who have recited it have attained to long life. You, my lord, should when walking, standing, sitting, or reclining recite it two to three hundred times every day. The reason I say this is that if samurai, and monks as well, do not avoid disease and disaster and thereby attain to long life, they will find it difficult to bring their respective Ways to fruition.

In particular, a great general, when there is a crisis in the nation, uses the purport of the *Liu-t'ao*[21] to subdue the enemy host. He does not care from where the barbarian hordes come, but crushes the rebels and destroys the enemies of the throne as though he were taking up a heavy axe and splitting a dead tree. His majesty and bravery will reach beyond the regions of the eight barbarian tribes,[22] his fame will stir the depths of the four seas. Because it is his responsibility to protect the nation and bring ease to the common people, night and day without relaxing he polishes the martial arts and practices inner contemplation and the power of faith. If at the same time he recites this text, then by the strength of the natural overflow of the compassion of the gods and Buddhas, his military destiny will become strong, his life span long, his magnanimity broad, and his governing of the province will go as smoothly as if he were rowing a boat with the current.

Since ancient times the idiotic generals who set countries

---

[20] Hakuin gives the title of this work incorrectly. Although in this story he talks about the recitation of this sutra, Hakuin is undoubtedly referring to the *Emmei jikku Kannon gyō* in forty-two characters.

[21] A work on military tactics, traditionally assigned to Lü Shang of the Chou dynasty. The present version in six chapters dates probably to the Northern Sung dynasty.

[22] Here and above Hakuin refers to the Chinese concept that all tribes surrounding their nation were barbarians.

into turmoil, lose their nations, and destroy their bodies, have paid no attention to the vital matters of nurturing their military destiny, of spreading benevolence, alleviating the distress of the common people, and governing the country. They pride themselves in a luxury quite beyond their station and delight in splendor and elegance. With territories producing a hundred *koku* they live as though they possessed a thousand; with territories producing a thousand *koku* they act as though they own the authority ten thousand command. They clothe themselves in conspicuous garments of silk, quite inappropriate to the warrior. Sex they make the great principle of man, and where one wife is sufficient they surround themselves with five or even ten mistresses. These women flaunt their graces and presume upon their status as favorites until every day is filled with the turmoil of jealousy and intrigue. Wastefully they exhaust their money and possessions, while the farmers living on their domains are barbarously plundered and made to suffer. These men wallow in drink and give honor to pointless artistic entertainments and riotous dancing. The true mind, the true will are put to confusion. Day by day the physical body declines, eventually a serious disease difficult to cure sets in, and life itself is difficult to sustain. The clear character inherent in all is obscured and destroyed by base personal lusts and desires until the point is reached where the mind-as-master cannot be determined even for a moment.

Then when they become obsessed with thoughts of the recompense in store for them in their next lives they are overwhelmed with misery. The warrior is taught that a thousand days of training serve to save an emergency of brief duration. Yet these warriors are always accompanied by beauteous women, delight in fine wines, and are addicted to improper amusements and entertainments. They haven't the vaguest knowledge of how to train horses for war; they are inept in their martial accomplishments and they are unskilled with the bow. Should the nation be faced with an emergency and the cannon balls fly, the halberds and lances be poised, and the swords of battle be already crossed, they act like monks who, when called upon to recite a sutra they have not practiced, are unprepared to recite quickly when obliged to perform the various services. What accomplishments do they

have that will allow them to support the nation? When the lord
to whom they owe deep obligations over successive generations
is surrounded by enemy forces, and when their parents who raised
them and to whom they owe a deep debt, are seized by enemy
rabble, attacked, and murdered, they tremble in confusion and,
without even looking back, leap upon unsaddled horses and flee
in panic any which way. What would it be like, to still be a
laughingstock a thousand years from now?

Furthermore, these people make it their practice to neglect
military preparations, to dislike study and learning, never to pay
even the slightest attention to the worthiness of the way of
benevolence, and not even in a dream to know of the vital
matter of nurturing their military destiny. Careless and negligent
to an extreme, they end up as people who never for a moment
determine for themselves the mind-as-master. Even should they
live eight hundred years as did P'eng Tsu,[23] the time spent
protecting their country and putting their own houses in order
would be as fleeting as scenes flashing by momentarily in a dream.
They seek fame and wealth and take pride in authority. Possessions
and clothing they consider as mere mud and sand; the farmers to
them are mere clods of dirt. They delight in association with
honey-tongued, flattering, sycophantic ministers; they detest and
keep at a distance loyal and blameless wise ministers. Insatiably
they wring taxes from the people, and they torture and destroy
living things without the slightest compunction. Then in the end
their evil obstructions pile up, and after they are dead they fall
to the evil realms of the three painful paths and the eight difficulties[24] and receive a horrible recompense for eternal kalpas of
time. Truly a frightening prospect!

In the past when a prince of clear character[25] who abided
in the highest good wished to bestow his benevolence upon the
world, he gave priority to selecting and employing righteous
officials and greatly feared and kept at a distance tyrannical

[23] The Chinese Methuselah.

[24] The eight circumstances under which it is difficult to meet a Buddha. See
"Yabukōji," fn. 8.

[25] Based on the opening passage of *Great Learning*. Starting with this passage,
the text is virtually the same as that in the *Sashimogusa* (HZS, p. 124 ff.).

officials. Why should this have been so? The tyrannical official brings harm to the Imperial throne and cuts the continuity of the nation, just as, when a drop of poison from the Chen bird's[26] feather falls into a river, all the fish and turtles are killed, or when a drop of mercury is injected into the main trunk of a tree, it is quickly withered. The tyrannical official turns the mausoleums of generations of ancestors into a wasteland of thorn trees where foxes and hares dwell. Detested, and rightly so, is the tyrannical official. He turns the divine spirits of generations of ancestors into idle spirits with no one to make sacrifices for them, into wild demons[27] with no relatives to hold services for them. Feared, and rightly so, is the tyrannical official. Therefore, wise princes and rulers abhor and reject such officials as if they were rotting corpses, detest and keep them at a distance as they would filth and excrement.

Villainous princes and rulers hold these tyrannical officials in high respect and employ them. That is why it is said that when a wise ruler appears the tyrannical official withdraws, and when a villainous ruler comes forth the tyrannical official opens wide his eyebrows. What kind of person is this official? The *Tzu-wei*[28] says: "The official is a government employee whose function is to govern the people." But elsewhere we read: "The official is a government employee whose function is to harass the people." Among officials there are the benevolent and the tyrannical. The benevolent official always keeps in mind what is profitable and what is harmful to the farmer. He investigates the quality of the soil and is sensitive to the hardships farming entails. In times of crop failure he remits taxes and lessens the duties, and devotes himself to keeping the people from suffering because of hunger and cold. He makes it his prime function to see that the throne of the nation is stable and that his master will not be damned for his tyrannical rule for a thousand years to come. That is why the people think of him as they would their own parents. He can

[26] A fabulous bird whose feathers contain a deadly poison.

[27] Idle spirits and wild demons are creatures condemned to endless wandering because they have no descendants to offer sacrifices and prayers for them. They are frequently mentioned by Hakuin.

[28] Famous Chinese dictionary. Hakuin probably refers to a Japanese edition.

rightly be called a "government employee who governs the people." Respected and worthy of respect is the benevolent official. It is he who truly should be employed.

The tyrannical official is quite the opposite. The tyrannical official is one who cuts and strips. He plunders and makes the people suffer as though he were cutting them up; he robs them of their possessions as though he were stripping them. He does not take into account whether the crop is abundant or a failure; he does not give a second thought to the cold and hunger of the people. He considers his own loyalty to consist in the reckless plundering and looting he accomplishes. In days of old he was known as the "tax-gathering minister."[29] His plundering and looting surpass that of a wise gentleman.[30] Therefore it has been said: "It is better to have a minister who robs [the state treasury] than to have a tax-gathering minister."[31] When a suit involving bribery is made, it is like throwing a rock into water; when a suit that does not involve bribery is made it is like throwing water on a rock."[32]

Supposing Mr. X and Mr. Y have a dispute in which a suit is filed. But the issues are unclear; who is right and who is wrong cannot be determined and the winning party cannot be decided upon. Things continue unsettled and in confusion day after day. Then Mr. X, dissatisfied with the lack of progress, secretly offers a bribe to the official, and by exposing a weakness on Mr. Y's side, Mr. X causes Mr. Y to be censured to a degree. Mr. Y is surprised and afraid and he now secretly hands over a bribe to the official, exposing in turn a weakness on Mr. X's part, and the latter is also censured a bit. Now Mr. X and Mr. Y are both terrified. Each in turn continues to hand over bribes, but the

[29] This term derives from *Great Learning*, 2, 10, 22.
[30] Presumably he believes loyalty to his lord to be measured by his success in plundering others for the latter's benefit.
[31] *Great Learning*, 2, 10, 22.
[32] Based on the Fifth Article of the "Seventeen-Article Constitution" of Shōtoku Taishi. Should the person who determines suits do so with a view to gaining bribes for himself, then the suit of a rich man will be like throwing a rock into water. It will encounter no opposition. If a poor person who cannot offer a bribe files a suit it will be like throwing water on a rock. The rock will not move.

affair is never settled. The bribery continues on for five years, for ten years, until the one whose possessions and power are exhausted so that he no longer can pay a bribe is seized and adjudged the loser in the suit. Therefore the people fear and hate a tyrannical official as they would an evil tiger roaming in the village streets, or a pestilence that sweeps over the land. Frequently the ruler of a nation is not in the slightest bit aware of this and himself believes that if a country prospers the people are at ease. But before he knows it the ruler will become like a Chieh or a Chou,[33] the people will become like those who suffered under these tyrants. In such cases one can well say: "A government official is one whose function is to harass the people." Hated, and rightly so, is the tyrannical official.

In the past the Ch'in Emperor, wallowing in luxury and reveling in his power, erected a great platform at Hsien-yang[34] and constructed the vast palace of A-p'ang and gloated in his pride. For these projects he did not have sufficient resources, so he promptly dispatched tyrannical officials to plunder the riches of the land. His storehouses overflowed, while the common people were filled with anger and resentment. It was not long before the land was in turmoil, Hsien-yang was burned and the A-p'ang palace destroyed.[35] Such barbarous kings and evil rulers as Chieh, Chou, Yu, and Li[36] each favored and made use of tyrannical officials and oppressed the people. In the end they lost the wealth and fortunes of the nation and fell from their positions as emperors.

Around the beginning of the Genroku era [1688–1703] there was a tyrannical official, in the employ of a certain feudal lord in Central Japan,[37] who in his greed plundered the people and caused them to lament in their misery. At this time the village head settled disputes and determined judgments. This infuriated the tyrannical official. In secret he brought false charges before the lord, and as a result the village head was sentenced to death. At the time of his execution he raised his eyes to heaven and cried in

---

[33] Evil rulers who destroyed their dynasties.   [34] The Ch'in capital.
[35] The city was set afire by Hsiang Yü and is said to have burned for three months.
[36] The evil kings of Chou in the eighth century, who brought their nation into decline.   [37] Unidentified.

his distress: "If I have committed a crime worthy of death, then do not halt this execution. But if I have done no wrong and still you execute me, then within three years you, my lord, will have lost your life and the continuity of your fiefdom will be cut off. Let everyone here be witness to this!"

After he had finished talking he was put to death. The skies became misty and the trees and plants drooped. And who would believe that before a hundred days had passed the lord developed a severe pain in his heart. All varieties of medicines were tried but to no avail. Acupuncture and moxa treatment had no effect and the skill of many doctors could not cure him, and finally he passed away. The whole castle town lamented his death. The fact that his heir was four years old was reported to the shogunate office, together with a request that the supervision of the fiefdom might continue in the family. The elders all made the long journey to Edo, but they had scarcely been there a day when the heir suddenly passed away. How sad it was that in only two years' time this great family with an income of over a hundred thousand *koku* was cut off at the root. The several thousand inhabitants of the castle town, old and young, of high station and low, were dispersed throughout the country and the castle town became a deserted place. How true it is: when it is about to rain the mountains appear closer; when a country is about to fall, the people have first been made to suffer. This is proof of the remark I made before—that the tyrannical official harms a nation's ruler and cuts off the continuity of his line.

In the spring of the fourth year of Hōei [1707] I was on a pilgrimage and hung my staff in this castle town. One day, after we had finished our begging rounds, a few of my companions and I visited the personal temple of this lord, to pay our respects to the mausoleum of his ancestors. From long before no incense and flowers had been placed in offering. It was as though demons moaned and spirits lamented. Knitting our brows and sighing, our reaction was: "How hopeless it is! All this desolation that we now see arose from the barbarity of a single tyrannical official. The one thing that the lord of a province or the master of a castle town must fear is the tyrannical official." This serves as proof of what I said before of the tyrannical official: he turns the mausoleums of generations of ancestors into a wasteland of thorn trees where foxes and hares dwell; he turns the divine spirits of generations of ancestors into idle spirits for whom there is no one to make sacrifices, into wild demons with no one to hold services for them.

Supposing there is a robber-minister who devises secret plots and mysterious schemes in order to bring a country to confusion and destroy its families, to bring harm to the ruler, disperse the ministers in all directions, and to cut the continuity of the country. The people of the whole country become enraged, sound the drums of alarm, and press in upon him, saying that they will boil him in oil or tear him to pieces with oxen, and still this does not satisfy their anger. Yet it should be known that a tyrannical official is even worse than this robber-minister. Moreover, should a ruler acquire a fondness for such a man and make use of him, his country surely will not last for long. How dangerous this is!

Once a monk said to me while angrily shaking his head: "Cruelty is the shadow of extravagance. Extravagance is like a sound; cruelty is like its echo." I asked him what he was talking about and found out what he meant.

When an evil ruler gains control of a country he will without fail demand luxury. When he demands luxury he will most likely assemble women for his court. When he gathers together these women his finances will not suffice. When his finances do not suffice he will exhaust every means in seeking to supplement them. But you cannot ask for financial resources from trees and water. Thereupon the ruler will select a particularly notorious tyrannical official and send him out among the people to rob and plunder their monies and possessions. If he plunders ruthlessly and obtains wealth in great quantity the ruler considers him wise and calls him loyal. Thereupon he rewards him with court rank and confers an official post upon him. The other officials open their eyebrows wide—as Fei Lien straightened up his shoulders, Wu Lai squared his elbows, Wang Mang strained his eyes, Tung Cho[38] shook his head—then, on the pretense of gathering taxes

[38] Examples of evil ministers: Fei Lien and Wu Lai were evil ministers under King Chou; Wang Mang (33 B.C.–A.D. 23) is the arch-villain who usurped the Han throne; Tung Cho (d. 192) is the tyrant celebrated for his cruelty and arrogance during the Later Han.

or in imitation of the government revenue system, they rob and
plunder the people of their grain and clothing materials, as
though they were squeezing dry bones in order to get the juice.
Thereupon the country declines and the people are exhausted.
Even should the winter be warm, the children will weep because
of the cold; even should the crops be plentiful, the women will
cry out with hunger. Then later the people will in their resentment rebel. And when they rebel, if there is no judgment from
heaven, then there will be punishment by man. How then can the
nation be expected to endure for long?

This is why it is said: "When a bird is about to die, its song
is sad,[39] when a nation is about to fall, its greed is excessive."
How frightening this is! An official should think this over well
and act with restraint. Is borrowing the authority of the ruler
recklessly to harm the people and ruthlessly to rob and plunder
them, something that a righteous and benevolent warrior would
ever conceivably do? Is it something that you can just ignore?
Ah, and what happens to your descendants after you have died?
You may alone destroy the throne of another country and cut
off its continuity, but do you think you will be a person who can
rest at ease later on? Do you want your own family to have its
descendants cut off? And do you think that it will be only your
descendants that are cut off? There is nothing more disloyal than,
as a minister to a ruler, to do harm to the national throne. After
the official dies he falls without question to an evil realm and
receives its tortures for endless time, and must taste the bitterness
of fire, blood, and swords.

When you think about it well, there is an extreme difference
in rank between a lord and an official, and the noble and the base
are entirely different. Yet I assume that they all have ancestors.
Assuming that they do, then these ancestors, from their homes in
the underworld, seeing a descendant of theirs assume the position
of a government official in this world, will be sure to cry out
loudly saying: "If you burn grain there will be no buds; when
there is a tyrannical official he will have no descendants. We will

---

[39] *Analects*, 8, 4. The second half of the quotation does not appear in the
Analects.

shortly become idle spirits and wild demons with no relatives to say services for us. How we wish you would become a benevolent official! By no means become a tyrannical official!" It should be known that when the good and the evil of these two officials is compared, they are as far apart as heaven and earth. When we look at the descendants of those who have been officials, the families of benevolent officials always prosper in years to come; the families of tyrannical officials fall upon evil days and starve to death by the roadside.

Some forty years ago there was, in the town office of a certain place, a tyrannical official. The people despised and feared him greatly, and after not so long a time he was judged by his fellow men, quickly stripped of his post, attainted, and reduced to penury. The father begged in the city streets by singing songs from the Nō plays; the children recited the military tales and begged at the doors of peoples' houses, and when they had finished their storytelling they were completely dispirited.

Someone has said that cruelty has two aspects, extravagance and avarice. What emanates from extravagance is "public;" what stems from avarice is "private." The "private" is in abundance; the "public" is rare. There is nothing to fear about the "public;" publicly the official takes things. There is much to fear about the "private." Without fail the official will hold conversations in secret with the village head, come to an understanding with him, fix the plans, and under the guise of an official order will greedily plunder at will, robbing day by day, stealing month by month. Finally the profits will have doubled and the official and the village head will divide them. The "public" official, however, will not place his wealth in savings. That is why the house of the village head grows more luxurious day by day. K'ang I built a vast mansion; Shih Ch'ung[40] sat in splendor in the recesses of his establishment, the sound of music and song reverberating far into the distance, and loaded wagons groaning as they rumbled past.

The common people day by day grow feebler, month by month become more stunted. It becomes impossible to support

---

[40] K'ang I is not identified. Shih Ch'ung (d. 300) was known for his great wealth and luxurious living.

a wife and family. Each house moans under the suffering, each family falls into decline, until misery and starvation are everywhere. There is grain in the fields in abundance; thus hatred wells up within. At last there comes a time when life is no longer of any consequence. When things reach this point twenty or thirty thousand men gather together like swarms of ants and bees. Screaming their hatred, they first surround the village head's house, smash open the doors, and scatter his possessions. If they catch him they will be sure to tear him to pieces. Thoroughly aroused, they end up by storming the city, entering its gates, and creating a riot. Then the temples within the domains are called upon, and with deception and persuasion they bring things under control. Once peace is restored a spy is sent around in secret to search out and seize the conspirators. Then twenty or thirty men are crucified or executed, and their rotting bones litter the fields. But it must be known that the conspirators are not among the people. They are the official and the village head.

Supposing there are some poor men who, gathering together in a small group, set out on a long journey to a distant province. But when they get there the people of this other province talk about their lord in the most damning and insulting terms. Hearing this, the poor men become enraged and do not hesitate to kill the detractors. The people of all the various provinces are like this. If the official imitates an earlier benevolent official and takes into account the quality of the crops each year, investigates what is good and what is bad for the people, sees to it that the high and the low gain profit equally, and shares in the misfortunes and joys of the noble and the base, who will take an evil attitude toward the ruler of the province? Don't they say that a desperate rat will bite a cat? No, the conspirator is not among the people. How can you say that he is not the official and the village head?

In the past it has been said: "When wealth is dispersed [among the people] the people will gather [around the ruler]. When wealth is gathered [by the ruler] the people will disperse [away from him]."[41] "Dispersing the people" does not mean that the people in their resentment and hate, bearing the old on

---

[41] *Great Learning*, 2, 10, 9.

their backs and taking the children by the hand, cross the borders
in tears and flee to another country. Even though they do not
cross the borders and go to another land, in their hearts they will
shun and stand apart [from the ruler]. This is known as "dispersing the people." "Gathering the people" does not mean that
the people out of joy and longing leave another country, and
with their baskets of rice and vessels of congee[42] come to gather
in our country. When the hearts of the people are happy and they
feel friendly, this is called "gathering the people." If the ruler is a
man of benevolence and virtue who alleviates the misery of the
populace, despises tyrannical officials and keeps them at a distance, and does not in the least covet and plunder, then the people
will rejoice and draw close. They will sing in the streets and clap
their hands in the fields, saying: "May no disease afflict our lord;
may he live ten thousand years. For this ruler we would walk on
unsheathed blades; we would throw ourselves into raging flames.
May our lord live ten thousand years!" In this way the hearts
of the people are filled with respect and friendship. This is known
as "gathering the people."

But if the ruler of a country in his covetousness should honor
and employ exclusively tyrannical officials, plunder and rob the
people and make them suffer, gather together gold and silver in
huge quantities, and not only impoverish the nation but apply
financial pressure on the ministers about him as well, then the
people will fear and hate him as they would a tiger. In their
resentment they will curse him in anger, moan in the streets and
lament in the fields, beseeching heaven and praying to the Gods:
"Ah, if we could only have a benevolent man! May someone
come forth, in the way that Wen and Wu destroyed Chou;[43]
in the way that Liu Pang and Hsiang Yü[44] defeated Ch'in!
May he cross our borders, occupy our land, govern it, and bring

[42] *Mencius*, IB, 11, 3. Descriptive of a populace welcoming a ruler who will
relieve them from oppression. Here the expression must refer to the provisions
taken along on a journey.

[43] The virtuous kings of the Chou dynasty who displaced the tyrant Chou of
the Shang.

[44] Liu Pang (247–195 B.C.) was the founder of the Han dynasty. Hsiang Yü
(233–202 B.C.) was a leader in the revolt against the Ch'in.

peace! May he execute the tyrannical officials one by one! May he rescue and revive us and give us our ease both day and night! Ah, if we could only have a benevolent man!" To this extent is the heart of man rebellious. This is known as "dispersing the people."

When one comes to think about it, the most unenvied thing in this world is the family of the village head. In looking at what has happened to the heirs of village heads over the past fifty years in the area twenty miles to the east and west of here, we see that of several hundred such families, the large majority have been ruined. Of those that have not deteriorated at all and continue on to this day, there are at most eight or nine. These are the descendants of good people, who during their terms of office never once plundered the people out of avarice. Of the others, the families have to a large degree been completely cut off and no longer exist. The descendants of those families that still just barely manage to persist are, for the most part, blind and stone deaf.

But those who are harmed and distressed the most would seem to be the departed ancestors of the village head's family. While they were still obscure they underwent innumerable sufferings, weathering the winter's cold and withstanding the summer's heat. As time passed gradually their family enterprises began to prosper. Once they attained success, they were singled out by the people and encouraged to become village heads. Now people come from far and near to offer their congratulations, and their relatives and family rush happily in. Soon signs of haughtiness begin to show. Quickly rooms and buildings are repaired and gates erected. Putting on new socks (*tabi*), they spend on furnishings and clothing and gradually come to pride themselves in their prosperity and to delight in ornamentation. The resources of the house are lavishly expended at this stage. Then it is that they secretly hatch evil plans and set in motion ruthless schemes to plunder the people greedily. The people hate and resent this, but swallowing their tears and bearing up under the difficulties, they follow along. Although outwardly they may seem to accept the situation, inwardly they grieve and hurt. Then it is only a question of time until a disaster strikes.

This is why the people have riddles such as: "In what way are the plane of the barrelmaker and the head of the village the same? The barrelmaker shaves away unevenness (*mura*); the village head shaves away the village (*mura*)," or "How are a ripe persimmon deep in the mountains and the home of the village head the same? They both rot away without people knowing about it."[45] These are little jokes stemming from the intense resentment of the common people, but they can serve as unsurpassed offerings and prayers for the ancestors as well as the descendants of those who are village heads. The reason I say this is that, should a village head hear these riddles and act with restraint, then his descendants will without fail continue. And if he should suddenly develop a benevolent heart, and be moved to rescue people from their everyday misery, then his descendants will prosper. But most village heads differ little from those described in the riddles. They are censured by heaven and punished by man. Sadly enough, the possessions of their families, that have been handed down, are all forgotten; the four walls of their houses are broken down and become firewood for the stove. The grounds are hoed up into fields for the farmers, and their ancestors become wild demons with no one to hold services for them. With this their descendants are suddenly cut off. The family of a village head is certainly not something to be envied.[46]

In ancient China there was a man by the name of Yang Hu[47] who served as governor of Hsiang-yang. Benevolent by nature and warm of heart, he always refrained from drinking, limited his expenditures, and by distributing the surplus brought ease to the impoverished. The nation grew rich and prospered. The people were all impressed by his virtue and after he died they erected a stone inscription to him at Mount Hsien. So devoted and saddened were the people of the region that it is said that whenever they passed by the tablet they bowed before it and shed tears of emo-

---

[45] These riddles are also found at the conclusion of the *Yabukōji*.

[46] The parallel text in *Sashimogusa*, 2 ends here.

[47] Yang Hu (d. 278). A brave general, he was noted for his sympathy toward the common people. This story also appears in the first part of *Sashimogusa* (HZS, p. 112).

tion. For this reason, even to this day, it is known as "the Tablet of the Falling Tears."

Again, in the period of the Three Kingdoms, the General Kuan Yü[48] from Szechuan served as governor of Ching-chou. Always pure and simple, he forbade luxury, maintained economy, restricted frivolous expenses, and was well qualified, because of his natural abilities, to be a minister to a king. He lightened the tax burden, kept tax-gathering ministers away, and nourished the people. At no time did he ever allow the people to suffer another's greed. The people of Ching-chou were as fond of him as of their own parents and respected him as though he were a god. After the general died, the people, to honor his virtue, erected a large temple to which was given the name "The Mausoleum of General Kuan." Never was the offering of sacrifices neglected. To be thought of as the parents of the people even for one day is to leave behind a record worthy of envy indeed.[49]

Those who are known as benevolent rulers and wise kings are possessed of a heart deeply motivated by benevolence. Night and day their compassionate wisdom extends to the lowest commoner in the most distant corner of the land, not to mention those within their own families. At first they regulate luxury and use caution in the disbursement of the nation's expenditures. With luxury expenses are heavy, and when expenses are heavy tyrannical government is favored. Invariably such a government covetously plunders the people. When the people are plundered they resent and hate, and when a country is hated that country will surely fall.

The books on the nurturing of life[50] say: "The breath is like the people. When the people decline the nation is sure to perish. When the breath is exhausted man is sure to die." How true it is that the breath is the basis of the body and the people are the

[48] Kuan Yü (d. 219). China's greatest military hero.

[49] The following section is paralleled in the concluding part of *Sashimogusa*, 2 (HZS, p. 134).

[50] This does not refer to any particular book, but to Taoist works in general that deal with the subject.

trunk of the country. Supposing you had an ancient pine one thousand feet tall. Its roots reach to the bowels of the earth; its branches extend to the highest heaven. For a thousand autumns the sunlight has gleamed from its green branches. The sound of the wind sweeping through reverberates for miles into the distance, as though dragons were singing and scolding. Yet if its trunk were dug at from day to day, if its roots were laid bare, how long would this ancient pine continue to live? Be it known that to treat the people with kindness from day to day is to cultivate the trunk; to use the people with greed is to lay bare the roots of the state.

In general, from courtier to the lowest commoner, there are countless varieties of people: artisans, merchants, witch doctors, musicians, the hundred kinds of workmen. But there is not one among them who does not live because of the farmers' toil. If the farmer didn't exist wouldn't we all starve to death by the roadside? It must be known that the farmers are the great root of the nation. We must be thankful to Shōtoku Taishi for having called the hundred families[51] the hundred treasures. However, recklessly to use them with greed, to cause them to suffer, to afflict them and to do them harm, brings down the hatred and anger and resentment of the hundreds and thousands of spirits. Heaven will send down disasters, earth will snatch away life, exhaust the military destiny, and without fail cut the continuity of the nation. When you examine the reasons, they all stem from the greed and cruelty of the tyrannical official, the evil machinations of the robber minister. How sad it is that the gentlemen under the lords of all the provinces today do not know of this, if only in a dream. They always think to themselves: "If the country is at peace then the people are at ease. The times we have today are truly not inferior to the Engi and Tenryaku[52] eras." How dangerous this is!

---

[51] *Hyakushō.* They are so mentioned in Shōtoku Taishi's "Seventeen-Article Constitution." Shōtoku used the term in the sense of "the people"; by Hakuin's time the term refers specifically to farmers.

[52] The reign of Emperors Daigo and Murakami, a time of peace, approximately 901–956.

II

❀ The Divine Ruler[1] was in every respect a man of superb benevolence and virtue. The compassion and concern that he extended toward the people was, to my mind, far greater than those exhibited by the men who are known as gentlemen and sages in China. He always maintained that if good government was to be bestowed on the nation, it would be essential to attract and make use of loyal and upright wise ministers, to discard and keep at a distance sycophantic and insincere treacherous ministers, to keep constant watch lest the people suffer from hunger and cold, to show concern over the difficulties of farming, and never to neglect the martial arts. It is like knowing if a person is alive or dead by feeling the pulse. The extravagant ruler will be sure to covet; the greedy nation will always be in confusion. When the warrior abandons the warrior's way one may know that the pulse has died in the body. To covetously cause the farmers to suffer and to delight solely in the splendor surrounding one's own body is what Emperor T'ai-tsung[2] of the T'ang referred to when he said that the people and he were of one substance and that to covet their possessions and to cause them suffering was like cutting one's thigh while filling one's stomach. Even though the stomach is filled, if the flesh of the thigh is destroyed, will the body be able to stand?

If the military leader follows the teaching, "When in the midst of peace, do not forget danger; in the midst of a well-governed land fear disturbance," then night and day he must not be remiss, he must delight in and encourage the military arts, and must without neglect carry on the family calling. There is no greater disloyalty than to claim that to struggle for trifles, to exact exorbitant taxes, to bleed the people, to devote one's self to silver and gold, and to amass goods in the government store-houses, are signs of loyalty. The Divine Ruler said that the greatest

[1] *Daijū shinkun.* A name for Tokugawa Ieyasu (1542–1616), founder of the Tokugawa shogunate. *Daijū* [great tree], refers to the shogun.
[2] Li Shih-min (597–649), second emperor of the T'ang.

loyalty was to recommend and encourage good people, to give highest importance to the usefulness one can have to one's master, to sympathize with the people with compassion the basis of everything, and to govern the nation in such a way that all men will be at peace.

Recently I read by chance the Divine Ruler's *Legacy*[3] and was both amazed and delighted. Who would have imagined the depth of his benevolence; that his saintly wisdom has been so superbly handed down! With the splendor of benevolent government and the ceremonies for governing the world, the three terraces shine on the four seas, the five planets guard the center, and the whole world rests in security.[4] Indeed, [his work] surpasses the great accomplishment of the establishment by Han Kao-tsu[5] of a dynasty that endured for four hundred years. There has been nothing its equal since the creation of the world. Surely this is not in the ordinary run of things! Could it be explained by saying that a Buddha or a bodhisattva, out of sympathy for mankind in this degenerate age, used its powers of will and appeared for a short time in the manifestation of a political leader?[6] This *Legacy* has no equal in China or Japan. It contains golden words that I feel are superior to the Six Classics[7] and excel even the *Analects* and *Mencius*. Although it scarcely comes to a hundred pages it is superior, as far as the warriors of Japan today are concerned, to the secret recesses of the *Avataṁsaka Sūtra*, as well as the various dynastic histories, and the many tens of thousands of volumes in the writings of the hundred schools. Rather than pointlessly reading and remembering the *Shih-chi* and the *Tso-chuan* and becoming a person of vast knowledge, there is nothing that surpasses reading this book as an aid for governing

[3] *Goikun.* Known to western readers as the *Legacy of Ieyasu,* it is a spurious work, said to have been written a hundred years after Ieyasu's death. Hakuin, quite naturally, does not question its authenticity.

[4] A highly ornate passage, descriptive of the greatness of Ieyasu's rule. The "three terraces" are six stars forming a part of Ursa Major.

[5] Liu Pang (247–195 B.C.), the founder of the Han dynasty.

[6] A bodhisattva, by the power of his will, may appear in the world. A political leader is one of the thirty-three manifestations of Kannon.

[7] Variously given. Included are such works as the *Book of Changes, Book of Songs, Book of Documents, Li-chi,* etc.

the family and regulating the body. I wish that the lords of provinces and cities would read this book, considering it a substitute
for reading the teachings and reciting the sutras each morning and
night. The province where this book is read with veneration will
receive divine protection for all eternity and the Buddhas will
cast protective glances upon it. In a province like this disasters
such as floods, droughts, and epidemics will never occur. Especially
in the world of peace that we have today these golden words
must not be neglected even for a day. The province in which this
work is read with respect will without fail prosper and its
descendants continue for long.

But a province that goes against this book and does not
follow it, that province will surely encounter natural disasters
and will not be able to endure for long. How regrettable it is
that [many people, not knowing its nobility, have for a hundred
and fifty years] left this book lying idle, [buried] under piles of
old papers.[8] It is as though the jewel of Pien Ho and the beautiful
Wagon-illumining Pearl[9] were buried beneath the mud. But if
you piled up a thousand, even ten thousand pieces of the jewel
that itself was worth city piled on city,[10] how could the benefit
it would bring a nation and the solace it would bring the people
exceed the power of this book? As a prayer for peace in the
world and the eternal continuance of the nation, there is no
sutra or *dhāranī* that can surpass this book. If warriors would
read this work with veneration, rather than reciting at length
the sutras and calling the Buddha's name, which are at any rate
quite unsuited to them, they would gain benefit in this world and
the world to come. I wish that some wealthy person who longs
for a fortuitous rebirth in the next life would have blocks cut to
perpetuate this work, have it printed throughout the country,
particularly so that it may be read by the samurai. It would serve
the good root much better than the erection of any enormous
temple, filled with pagodas and halls.

[8] The above passage has been supplemented with the text of the Hosokawa
edition.
[9] Pien Ho was the owner of a fabulous jewel. The "Wagon-illumining Pearl"
is a gem with such brilliance that it can illumine a distance of twelve wagons
to front and rear.   [10] Pien Ho's jewel was worth fifteen cities.

We Buddhists recite each morning and evening the teachings as handed down by Shakamuni, our ancestral Buddha. In the same way, for the Japanese samurai of today, can any one surpass the Divine Ruler, be he Buddha, God, or ancestor? Is not this book the one to which the highest honor must be paid? There is no one, be he samurai, farmer, monk, or mendicant priest, who has not benefited from the many years of peace. It all owes itself to the virtue and the power of the fine government of the Divine Ruler, that makes compassion the basis of everything, and has extended unchanged since it was established. How fortunate it is that a text in the kana syllabary has been left. Now it can be read by any samurai or dharma master, no matter how inept at Chinese characters or lacking in talent he may be. And people who are completely illiterate, such as farmers, artisans, or merchants can install a volume in the Buddhist shrine in their own homes. Giving reverence to it morning and night will serve as an unsurpassed prayer for safety within the household.

There is a certain person who invariably says to me: "You are quick to praise this book and say it is superior to the Six Classics. Isn't this the height of stupidity? You seem always to be seeking adulation."

If I seem to be seeking adulation with all sorts of strange calculations and manipulations, why would I limit my praise to this one book alone? I myself have occasion to laugh at the great stupidity of others. It is just like a good doctor preparing a prescription. It may be just a dash of akebia, but for a person suffering from an obstruction of the bowels, seriously ill and on the verge of death, its marvelous effectiveness surpasses that of wolfsbane, ginseng, Chinese milk vetch, or the dotted bell flower. But if, because of this, people were to say in praise that akebia is superior to wolfsbane and ginseng, wouldn't this be the epitome of stupidity? Don't the people of today know that this book is like the wolfsbane and ginseng? Why are they so abysmally stupid? Even if I were setting evil schemes to gain adulation, what would it profit me, who am close to the end of my life?

Admittedly I am the dregs among monks, but I am not without motivation to bring benefit to the world. But even with this motivation, how can my meager talents approach to the power that this book possesses? That is why when I meet the

right person I have him read this book. If this book is made use
of in a province, then that province will have nothing but great
felicity. It is regrettable that unless there is someone who knows
about swords, refined steel and ordinary steel are likely to get
mixed.[11] If in the future someone sees this book put to use throughout the country, and is struck with joy and veneration, his reaction would be comparable to finding a precious jewel on the
road at night or to obtaining a compass in fog-bound seas. If in
the future someone sees this book put to use throughout the
nation and is struck with fear and hatred, his reaction would be
like meeting the demon of pestilence in a narrow alley or an evil
tiger in a secluded valley. Is there a ruler of men or a minister
of the people who does not delight in and venerate this book? Is
there a ruler of men or a minister of the people who hates and
fears this book? Such superior rulers as Yü and T'ang, Wen and
Wu, such wise ministers as the Duke of Chou and the Duke of
Shao,[12] would have respected and rejoiced in this book. Such
tyrannical rulers as Chou of Yin and Chieh of Hsia, such robber-
ministers as Chao Kao and Li Ssu,[13] would have feared and
despised this book.

The Ch'in burning of the books must not be carried out
again.[14] A long time ago under the Ch'in, a tyrannical government ran things as it pleased. Chao and Li seized the powers of
government. They plundered and looted and destroyed the books
and violated greatly the teachings of the sages. While they were
committing these crimes they feared that resentment and blame
would be heaped upon them for a thousand years to come, so they
sealed the mouths of the Confucianists and burned their books.
It was the same thing when the tyrant Emperor Wu of the T'ang,[15]
despising greatly the concept of cause and effect, hated it when

---

[11] The Hosokawa text adds here: "It is regrettable that this book was so late
in being promulgated throughout the world."

[12] Legendary good emperors and ministers.

[13] Evil kings who brought their dynasties to an end. Chao Kao (d. 207 B.C.)
and Li Ssu (d. 208 B.C.) were evil ministers under the Ch'in.

[14] In other words, Ieyasu's *Legacy* must not be destroyed by evil ministers in
the way that the books of the Confucianists and other philosophers were
burned under the Ch'in.

[15] Reference is to the persecution of Buddhism in the Hui-ch'ang era (842–845)
under Emperor Wu of the T'ang.

monks preached on the subject, and therefore forced them to return to lay life and live in thatched huts.

In years to come treacherous retainers and thieving samurai, detesting the thought that the *Legacy* will come into use, will be sure to say: "How can the testament of clear virtue and the highest good of our Divine Ruler be imprudently distributed throughout the country and be touched by the hands of base and common people! It must be wrapped up ten times in cloth, be stored away in the recesses of libraries, and never recklessly be shown to others."

This may be so, but consider our Tathāgata Shakamuni Buddha, son of Śuddhodana, king of all India, this prince whose virtue was so great that he became teacher to the three worlds and six paths. Brahmā pressed together his palms, the Dragon Kings venerated him; no greater respect and honor than this could be shown. The sutras that he preached were distributed without question among the common people and amidst the market stalls. In fact, the only fear was that these scriptures might not gain a wide distribution. That is why, if you open a volume of the scriptures, you will frequently find a notation indicating that the work is to be handed down to later generations. Even slaves and menials render them honor by handling or reciting them.

The benefit that this *Legacy* can bring to the world and the people it can save are like torrential rains relieving an intense drought; finding it is better than finding a bamboo raft at the crossing place of a wild stream. How can anyone despise the breadth of the blessing brought by the Divine Ruler who, making benevolence the basis of all things, carried on work equal to that of a bodhisattva! Furthermore, if you make this *Legacy* secret and hide it and vainly consign it to the bellies of silver fish, will this not be violating the will of the Divine Ruler? There is no greater disloyalty for a samurai of today than to violate the will of the Divine Ruler.

In your domains your ancestors for many generations now have possessed deep benevolence. There have been many compassionate and modest gentlemen and no lack of loyal and honest persons, who have contributed their talents to their lord, and one after the other rendered assistance to benevolent government.

Thus your domains flourish, the people are gentle, the farmers have an abundance of millet, and the women possess sufficient cloth. One has but to step over the boundaries of your domains to be struck by the brilliance of the mountains and the colors of the waters, and to notice the smoke wafting up from the hearths in villages near and far. Yours may rightly be called the Gentleman's Province of Japan. Because of this there has been no accusation of tyrannical government leveled against you by the people.

When you think this over, the blessings you have had, and the fact that you were born to be ruler of a felicitous and benevolently governed domain, all owe themselves to the fact that in a former life you reached to a point where you had accumulated considerable virtue through your practice of the disciplines. You must exercise restraint and concentrate on establishing an attitude in which neither the blessings acquired from all the good actions of the past are exhausted nor are you caught up in evil causes of crimes and obstacles leading to karmic suffering. As everyone knows, fortunate, noble, and free people, who in the present life are princes, generals, feudal lords, or members of great families, were in a previous life all people who strove to be born in the Pure Land or endeavored to become Buddhas. For two or three lives they struggled and practiced painfully, followed the eating regulations, maintained the precepts, recited and copied the sutras, and exhausted themselves in various spiritual endeavors. They represent the second coming of famous and noble monks and the general run of Buddhist practitioners.

But even if they have practiced the mysteries of the three worlds, until they have opened the eye to see into their own natures and unless they have practiced the great practice of the bodhisattva, it will be difficult for them to meet the conditions for becoming a Buddha. However, rewards for the various good things done in former lives have not been lacking and they have been born as people of noble and high estate, well endowed and possessed of freedom. But with each new birth the past is forgotten, so that they end up by losing their past aspiration for enlightenment and their compassion. Relying on their blessings and fortune, they take pride in their power, cause the common people to suffer, extort taxes, and, piling up limitless evil karma, fall inevitably at their deaths into hell. For this reason it is said, "Worldly blessings are the enemies of the three periods." At any rate, one must recognize that the most important point of discretion is not to make an error in the conduct of government. The lord of any province, even if he does not have the power to spread benevolence, alleviate the suffering of the people and bring them good fortune, should outlaw luxury, regulate frivolous expeditures, and strictly maintain frugality. If this is done should the relief of the peoples' suffering be so difficult a thing?

Some time ago two brothers were abbots, one at Mount Kōya and the other in Kyoto.[16] One day the abbot from Mount Kōya paid a visit to his brother in Kyoto, and in the course of a rambling conversation remarked: "Living in that place way out in the country, things don't go as one would want them to most of the time. It is especially bad because the temple domains are so small. We are always running short of things and time hangs heavily on my hands as the days pass." As he spoke tears filled his eyes and he became quite despondent.

The Kyoto abbot replied: "That may well be, but as I watch the people around me, I see many who delight in poverty, and the thought that they lack for things does not bother them at all."

The abbot from Mount Kōya exclaimed: "I can't believe you said what you did! What person with human emotions could possibly like poverty and not be bothered by the lack of things?"

To this the abbot from Kyoto replied: "Those who desire luxury and delight in beauty are ultimately people who like poverty and want. Where they need only three attendants they

---

[16] The terms used are *Kōya no omuro* and *Kyō no omuro*. "Omuro" is a place name in western Kyoto and the name is used here to refer to the Ninna-ji, a temple located there. In the ninth century it became the custom for imperial princes to enter this temple, so that we may assume that the brothers mentioned here are of the imperial household. *Kōya no omuro* probably refers to the Kongōbu-ji on Mt. Kōya and *Kyō no omuro* to Ninna-ji, or possibly Tō-ji in Kyoto. I have arbitrarily designated them as abbots for the sake of translation. Their exact rank is unclear.

employ five; where they need five servants they hire ten. Then there are clothes and furniture to buy. It may be a simple visit to a shrine or temple to which one could just as well walk, but nevertheless a great procession of palanquins and carts is required. Although such a one may be a lord who controls a fief of ten thousand households, he never thinks that things suffice. Monks such as we, who have left our homes or retired to seclusion, can reduce our needs by half, and still not think that things are not sufficient. Nowadays it is no trouble at all to alleviate the suffering of beggars and outcasts and to assist the old and the ill."

The abbot from Mount Kōya was deeply impressed and in a voice choked with tears remarked: "Not only is the eloquence of your language superb, but I envy you too for the wisdom you possess concerning the world at large." Isn't this a fine story that will endure for a thousand years?

This is something that happened in the summer of the *ki-shi* year of the Kampo era.[17] A group of seven or eight respectable old women knocked on the door of my room and announced: "We are lowly females from the isolated mountain village called Katsurayama, some ten miles to the north of here. We have come to visit you for a strange reason. Please show compassion and explain something to us, for we have ears like deer and monkeys and have never heard the Law of the Buddha. Even if you have but one word of explanation, please illuminate for us the road of darkness that has continued so long."

Hereupon they told the story of the daughter of one of their group, who in the winter of the year before had become seriously ill and had taken to her bed. Gradually she had grown weaker and more exhausted until eventually she passed away. But because a slight warmth still lingered in the region about her chest, they were in no hurry to carry out the funeral. Then some ten days later, suddenly one night she returned to life, and raising herself up, cried out aloud. This is the story she told:

"A little while ago I was marched off by some strange people. I recall having gone some miles through a dark and

---

[17] There is no sexegenary designation *ki-shi* in the Kampo era. The second year of Kan'en (1747) is doubtless meant.

frightening place that seemed somewhat like the rim of a valley. I could scarcely stand the suffering as I saw about me on all sides a terrifying world that I supposed to be hell. Everywhere was total darkness, for there was no light from the sun and moon. From amidst the flames[18] shooting forth from the hells of Incessant Suffering and Searing Heat I could hear the screams and wails of the sinners being tortured there. Famous men and people of high station, beggars and outcasts, were all packed in together. Among those who were undergoing this unspeakable torment were quite a number of people who were known to me. Monks were also mixed in among them and they too were suffering intensely.

"There was a huge plain that extended farther than the eye could reach. Here were numberless beings, who seemed to be suffering from leprosy. They had the shape of human beings but were so emaciated that they looked like stakes burned black; stooped over, they wailed and wept in their pain. After I had proceeded a vast distance beyond this place, I eventually reached a huge iron gate that towered a hundred feet in the air. Looking up, I noticed about twenty feet above me a large plaque attached to the gate, with the words 'The Palace of Emma' inscribed. Brawny jailers formed an endless procession as they dragged the sinners through the gate. Trembling with fear, I peered inside and everywhere I looked was a vast expanse filled with sinners in uncountable numbers, crouched on small rock piles weeping and wailing. What they were saying was: 'How awful it is that we did not have the slightest conception of this frightening place while we were still in the ordinary world. What we learned from the talks on Buddhism we heard was pointless nonsense prated by ignorant nuns and the like, who were only looking to gain things for themselves. How utterly contemptible and useless they were. Some time the day must come when we can escape from this awful place.' Their miserable appearance and the sound of their wailing, screaming voices sent a stab of fear to my vitals.

[18] The flames of hell are black.

"The appearance of these hells: [19] the Hell of Wailing, the Hell of Great Wailing, the Hell of Searing Heat, the Hell of Great Searing Heat, the Hell of the Black Chains, the Hell of Mass Suffering, is beyond the power of the mind to conceive or of words to describe.

"In a dark and terrifying place under the dank shade of ancient trees stood a rotting and decaying prison, its walls leaning crazily. Within were some seven or eight people who appeared to be of the samurai class. Wasted and exhausted, they clutched tattered silken garments about their shoulders, and crouching in agony, stretched forth trembling arms as thin as hemp stalks to beg from people passing by. These were people who eighty years ago served as officials in a town office in Izu. When one looked at the prisons that stood in rows beneath the trees in the area, they were filled with beings, some of whom had been there long and others who had only recently arrived. There were the noble and the great, some in unfamiliar costume, but all with their necks bent in pain. Some even sat and slept. Others, covered with hair like a tiger's, squatted with terrifying expressions on their faces. There were kings and ministers from Japan and China who had mercilessly tortured the common people in their greed. When I recollect these and other scenes of hell my hair stands on end in terror."

The old women went on to say: "Since having heard the daughter describe these events in her choked voice we are no longer able to sleep with ease at night. If there is a way for us to be saved, please teach it to us. The daughter wanted very much to come herself on this pilgrimage, but because of her long illness she was not in fit condition to make the journey here. Before we had even finished hearing her story, we were struck with fear

---

[19] There are eight hot hells described in the scriptures, one below the other, and each more fearsome and dangerous and longer in duration than the other. Hakuin, while frequently mentioning them, does not list all of them or put them in their correct order. They are, in descending order: the hells of Repeated Misery, Black Chains, Mass Suffering, Wailing, Great Wailing, Searing Heat, Great Searing Heat, and Incessant Suffering. There are also eight cold hells, to which Hakuin does not refer.

and so came to ask you for the name[20] or if you would be good enough to write something for us."

Nowadays, when people hear stories such as this they frequently take them as empty theories and deluded talk, and they will clap their hands and roar with laughter, saying: "For man, with the good functioning of Yin and Yang, death is like the extinguishing of a lamp. What heaven can there be? How can there be a hell?"

This is the heresy that everything ends with death, and it is a frighteningly evil view. There is no idiocy that exceeds this. One can characterize such people with the phrase: "a small amount of wisdom blocks enlightenment." If heaven and hell really did not exist, then "there is no land under heaven that is not the king's land." What place would there be for Buddhas and gods to stay? "To the farthest boundaries of these lands there is none but is the king's slave." What need would there be for priests and nuns?[21] Yet in India there are the famous gardens at Jetavana and Veṇuvana, and the temple at Nālandā.[22] In China there are the five mountains and the ten monasteries.[23] It need not be mentioned that in our country there are numerous Caves of the Dharma and holy places. If heaven and hell do not exist, of what possible use are they? What sort of worthless implements are such things as Buddhist statues and sutra rolls then?

In the past there have been numerous examples of venerated rulers who put aside their royal garments to don the habits of monks. Far away in India we have such men as King Subhavyūha and his two sons, the princes Vimalagarbha and Vimalanetra as

[20] Most commonly, the six characters *Namu Amida Butsu* [Reverence to Amida Buddha]. If given to a believer they will assist him on his path to the Pure Land. Presumably the old women wished Hakuin to write out the characters for them.

[21] See "Yabukōji," fn. 25.

[22] Jetavana is the park in which a monastery was built, a favorite resort of Shakamuni. Veṇuvana is also a park associated with the Buddha. Nālandā is a celebrated monastery. Hakuin mentions another place here that cannot be identified and may well represent a slip of his memory.

[23] Five major temples and ten other monasteries associated with Zen. They represent a system of grading temples established during the Sung period. This system was also adopted in Japan.

well as Siddhārtha.[24] In our country Emperor Kazan[25] and other historical worthies, emperors equipped with the ten virtues, shaved their heads and put on Buddhist robes and were known as cloistered emperors. What of them? Among those of the coiffured and beauteous hair there were Shinnyo Daitoku,[26] Chiyono,[27] Chūjō hime,[28] Giō, Gijo, and Hotoke Gozen,[29] and Eshun-ni;[30] among ministers and warriors there were Madenokōji Chūnagon Fujifusa,[31] Saimyōji Nyūdō Tokiyori,[32] Karukaya Nyūdō Shigeuji,[33] Satō Hyōe Norikiyo,[34] Kumagai Shōjirō Naozane,[35] Endō Musha Moritō,[36] Okabe Rokuyata Tadazumi,[37] and other brave heroes. What of these people, as well as the men of wisdom and famous priests of the past and present, who gave up official positions difficult to surrender, who cast aside love and affection so difficult to turn away from, all in order to undergo indescribable suffering? Are you going to say that they were all crazy?

[24] Reference is to a story in the *Lotus Sūtra* (T9, p. 59c) in which these two princes performed miracles in order to convince their father, the king, of the value of the Buddhist teachings. Siddhārtha is the personal name of Shakamuni.

[25] Emperor Kazan (968–1008), the sixty-fifth Emperor.

[26] Shinnyo Daitoku is the famous prince, Shinnyo Shinnō, who went to China and is said to have been eaten by a tiger while on his way to India. "Those of the coiffured and beauteous hair" refers to people associated with the court.   [27] Unidentified.

[28] Legendary figure who fled the court to become a nun. She is mentioned also in "Yabukōji."

[29] These three women appear in the *Heike monogatari*, associated with Taira no Kiyomori. Their story appears below in the text.

[30] Famous Sōtō Zen nun of the early Muromachi period.

[31] Madenokōji Fujifusa (n.d.). Loyalist of the Yoshino period who became a monk in 1334. The story that he later became the second abbot of Myōshin-ji, Jūō Sōhitsu, is incorrect.

[32] Hōjō Tokiyori (1227–1263). Shogun in the Kamakura military government and a devout Zen follower.

[33] Karukaya Shigeuji is the subject of elaborate stories and legends, used in Nō and puppet plays. He is more commonly known as Karukaya Dōshin.

[34] Satō Norikiyo. The lay name of the late Heian poet Saigyō (1118–1190).

[35] Kumagai Naozane (1141–1208), warrior-hero of the Kamakura period.

[36] Endō Moritō, lay name of the monk Mongaku, who flourished in the early Kamakura period. He appears as the subject of Nō drama and puppet plays.

[37] Okabe Tadazumi (n.d.). Warrior-hero associated with Minamoto no Yoshitsune.

Do you still want to say that they didn't know whether heaven and hell existed?

In Buddhism, to believe in cause and effect, to know that rebirth occurs, to fear a painful recompense are known as being possessed of great wisdom. Man is called the spirit-possessed of all beings because he differs from horses, cows, dogs, pigs, wolves, and deer. He knows that there is a rebirth; he fears the painful recompense of evil deeds. If you now accept the view [of people who do not believe in heaven and hell] and take all people to be the same as these animals, are you going to be satisfied with this view later?

You, my lord, in your ruling of your land and protection of your domains—be it for a hundred years, be it for fifty years—must be very circumspect and recognize that the essence of virtuous action is to forbid luxury, regulate extravagant expenditures, and, when you have a surplus, to use it for the benefit of the farmers. When you read the ancient honored texts and writings, all speak of the Kingly Way as being of first importance. If it does not discuss the Kingly Way it is not an honored text. If you inquire into what the principal message of this Kingly Way is, it is nothing more than to give priority to dispensing benevolence, to rescue the common people with compassion, and thus to govern your domain. In the world of today dispensing benevolence and succoring the common people require no methods other than to forbid luxury, regulate excessive expenditures and, to touch upon a rather difficult subject these days, to reduce the number of women in the inner chambers, and to simplify all matters in general.

The people in the womens' quarters will for a while feel a loneliness and a certain empty desperation, but when it is explained to them that it is for the benefit of the lord, of the nation, and of the people, as well as for the life to come, a wise person cannot but agree. The more people there are in the women's quarters the less chance will there be for a moment's peace from the jealous feuding. All that will result is deep crimes and much evil in the world to come. The ruler, too, must think about this well. These women are, after all, human beings. If the lord prides himself in his luxury and behaves capriciously, he will make a hell on earth for the women, as Pan Chieh-yü[38] was forced to bear the resentment of the womens' quarters and Fujitsubo[39] was made to cry throughout the night. Is this something that someone with even a modicum of benevolence in his heart would do? Isn't the custom that a chaste woman does not take a second husband really an unfair proposition? I would rather have it that a wise husband does not maintain two wives.

In the past, while the Daishōkoku Nyūdō Kiyomori[40] was attended on by just the two sisters Giō and Gijo, everything was on the friendliest of terms. But when Hotoke no mae was added to the group, night and day there were nothing but unpleasant incidents, so that, no longer able to stand the situation, Giō and Gijo crept out of the castle and both became nuns. At any rate, as far as the womens' quarters are concerned, the fewer the women the quieter things are and the better it is. A wise person, no matter how much importunity he may have from the womens' quarters, will reduce the number of people, simplify things, and live quietly. When he has spare time he will devote himself intensively toward affairs of the next world. What more felicitous conduct could there be?

I hear from time to time of various easygoing lords who pay out sums of from three hundred to five hundred pieces of gold to buy singing and dancing girls or other so-called women of pleasure from the Kyoto area. They amuse themselves with them for two or three years and then exchange them for other girls, much as they would fans or pipes. There are reports that in some households one third of the total expenses go for the needs of the womens' quarters. This does not matter so much for a house

---

[38] The chief favorite of Emperor Ch'eng of the Han, who was supplanted by Chao Fei-yen.

[39] In the *Tale of Genji* Fujitsubo, as the emperor's consort, bears a child by Genji. She appears in other works as well.

[40] Taira no Kiyomori (1118–1181). The story is found in *Heike monogatari* and *Gempei seisui ki*. Giō and Gijo were *shirabyōshi* [dancing girls], who had come to Kyoto with their mother. They became favorites of Kiyomori, who installed them in a mansion. Later another dancing girl, Hotoke Gozen (Hotoke no mae), attracted Kiyomori's fancy. Giō and Gijo fled to become nuns. Later Hotoke Gozen joined them and they all devoted themselves to seeking rebirth in the Pure Land.

blessed with a splendid fortune, and possessing an overflow of wealth, but very frequently people not so well provided for will pile up two thousand *ryō* of debts on an income of a thousand *koku*, twenty thousand *ryō* of debts on an income of ten thousand *koku*. Then they will ignore, impoverish, and bring suffering to their hereditary retainers, whose duty it is, when an emergency arises, to ward off the flying arrows and sacrifice their very bones and flesh for their lord. In a time of need these lords will expend their money on people who are unfit even to carry a raincoat box. In the end isn't it the people as a whole within the domains who suffer? What state of mind is it that allows for the concentration of luxury in one person, while causing many to suffer? What will happen in the next world? A frightening prospect indeed!

When one watches the *sankin kōtai*[41] processions of the lords of the various provinces, a huge number of persons surround them to front and rear, bearing countless spears, spikes, weapons of war, horse trappings, flags, and curtain poles. Recently, even for trivial river crossings, depending on the status of the family, a thousand to two thousand *ryō* are used without even thinking about it. In the Tenshō and Bunroku eras[42] when the country was not yet at peace this was an established precautionary procedure.

But the Divine Ruler brought order to the world, and now as the various lords go back and forth, there is no one even to shoot a rusted arrow at them. If under the motto "a humane man has no enemies"[43] you take the true precautions of being extremely benevolent, worrying about the people, and governing your domains well, then ten good hereditary retainers to front and rear will do. It will be far more profitable than employing a horde of several thousand insincere flatterers. But if you are wealthy and powerful and do not bring pain and suffering on the people, how many thousands of people you employ should be at your own discretion. Yet from what one hears from all the

[41] The system established in the Tokugawa period by which certain feudal lords were required to travel to Edo and spend half the year there, leaving their families behind as hostages when they returned to their own domains.

[42] The years 1573–1595, before the establishment of the Tokugawa shogunate.

[43] *Mencius*, IA, 5, 6.

provinces everywhere, the sadness of life lodges itself among the common people.

If you should have the desire to study Zen under a teacher and see into your own nature, you should first investigate the word *shi*.[44] If you want to know how to investigate this word, then at all times while walking, standing, sitting, or reclining, without despising activity, without being caught up in quietude, merely investigate the koan: "After you are dead and cremated, where has the main character [45] gone?" Then in a night or two or at most a few days, you will obtain the decisive and ultimate great joy. Among all the teachings and instructions, the word *death* has the most unpleasant and disgusting connotations. Yet if you once suddenly penetrate this "death" koan, [you will find that] there is no more felicitous teaching than this instruction that serves as the key to the realm in which birth and death are transcended, where the place in which you stand is the Diamond indestructible, and where you have become a divine immortal, unaging and undying. The word *death* is the vital essential that the warrior must first determine for himself.

The warrior who has not investigated the "death" koan is weak and timid in body and mind and in the end is unable to determine the mind-as-master. Then when an emergency occurs, he is surprisingly cowardly and unprepared, and thus unable to stand by his lord to the end. This is why it is said that if a person gives rise to a panic-striken terror, the mind-as-master has not yet been determined. Even if a person is well trained in the usual military arts, can wield the sword of Kurō or the spear of Sanada,[46] if the mind-as-master is not determined, when an emergency

---

[44] Meditation on the character *shi* [death]. In other words, meditation on the koan given below in the text. I do not find this koan given in any of the major collections. Hakuin, in the *Oniazami* (HZS, pp. 182–84), devotes considerable space to a discussion of meditation on the subject of death. He quotes Suzuki Shōsan to the effect that the aspiring warrior should write the character for "death" on his chest twenty or thirty times each morning.

[45] *Shujinkō*. The main character, chief actor. Used in the same sense as "original face," "true man without rank." That which can be realized only by someone who has gained enlightenment, and which is inexpressible in words.

[46] The "sword of Kurō" refers to Minamoto no Yoshitsune. "The spear of Sanada" refers most likely to Sanada Yukimura (1566–1615).

arises he trembles with fear and is not of the slightest use whatever.

However, to be superior in all abilities is to possess the mind-as-master. If one wishes to determine this mind-as-master then one must concentrate solely on the resolution of the "death" koan. Once this koan is even to a small degree determined, the mind-as-master is fixed as firmly as a huge rock. It may be described as being as solid as a range of mountains, as vast as the great sea. For the person who has determined this "death" koan even to a small degree, the great matter of seeing into his own nature and attaining awakening is as obvious as looking at the palm of the hand.

It is always my humble wish that you will constantly set firm this mind-as-master and with sincerity and straightforwardness regulate your own body. From now on just set far away to rest this young lord with an income of a million *koku*, dwelling amid the jeweled blinds and golden screens, the brocade hangings and embroidered curtains. It is essential that you do not keep yourself in a lofty position, but that from today you withdraw from it, as if from a dangerous place you despise, and become a person devoted to humane government and filial compassion. Gain an understanding of the lowly official and servant, whose estate is so different from your own, and of the debased position of the lackey. When the mind-as-master is fixed with a certainty, do not even for a moment adopt the airs of a great ruler, but keep your morning and evening meals simple, wear mostly cotton clothing both summer and winter, and avoid being seen by others. Clean up the garden, change the water in the basins, and with a laughing face wash the feet of the retainers' horses. Even if it be the work of the most debased menial, practice and learn it. Then with your inner awakening, if you follow the principles set forth by the Divine Ruler and spread compassionate blessings among the common people, Heaven will reward you with a long life and earth will favor you with abundant blessings. You will not differ in the slightest from the benevolent man of long life described in the ancient texts, and will live as long as did Urashima. For all generations to come you will be venerated as a famous general of clear virtue and superlative goodness.

There is an ancient saying that even a gentleman will make one error in a thousand words and even an inferior man will have one worthwhile thing to say in a thousand words. If I have written something even half worthwhile in a thousand words, I hope it will be of some help, no matter how insignificant, in the conduct of your government. That I have kept writing so long does not mean that I am fishing for gain beneath the waves of the world. I certainly am not one to enter my claim to fame in the foot paths of the Deer Park.[47]

Since the year I had the honor of meeting you at the Kokusei Temple,[48] I have heard reports from time to time that you have spoken of me, and this has moved me greatly. While it may not accord with your lofty thinking, what I have written here merely follows the dictates of my heart. I am ancient and decrepit, past seventy years of age, an old man on the brink of death, who does not concern himself with the time of day. All of my worldly hopes have been cut off and it is certainly without any attempt at insincere flattery that I sit writing throughout the night by the light of a single lamp, rubbing these tired old eyes. "Not praying that things will be wrong, I wonder whether or not I am a slightly useful scarecrow standing in the fields."[49] They say that Yü bowed to the speaker when he heard good words.[50] And later when he came to be called Great Yü, even though he was a great sage, who knew the principles at birth and practiced them with innate assurance,[51] when he heard good words, even if they were spoken by woodcutters, fishermen, and slaves, he bowed and

---

[47] The meaning is unclear. Reference is possibly to the park where the Buddha preached his first sermon.

[48] The Kokusei-ji in Okayama.

[49] The verse here is defective. In the Hosokawa text it reads: *Ashikare to / Omo-wan mono o / Koyamada no / Itazura naranu / Sōzu narikeri,* "Not wishing that things will be bad, A slightly useful scarecrow standing in the fields." It is an adaptation of a verse on the subject of meditation sitting by Dōgen, that runs: *Mamoru to mo / Omowazu nagara / Koyamada no / Itazura naranu / Kagashi narikeri,* "Guarding, but unaware of it, A slightly useful scarecrow standing in the fields." Dōgen's verse is found in *Sanshō dōei shū (Kokubun Tōhō Bukkyō sōsho* [Tokyo, 1925], 8, 229). In Hakuin's verse there is a pun on the word *sōzu* [priest; scarecrow]; Dōgen reads the word *kagashi* [scarecrow].

[50] *Mencius,* 2A, 8, 2.   [51] A paraphrase of *Doctrine of the Mean,* 20, 9.

regretted only that he had heard them too late. Although my words are only those of a wild monk, if they prove of value to the conduct of your governmental duties, read them again and again and think of them no less than did Yoshitsune of the "country strategy" military work that he treasured as his secret guide-book.[52] But on the other hand, if you find my words pointless, then throw them at once into the stove and consign them to the flames.

With respect,

The fourth year of Hōreki [1754]

[52] Based on a story in *Gikei-ki*. Minamoto no Yoshitsune visits Oniichi Hōgen at his home in Kyoto, seeking to learn military methods handed down in Oniichi's family. He is refused, but Yoshitsune makes an agreement with Oniichi's third daughter, so that when her father is away on a pilgrimage to the Kumano shrines, Yoshitsune is shown the book and gains knowledge of military strategies.

THE WORKS OF HAKUIN

❀ Hakuin's writings are voluminous; many were printed during his lifetime, others were published by his disciples after his death, and still others remained in manuscript form until Hakuin's collected works were published. No attempt at an exhaustive bibliographic study will be made here, although such a study might shed light on some works that may be attributions and on others that were published under varying titles. This applies especially to some of Hakuin's short pieces that are often gathered together and published under titles assigned arbitrarily by different editors.

In listing Hakuin's works, I have largely followed the dating and chronology given by Rikukawa Taiun in his *Kōshō Hakuin oshō shōden*, with reference to the editions appearing in the *Hakuin oshō zenshū*. There are a large number of brief works whose date of composition is uncertain. The dates of publication, when known, are based on the *Shinsan Zenseki mokuroku*.

1. *Nunotsuzumi*

This work exists in two versions: a one-volume printed edition with preface dated 1714, issued at Izusan (HOZ5, 1–18); and a five-*kan* edition in three volumes published in Kyoto in 1753 (HOZ5, 19–86). The second version is revised and greatly enlarged. The work was originally written in behalf of an acquaintance of profligate and unfilial tastes, who is said to have been reformed on reading the text. It contains a series of stories that detail banishments or other misfortunes that befell unfilial sons and perpetrators of evil in both China and Japan. A *nunotsuzumi* is a cloth drum; that is, a useless article. The title of the revised version is given as *Saiben nunotsuzumi* (*Nunotsuzumi* reappraised or revised) in *Hakuin oshō zenshū*.

2. *Kanrin ihō*

Published by Tōrei in 1769, shortly after Hakuin's death. Said to have been composed in 1715, the work is a brief selection of verse, and of phrases from famous Zen texts that Hakuin considered important for his students. HOZ4, 367–83.

3. *Satsujo ni atauru sho*

A letter to a certain Osatsu, the daughter of Shōji Yūtetsu. It details the attitude that one who is caring for a sick person should adopt toward the patient. Dated 1737. HOZ6, 396–406.

4. *Jōzan hyakuin*

Composed in 1737 on the first occasion on which Hakuin delivered lectures at the request of another temple, here the Rinzai-ji in Kawatsu, Izu. *Jōzan hyakuin* contains a hundred poems, ninety-nine by monks present on the occasion, and one by Hakuin. The work is important in that it gives the names of the participants and the temples from which they came. HOZ6, 305–22.

5. *Sokkō-roku kaien fusetsu*

One of the most important of Hakuin's works, it was composed in 1740 and first published in 1743. It consists of material introductory to a series of lectures on the *Hsü-t'ang ho-shang yü-lu* (the Record of Hsü-t'ang Chih-yü). The work contains talks on the old heroes of Zen and urges contemporary Zen students to emulate them and to restore Zen to its former greatness. Included are detailed attacks on "Silent-illumination" Zen and the practice of Pure Land Buddhism and Zen together. The work was recorded by Hakuin's disciples. "Sokkō" is a pseudonym used by

Hsü-t'ang.[1] For lectures on this work, see Mineo Daikyū, *Sokkō-roku kaien fusetsu kōwa*, Tokyo, 1934. HOZ2, 365–450.

6. *Kanzan shi sendai kimon*

Composed in 1741, printed in three *kan* in 1746. Lengthy commentary on the poems of Han-shan, as recorded by Hakuin's disciples. This work is still used extensively in Rinzai monasteries today. As Rikukawa notes, an early version of *Yasen kanna* is contained within the text. HOZ4, 1–364.

7. *Dokugo shingyō*

Written 1741 and said to have been printed in 1760. One of Hakuin's most popular works, it contains verses and comments on the *Heart Sūtra*. It is also known as *Hannya Shingyō dokugo chū*. For a text with commentary see Shibayama Zenkei, *Dokugo shingyō*, Kyoto, 1964. HOZ2, 305–28.

8. *Kabe soshō*

Written 1748 but not printed during the Tokugawa period. It contains brief passages in praise of the Governor of Mishima, in whose domains good government has prevailed, in contrast to other areas that have fallen on evil times. HOZ6, 155–62.

9. *Orategama* and *Orategama zokushū*

The *Orategama*, containing three letters, was first published in 1749. The *zokushū* appears, together with the main text, in an edition of 1751. There are several other Tokugawa period printings and numerous editions in the post-Meiji era. The title is said to be the name of Hakuin's favorite tea-kettle, but this has not been verified. HOZ5, 107–246.

---

[1] ZD (p. 404) states that Hakuin is the only source for this information; however, a poem using this name in its title is found in *Hsü-t'ang ho-shang yü-lu*, 7 (T47, 1038c).

10. *Kaian koku go*

In two *kan* and three volumes, completed in 1749 and published in 1750. The present version is in seven *kan*, containing Hakuin's comments and verses on the *Daitō-roku* (the Record of Shūhō Myōchō (Daitō Kokushi)). Kaian koku is the locust-tree land of tranquility, a never-never land of dreams. For a useful commentary see Iida Tōin, *Kaian koku go teishō-roku*, Kyoto, 1927. HOZ3, 15–378.

11. *Neboke no mezamashi*

Written in 1749 but not printed until the Meiji period. A popular work directed toward those who seek profit in the floating world. Composed in a light verse form, it urges people to awaken from their dreams (*neboke no mezamashi*) to the essentials of Buddhism, especially to Zen. HOZ6, 291–99.

12. *Hōkyōkutsu no ki*

Written in 1750 and printed during the Kaei period (1848–1853). The story of miracles seen by a fisherman of the Pure Land faith in a cave into which he had rowed his boat. Hakuin takes the occasion to return to his familiar theme of the need to see the Pure Land of one's own mind. HOZ5, 247–56.

13. *Oniazami*

Dated 1751, this is a draft of a letter outlining the essentials of Zen. A large part of the work is reminiscent of *Orategama*, although much additional material is included. The text in *Hakuin Zenji shū* (pp. 181–98) contains a letter dated 1752 that is not found in the *Hakuin oshō zenshū* version. The *oniazami* is the horse thistle, *cirsium spicatum*. HOZ5, 257–318.

14. *Yabukōji*

Composed in 1753 and printed in 1792. Letter to the lord of Okayama castle on the practice of Zen, with emphasis on the

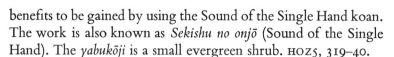

benefits to be gained by using the Sound of the Single Hand koan. The work is also known as *Sekishu no onjō* (Sound of the Single Hand). The *yabukōji* is a small evergreen shrub. HOZ5, 319–40.

15. *Hebiichigo*

Composed in 1754 and printed in 1862. Letter to Lord Nabeshima detailing the virtues of a beneficent ruler, with many cautionary examples of the fate in store for tyrannical officials. Apparently because the work mentions Tokugawa Ieyasu, although in an extremely laudatory manner, its publication was for many years forbidden.[2] The *hebiichigo* is *duchesnea indica*, literally the snake-strawberry. HOZ5, 401–450.

16. *Yasen kanna*, gekan.

Written in 1755. This differs from the famous work known under this title and is unrelated in contents. It is a typical cautionary letter to the retainer of a feudal lord, upholding benevolent government for the benefit of the people, and warning against the imposition of heavy taxes. It is much in the manner of *Hebiichigo*. The work concludes with an exhortation to practice ultimate good through seeing into one's own nature. It includes a discussion of Buddhist compassion and wisdom. HOZ5, 367–400.

17. *Keisō dokuzui*

Completed in 1756 and published in nine *kan* in 1758. Hakuin's *goroku*, or recorded sayings, compiled by his disciples. It contains sermons, talks, verse and prose comments on old koans, homilies, letters, prefaces, postfaces, inscriptions, verses, poems, and other miscellaneous materials. The title may be translated as *Poison Flowers from a Thicket of Thorns*. HOZ5, 1–302.

18. *Fukura suzume*

Dated 1757, this salvationist tract is intended for the general populace, and warns against the evil tendencies in man. The title refers to a sparrow with its feathers fluffed out. HOZ6, 149–54.

[2] See Rikukawa Taiun, *Kōshō Hakuin oshō shōden*, pp. 308–309.

19. *Yasen kanna*, jōkan

First printed in 1757, with numerous later editions. This is probably Hakuin's most famous work. It details his encounter with the hermit Hakuyū, and gives recipes for curing the "Zen sickness." A large number of editions have appeared and its appeal is not limited to Zen followers alone. The best English translation is R. D. M. Shaw and William Schiffer, "Chat on a boat in the evening," *Monumenta Nipponica* XIII, no. 1/2 (1956), pp. 101–127. HOZ5, 341–66.

20. *Hōkan ishō*

Printed in 1758. Hōkan Kokushi is the posthumous title of Gudō Tōshoku; the title may be translated, then, *Remaining Illumination of Gudō*. The work was written following a visit to the Rurikō-ji in Mino, where Hakuin lectured on the hundredth anniversary of Gudō's death. Hakuin took the occasion to promote the publication of Gudō's "records," but encountered indifference on the part of the temple priests in the area. Angered, he composed this piece in seven-character verse form. It starts with a few words in praise of Gudō and then proceeds to attack, often in intemperate language, contemporary Zen practitioners. Included is a discussion of T'ung-shan's theory of the "Five Ranks," used today in Hakuin's Zen teaching. HOZ1, 231–66.

21. *Keisō dokuzui shūi*

Dated 1759, this work contains material supplementary to the *Keisō dokuzui*. It includes the text of *Dokugo shingyō*, as well as an essay entitled "Jinjakō bengi o yomu," that concurs with and augments the *Jinjakō bengi* by the Shingon priest Jakuhon (1631–1701). The latter work is sharply critical of the famous book on Shinto shrines, *Honchō jinja kō*, by Hayashi Razan. Jakuhon wrote his work in response to the anti-Buddhist sentiments that Hayashi had expressed.[3] HOZ2, 305–364.

[3] *Ibid.*, pp. 251–58.

22. *Yaemugura*

Written in 1759, this work is composed of two entirely un-related volumes. The first *kan* is entitled *Takazuka yonjō kōki* (Record of the Filiality of the Four Daughters of Takazuka). It contains elaborate descriptions of hell and the sufferings of those who fall there. The piece concludes with the story of Onoda Hisashige's four granddaughters, who made a copy of the *Lotus Sūtra* in kana script as an act of filial duty. *Kan* two is the *Emmei jikku kannon-gyō reigen-ki* (Account of the Miracles of the Ten-Phrase Kannon Sūtra for Prolonging Life). It cites examples of those saved from disaster and death through the virtue gained from the recitation of this text.[4]

The version given in *Hakuin Zenji shū* adds a third *kan*, (pp. 389–442) dated 1761. This includes a supplement entitled *Osana monogatari* (Tales of Childhood). This latter piece is a detailed autobiography, roughly paralleling the *Itsumadegusa*. *Yaemugura* is the goose grass. HOZ6, 1–120.

23. *Moshio gusa*

Published 1759, this work is a collection of Hakuin's *waka* poetry. *Moshio*, meaning "salt from seaweed," is taken from the first poem of the collection, where the word is used. HOZ6, 333–44.

24. *Sashimogusa*

Written in two *kan* in 1760. It contains two letters dealing largely with the necessity of nurturing health and the virtues of good officials and the evils of tyrannical ones. The text is in places virtually identical with *Hebiichigo*. The meaning of the title is unclear. HOZ5, 451–511.

25. *Kana mugura*

Composed 1762, the printed editions are not dated. It contains two unrelated works: *Shin dangi* (New Preachings), and *Tsuji*

---

[4] For details see Translation, "Hebiichigo I," fn. 16.

dangi (Preaching at the Crossroads). The *Shin dangi* is meant for the general reader and largely concerns descriptions of hell and paradise. It was published by Tōrei together with other pieces by Hakuin in 1770 under the title *Tsuji dangi*. It is included in some modern popular collections of Hakuin's works under the latter title.

The *Tsuji dangi* is a lengthy piece of unusual content. It starts by extolling the virtues of Buddhism and repeats a passage on a specific contemplation, found also in the *Orategama* and *Yasen kanna*. There follow examples of famous Buddhist believers, stories of the relationship between Shinto and Buddhism, and stories of the fate of Confucianists who attacked Buddhism. Many of the episodes do not appear elsewhere in Hakuin's works. *Mugura* refers probably to the weeds in an untended garden. HOZ6, 163–217.

26. *Anjin hokoritataki*

Dated 1764. This brief piece is written in imitation of the Ahodara-kyō, popular at the time,[5] which consisted of nonsense verses, recited to the accompaniment of the wooden drum by begging priests. They dealt with strange events and current sensations, and were recited at great speed. Such recitations developed in the Kyoto-Naniwa area, spreading later to Edo.[6] According to the preface this work was written for a Pure Land priest who had demonstrated his understanding of the Zen teachings. It talks of Buddhism in terms of a merchant selling his wares. *Anjin* "means the mind at peace"; a *hokoritataki* is a duster. HOZ6, 243–50.

27. *Itsumadegusa*

Written 1765–1766 in three *kan*. In seven-character verse form (not without irregularities and errors), it is largely autobiographical in character. The first *kan* details Hakuin's experiences through

---

[5] See Rikukawa Taiun, *Kōshō Hakuin oshō shōden*, p. 209.
[6] See Makimura Shiyō, *Ōsaka hōgen jiten*, Osaka, 1955, p. 20.

his visit to Shōju Rōjin; the second treats the period afterward, and includes frequent attacks on "heretical Zen gangs"; *kan* three is devoted to Hakuyū and contains much of the material found in *Yasen kanna* and the section of *Orategama* that parallels *Yasen kanna*. *Itsumadegusa* is another name for *kizuta*, the ivy. HOZI, 149–230.

The date of composition of the following works is uncertain.

28. *Kana innen hōgo*

Printed 1827. Preachings on causality in the kana syllabary. The work consists of five tales of causality drawn from stories current in the area around Hakuin's temple. HOZ5, 87–104.

29. *Usen shikō*

Reading and meaning of title are uncertain. A letter dealing with the need of the Confucianist to meditate and to see into his own nature if he is to understand the essentials of the Confucian teaching. HOZ6, 121–47.

30. *Otafuku jorō kohiki uta*

"The Grain-Grinding Song of the Ugly Prostitute," published 1760. It is written in the fashion of grain-grinding songs popular at the time. It treats of Buddhism in general, and, although written in a popular form, is directed toward those well versed in Zen. HOZ6, 219–30.

31. *Shushin obaba kohiki uta*

"The Grain-Grinding Song of the Old Woman, Mind-as-Master." Printed in 1770, it is written in the same style as the above work. A brief piece, it begins with a sermon on the Four Vows and then turns to comments on Zen. It is directed toward advanced students. HOZ6, 231–38.

32. *Zazen wasan*

This brief song in praise of meditation is one of the most popular works of Hakuin and is in constant use at all Rinzai temples today. An English translation appears in Miura and Sasaki, ZD, pp. 251–53.

33. *Segyō uta*

A song in praise of charity, dealing with Buddhism and common morality, and meant for the populace in general. HOZ6, 239–42.

34. *Daidō chobokure*

A *Chobokure* is a kind of popular song, sung to the accompaniment of two small wooden gongs. A brief piece in praise of the Great Way (*Daidō*), it is a preaching on Buddhism for the public. HOZ6, 251–56.

35. *Kusatori uta*

Weeding song; cautionary words on Buddhism. HOZ6, 263–68.

36. *Zen'aku tanemaku kagami wasan*

A printed edition appeared in 1837. "Verse on the Mirror in which the Seeds of Good and Evil Sown are Reflected." A discourse on cause and effect. HOZ6, 269–82.

37. *Kōdō wasan*

"Verse on the Obligations of Children Toward Their Parents." HOZ6, 362–65.

There are numerous other short pieces by Hakuin, many of which appear in popular editions of his works. A large number of these can be found under the title of *Zassan* in HOZ6, 357–78. Another collection, known as *Kokurin sekidoku* (HOZ6, 379–539), contains a large number of individual letters addressed to a variety of people, many unidentified. There are also poems that do not appear elsewhere, verses inscribed on pictures, and other materials in addition to those discussed above.

❀ BIBLIOGRAPHY OF WORKS CITED

A. Works in Tripitaka collections (by title)

A-mi-t'o ching shu-ch'ao (Amida-kyō shōshō), by Chu-hung. ZZI, 33, 2–3.

Avataṁsaka Sūtra (Kegon-kyō). T9 (no. 278), pp. 395–788.

Cheng-tao ko (Shōdō-ka). T48 (no. 2014), pp. 395c–96c (also contained in *Ching-te ch'uan-teng lu*, T51, pp. 460a–461b).

Chia-t'ai pu-teng lu (Katai futō-roku). ZZ2B, 10, 1–2.

Ching-te ch'uan-teng lu (Keitoku dentō-roku), by Tao-yüan. T51 (no. 2076) pp. 196–467.

Daitō Kokushi goroku. T81, pp. 191–242.

Diamond Sūtra (Vajracchedikā; Kongō-kyō). T8 (no. 235), pp. 748–52.

Fa-yen ch'an-shih yü-lu (Hōen zenji goroku). T47 (no. 1995), pp. 649–69.

Fan-wang ching (Bommō-kyō). T24 (no. 1484), pp. 997–1010.

Fo-tsu li-tai t'ung-tsai (Busso rekidai tsūsai). T49 (no. 2036), pp. 477–735.

Fo-tsu t'ung-chi (Busso tōki). T49 (no. 2035), pp. 129–475.

Hsin-hsin ming (Shinjin mei). T48 (no. 2010), pp. 376–77. (Also contained in *Ching-te ch'uan-teng lu*, T51, pp. 457a–b).

Hsü-t'ang ho-shang yü-lu (Kidō oshō goroku). T47 (no. 2000), pp. 984–1064.

Kaimokushō, by Nichiren. T84 (no. 2689), pp. 208–33.

Kao-wang Kuan-shih-yin ching (Kōō Kanzeon-kyō). T85 (no. 2898), pp. 1425–26.

Kuan P'u-hsien P'u-sa hsing-fa ching (Kan Fugen Bosatsu gyōbō-gyō). T9 (no. 277), pp. 389–94.

Kuan wu-liang-shou ching (Kammuryōju kyō). T12 (no. 365), pp. 340–46.

Lin-chi lu (Rinzai roku). T47 (no. 1985), pp. 495–506.

Lotus Sūtra (Saddharmapuṇḍarīka; Hoke-kyō). T9 (no. 262), pp. 1–61.

Mo-ho chih-kuan (Maka shikan), by Chih-i. T46 (no. 1911), pp. 1–140.

Nirvāṇa Sūtra (*Nehan-gyō*). T12 (no. 374), pp. 365–606.

P'ang chü-shih yü-lu (*Hō koji goroku*). zz2, 25, 1, 28–41.

Pao-ts'ang lun (*Hōzō ron*). T45 (no. 1857), pp. 143–50.

Pi-yen lu (*Hekigan roku*), by Yüan-wu K'o-ch'in. T48 (no. 2003), pp. 139–225.

Shan-hui ta-shih yü-lu (*Zenne daishi goroku*). zz2, 25, 1, 1–27.

Shih-shuang Ch'u-yüan ch'an-shih yü-lu (*Sekisō Soen zenji goroku*). zz2, 25, 1, 81–93.

Shōshitsu rokumon. T48 (no. 2009), pp. 365–76.

Ssu-shih-erh chang ching (*Shijūnishō gyō*). T17 (no. 784), pp. 722–23.

Ta-ch'eng ch'i-hsin lun (*Daijō kishin ron*). T32 (no. 1666), pp. 575–83.

Ta-hui P'u-chüeh ch'an-shih yü-lu (*Daie Fukaku zenji goroku*). T47 (no. 1998), pp. 811–957.

Ta-hui shu (*Daie no sho*). T47 (no. 1998), pp. 916–43.

Ts'ung-jung lu (*Shōyō roku*). T48 (no. 2004), pp. 226–92.

Vimalakīrti Sūtra (*Yuima-gyō*). T14 (no. 475), pp. 537–57.

Wu-chia cheng-tsung tsan (*Goke shōshū san*). zz2B, 8, 5, 452–98.

Wu-liang-i ching (*Muryōgi kyō*). T9 (no. 276), pp. 383–89.

Wu-liang-shou ching (*Muryōju kyō*). T12 (no. 363), pp. 318–26.

Wu-men kuan (*Mumonkan*). T48 (no. 2006), pp. 292–99.

Yüan-chüeh ching (*Engaku kyō*). T17 (no. 842), pp. 913–22.

Yüan-chüeh ching ta-shu (*Engaku kyō daishō*). zz1, 14, 2.

B. Other works

Akizuki Ryūmin. *Kōan.* Tokyo, 1965.

Dōgen. *Sanshō dōei shū. Kokubun Tōhō Bukkyō sōsho,* ser. 1, vol. 8, Tokyo, 1925, pp. 225–33.

Echū. *Zenso nembutsu shū. Dai-Nihon Bukkyo zensho,* vol. 70. Tokyo, 1918, pp. 252–88.

Fujita Genro, ed. *Kattō shū. Zudokko,* Kyoto, 1957, pp. 109–197.

Fukunaga Shūho. *Gendai sōji-Zen hyōron.* Tokyo, 1926.

Furuta Shōkin. *Nihon Bukkyō shisōshi no shomondai.* Tokyo, 1964.

Hurvitz, Leon, "Chih-i," *Mélanges Chinois et Bouddhiques,* XII (1962).

Hyakurenshō, Kokushi taikei 11. Tokyo, 1931, pp. 1–257.

Iida Tōin. *Kaian koku go teishō roku.* Kyoto, 1927.

Injō, *Tōdo yawa.* 2 vols., 1762.

Itō Kazuo. "Hakuyūshi no hito to sho," *Zen bunka*, no. 6 (November, 1956), pp. 40–48.

Kanzan shi. Kyoto, Ogawaraya Hyōe, 1759. 2 vols.

Kōchi Eigaku. "Keizan Zenji no Mikkyōteki hairyo to sono raiyu," *Shūgaku kenkyū*, no. 2 (1960), pp. 42–49.

Komazawa Daigaku Toshokan. *Shinsan Zenseki mokuroku*. Tokyo, 1962.

Makimura Shiyō. *Ōsaka hōgen jiten*. Osaka, 1955.

Mineo Daikyū. *Sokkō-roku kaien fusetsu kōwa*. Tokyo, 1934.

Nogami Toyoichirō. *Yōkyoku zenshū*. Tokyo, 1935–1936. 6 vols.

Ogisu Jundō, "Nihon Zenshū nijūshi-ryū shiden kō," *Nihon Bukkyō gakkai nempō*, no. 21 (1955), pp. 273–89.

Okada Minoru. *Jikkinshō shinshaku*. Tokyo, 1930.

Ōkubo Dōshū. "Dōgen zenji no genshi sōdan to Nihon Daruma-shū to no kankei," *Dōgen Zenji kenkyū*, Tokyo, 1941, pp. 77–125.

Rikukawa Taiun. *Kōshō Hakuin oshō shōden*. Tokyo, 1963.

Shaw, R. D. M. and Schiffer, William, "Chat on a boat in the evening," *Monumenta Nipponica*, XIII, no. 1–2 (1956), pp. 101–127.

Shibayama Zenkei. *Dokugo shingyō*. Kyoto, 1964.

Shimizutani Zenshō. *Kanzeon bosatsu no shinkō*. Tokyo, 1941.

Shiban. *Honchō kōsō den. Kokuyaku issai kyō: Wa-Kan senjutsu-bu*, Tokyo, 1961. Vols. 89–91.

Shiren. *Genkō shakusho. Kokuyaku issai-kyō: Wa-Kan senjutsu-bu*. Tokyo, 1963–1966. Vols. 87–88.

Suzuki Daisetsu (Teitarō), ed. *Daitō Kokushi hyakunijissoku*. Tokyo, 1944.

——— *Zen shisōshi kenkyū*. Tokyo, 1943–51. 2 vols.

Suzuki Taizan, "Sōtō Zen no gufu to sono gegosha," *Kokumin seikatsushi kenkyū*. Tokyo, 1960, IV, 223–76.

Tokugawa jikki. Kokushi taikei, 1929–1935, vols. 38–47.

Uji shūi monogatari. Kokushi taikei 18, Tokyo, 1932, pp. 1–290.

Waley, Arthur. *Book of Songs*. New York, 1960.

Yampolsky, Philip. *Platform Sutra of the Sixth Patriarch*. New York, 1967.

Yanagida Seizan. *Rinzai no kafu*. Tokyo, 1967.

——— *Kunchū Rinzai roku*. Kyoto, 1961.

Yokozeki Ryōin. *Edo jidai Tōmon seiyō*. Tokyo, 1938.

Zen Taiheiki. Zoku Teikoku bunko, Tokyo, 1898, pp. 375–1079.

C. The following popular editions of selections
from Hakuin's works were consulted

Karaki Junzō, ed. *Zenke goroku shū. Nihon no shisō*, vol. 10. Tokyo, 1969.
Miyauchi Sotai. *Hakuin zenji hōgo shū*. Tokyo, 1942.
Nomura Zuijō. *Hakuin to Orategama*. Kyoto, 1931.
—— *Hakuin to Yasen kanna*. Kyoto, 1926.
Takahashi Chikumei. *Hakuin zenji gongyō-roku*. Tokyo, 1937.
Takeshita Naoyuki, ed. *Hakuin hōgo shū*. Tokyo, 1953.
Tsukamoto Tetsuzō, ed. *Zenrin hōgo shū*. Tokyo, 1928. (*Yūhōdō bunko*).
Yamamoto Isao, ed. *Hakuin zenji hen. Kōsō meicho zenshū*, vol. 12. Tokyo, 1930.

❀ INDEX